Emerging Form in Architecture

Emerging Form in Architecture: Conversations with Lev Zetlin

Forrest Wilson, A.I.A.

Professor and Chairman of the Department of Architecture and Planning
School of Engineering and Architecture
The Catholic University of America

Cahners Books
A Division of Cahners Publishing Company
89 Franklin Street, Boston, Massachusetts 02110

Library of Congress Catalog Card Number: 75-8912
ISBN: 0-8436-0150-7
Designed by Jennie Bush/Designworks, Inc.
Printed in the United States of America

Library of Congress Cataloging in Publication Data

Wilson, Forrest, 1918–
    Emerging form in architecture: conversations with Lev Zetlin.

    Includes index.
    1. Structural engineering.   2. Zetlin, Lev,
1918–   I. Title.
TA636.W54   624′.1′0924   75-8912
ISBN 0-8436-0150-7

". . . when we do have fuller knowledge [of the brain] our whole picture is bound to change radically.

"Much that is now culturally acceptable will then seem to be nonsense. People with training in the arts still feel that in spite of the alterations made in their lives by technology; by the internal combustion engine, by penicillin, by the bomb, modern science has little to do with what concerns us most deeply. As far as today's science is concerned, this is partly true, but tomorrow's science is going to knock their culture right out from under them."

—Sir Francis Crik, "The Computer, The Eye, The Soul," *Saturday Review of Literature,* September 3, 1966.

Contents

Editor's note

This book is the result of interviews and conversations held over a period of nearly ten years between Forrest Wilson and Lev Zetlin. Some of the material is written by Wilson; other words are Zetlin's—organized and edited by Wilson. To differentiate between Wilson's and Zetlin's words this book has been set in two different typefaces.

This one is used to indicate Wilson's words.

This one is used to indicate Zetlin's words.

Preface

A decade ago, as an editor of the architectural magazine *Progressive Architecture,* I was assigned to work with Dr. Lev Zetlin in preparing an article on the future of engineering. What began as a routine assignment continued for the next ten years as a personal project. The result was a series of intermittent interviews, casual conversations, question and answer sessions, which I recorded, transcribed, and edited.

The purpose of this book is to describe the frame of reference within which a talented engineer solves problems. More important, the attitudes he holds are reshaping our world.

At a time when many university professors do not understand the workings of an electric can opener it is refreshing to hear an engineer describe the way he thinks and the reshaping of the built environment in simple comprehensible terms. Zetlin can make complex engineering concepts clear, with a sense of humor and a remarkably original turn of mind. His ability to visualize problems in terms of universal force systems and describe solutions as clearly as the analogies of a Russian peasant seemed to me to be an experience worth sharing.

The best technique, it seemed to me, was to use his own words. The method was to record conversations and then edit and return them to Zetlin for his comments and elaboration. If there is sometimes a confusion of tone, it is because my writing habits have intruded on Zetlin's style of expressing himself. The ideas are his. From time to time I have put his remarks into what I perceive to be their historic perspective, through introductory paragraphs.

Technical descriptions were gathered from men in his office and contemporary architectural and engineering journals. I wish to thank the editors and publishers of *Architectural Record, Civil Engineering, Progressive Architecture, Architectural Forum,* and *Engineering News Record,* as well as Lev Zetlin's associates for permission to quote from their descriptions of his projects.

A brief interview with architect Philip Johnson clarified aspects of productive collaboration between a talented architect and engineer. Johnson commissioned Zetlin early in Zetlin's career. Some of the most exciting projects of both men were the result. Unfortunately the length of the book did not allow me to dwell on this aspect of Zetlin's work.

The book is organized into five sections entitled Introduction, Incremental Change, New Forms, The Future and The Self-Fulfilling Prophecy. In the first section Zetlin talks of his ideas of creativity and his approach to engineering problems. The second describes a group of projects in which innovation is concealed within the form of traditional building. In the third, New Forms, innovation emerges in its own right to assert radical changes in the shape of the built environment. The fourth section, The Future, deals with some of Zetlin's predictions for our built environment, and the fifth, The Self-Fulfilling Prophecy, describes a series of theoretical studies.

The divisions are not clearcut. Incremental change often pushes through to become new building form and theoretical studies become reality as part of current building vocabulary.

9

All the work of Zetlin and his associates is not included. Projects were selected for the way they illustrate Zetlin's mode of thought and problem-solving attitudes. As the book progressed his office was increasingly engaged in startling new projects more rapidly than they could be recorded. The selection of work however, does chronicle a progression of designs increasing in size from the time Zetlin opened his office as an obscure Doctor of Philosophy two decades ago until today when he is internationally recognized.

Early commissions tended to be single buildings or unique building solutions. Later commissions became larger prototype solutions for systems of construction and series of buildings. Yet his work cannot be listed in an orderly progression. The development of ideas does not have a linear chronology. For example, one of Zetlin's first commissions, the modest yet startlingly original Nuclear Reactor built at Rehovot, Israel engineered as part of Philip Johnson's design for the complex, featured an ingenious use of hyperbolic parabaloid walls. This form emerges almost twenty years later as the cantilevered roofs of gigantic "superbay hangars" built in Los Angeles and San Francisco as prototypes and scheduled for many locations throughout the world. Zetlin was no longer working for an architect but was instead the prime designer. The self-dampening cable system of the Utica Auditorium was developed, patented and ends momentarily as a proposed system of transporting ships across the isthmus of Panama to replace the present canal.

This is not a book meant necessarily to be read in an ordered sequence. It can be opened in the middle and read in both directions, which seems apropos, given the dispersed way that we now acquire information and the way Zetlin's ideas seem to proliferate.

This is also not meant to be a "pretty book." The forms emerging today in our built environment are more and more the result of engineering optimization. They do not necessarily appeal to the cultured sensibility as did the work of traditional virtuoso architects and engineers. Such rational solutions do not always coincide with our aesthetic prejudices. These new forms may eventually be appreciated aesthetically, but by then other forces and motivations will probably be at work changing the shape of the world. Aesthetic ideas and the men they are built around seem to be most admired when both are dead.

Zetlin's ideas are very much alive. They have the vitality to change the shape of our world and are doing so. We ignore them at our peril.

10

Lev Zetlin–a chronology

July 14, 1918: Born in Namangan, Russia

1939: Graduated from the Higher Technical Institute, Palestine, Civil Engineering Diploma. Other education: elementary and secondary, American College, Tehran, Iran; High Schools, Palestine; London University matriculation.

1940: City and Guilds College, London (First Class).

1941–1943: Commissioned, British Army.

1944: Established one-man engineering consulting office, Tel Aviv, Israel; maintained until 1950.

1944–1948: Chief structural engineer for Israel's Department of Agricultural and Industrial Settlements; continuing as independent consultant.

1948–1950: Commanding officer, Civil Engineering Division, Israeli Air Force, Rank Captain.

1950: Left Israel to study at Cornell University.

1951: Masters of Civil Engineering, Cornell University.

1953: Doctor of Philosophy (Structural Engineering, Applied Mechanics, Soil Mechanics), Cornell University.

1953–1955: Assistant Professor of Civil Engineering; Cornell University.

1954: Elected to The Society of American Military Engineers.

1956: Founded Lev Zetlin Associates, consulting engineers, New York City.

1960: Became Fellow of the American Society of Civil Engineers.

1961–1967: Professor of Civil Engineering, Pratt Institute, Brooklyn, New York.

1963: Design Award from *Progressive Architecture* for Medium Security Prison, Leesburg, New Jersey.

1964: Award of Merit by Prestressed Concrete Institute for New York World's Fair Observation Towers; Design Award from *Progressive Architecture* for Kline Science Center, Yale University; Special Award from the Concrete Industry Board, Inc. for the Eastman Kodak Pavilion at the New York World's Fair.

1964–Present: Consultant on research to Union Carbide Corporation.

1965: Member of Manhattan College's Board of Consultors in Civil Engineering.

1966: Elected to Executive and Professional Hall of Fame; Received medal for Hadassah Hebrew University Medical Center, Jerusalem.

1967: Architectural Critic, College of Architecture, City College, New York; Elected to Editorial Advisory Board of *Building Construction* magazine; Certificate of Merit for "Distinguished Service to Civil Engineering" from *Dictionary of International Biography;* Elected Member of Public Advisory Panel on Architectural Services for the General Services Administration.

1968: "Honor Award" from U.S. Department of Housing and Urban Development (HUD) for Bluebeard's Hill Apartments, St. Thomas, Virgin Islands.

1968–Present: University Professor of Engineering and Architecture, University of Virginia.

1968–Present: Director of the Center for Research and Innovations for Buildings (CRIB), University of Virginia.

1969: Awarded Gold Medal by Société Arts, Sciences, Lettres (Under the Sponsorship of the French Academy); Award: "The Two Thousand Men of Achievement".

1970: Certificate of Merit for Excellence in Design for Yeshiva University Library, New York, by the New York State Association of Architects; "Honor Award" from Department of Housing and Urban Development (HUD) for Charles Center Apartments, Baltimore.

1971: Award of Merit from the Chemical Industry Association; Architectural Award of Excellence, AISC for Superbay Hangar Maintenance Facility.

1972: Elected "Member of Eminent Distinction": *The National Register of Prominent Americans;* Elected to "Personalities of the South" by the Editorial Board of American Biographical Institute; "Award of Merit" from the Concrete Industry Board for the Jewish Institute for Geriatric Care, New York; "Honor Award" from the Long Island Association of Commerce and Industry for the Security National Bank, New York.

1973: Knight of Honor bestowed by the Knights of Malta for distinguished achievement; Chairman, Consultor Committee, Manhattan College of the Sacred Heart.

1 Introduction

The changing shape of our physical world challenges our atavistic memories of form and shape. As our built environment is increasingly dominated by the rational forms of engineering, we are haunted by a nebulous perceptual disquiet.

Since childhood we have been conscious that the buildings that surround and protect us from the elements are composed of overwhelming, delicately balanced, man-crushing weights of timber, stone, steel, and concrete. We know that it is this precarious equilibrium that prevents our buildings from tumbling down upon our heads. The logic of force and counterforce was verified with our first tottering infant steps as we attempted to hold ourselves upright upon our wobbly ankles. Since then we have assured ourselves countless times, consciously and subconsciously, that gravity pulling toward the center of the earth is the force that holds together the shells of man-made space. We have, over time, developed a sense of the rightness of size for structural members and the logical geometries of building.

This assurance has been challenged by modern engineering. The silhouettes, sections, façades, and profiles of modern structures do not resemble the outlines stored in our memories. Lacking a reassuring familiar geometry they threaten our sense of well-being.

This profound sense of unease is reminiscent of that generated by the Mannerist architects four centuries ago. The sensibilities of the observer were willfully outraged by the assault on the logic of the classical forms of Renaissance structures. The Mannerists playfully destroyed the logic of the arch with absurdly large and ridiculously small key stones. They derided the upright integrity of the column by turning it into a ludicrous corkscrew and transformed the stout bearing wall into a frivolous undulating curtain. The impact of Mannerist design depended upon the perversion of the sense of structural correctness affirmed by the Renaissance.

The structural appearance of many of today's buildings is as disturbing to our inner sense of well-being as were Mannerist buildings to Renaissance perceptions. But the disquiet that plagues us originates in the logic of engineering optimization rather than design egocentricity.

Buildings have become larger and larger during the past 20 years, and, with an increase in size, a new aesthetic has emerged. Compare, for example, the Chicago Tribune Tower, a 1920s skyscraper, with the recently completed John Hancock Building. The steel frame of the Tribune Tower is clothed in Gothic stone caricature. The aesthetic model for the Hancock building is the naked profile of an electric transmission tower.

As buildings become larger, building labor changes its character, and economy and industrialization become larger factors. Building form is less controlled by the arbitrary aesthetic dictates of prevailing architectural styles. Almost anyone can design a building with spans between columns of 40 or 50 feet. Little engineering skill is required to devise such a structure and it can be almost any form its designer chooses. But a building with a clear span of 200 or 300 feet demands that the structural form follow a logic dictated by the control of physical forces. The engineering industrial process and the mobilization of labor that makes such a structure possible is complex, difficult, and clearly expressed in the form of the building no matter what its decoration.

We have not yet learned to live comfortably with such structures. The tenants of the Hancock building in Chicago must accustom themselves to life above the clouds out of contact with the streets or the world below. Yet they retain an atavistic cave memory. High buildings drift with wind pressures. Such movement is not structurally dangerous. Yet the building must be stiffened at great cost in material and labor to eliminate the slight sway. These same building occupants would be at ease driving 100 miles an hour on a thruway. As buildings tend more and more to lose their ties with the past and assume the forms of efficiently engineered machines, as the rational philosophy of the engineer supplants the aesthetic egocentricity of the architect, we experience a nameless anxiety.

15

We have always thought more of practical engineers than we have of cultured architects. There are approximately ten times the number of registered civil engineers as registered architects in America. In the folklore of the professions the architect is pictured as an impractical dreamer, while the engineer is motivated by the no-nonsense practicality of the common sense. The engineered form of the living quarters in a space station or an undersea laboratory is unquestioned, yet a modest modern house built in a neighborhood of traditional homes causes immediate and sometimes violent reaction.

Engineering form is taken for granted and may well, therefore, be a truer indication of our civilization than architecture because engineering is practiced by men who are not necessarily influenced by the implication of their acts.

Artifacts, not art, are the true plastic expression of the beliefs and convictions of a society. For they are the unconscious expression of the intelligence, technical sophistication, and artistic comprehension of the civilization assimilated and unconsciously expressed by the artificer who created them.

The engineer fashions his work with unquestioning assurance as part of the total value system in which he lives. The engineers who design skyscrapers are as unconcerned with the social, political, economic, and aesthetic implications of their structures as were the designers of the pyramids. For this reason an objective examination of the

16

engineering of any man-made structure reveals the entire range of prevailing human values existent in the society in which it was created.

It was once said that an idea in good currency is no longer relevant. Most of the ideas that motivate our society go unquestioned although we are fond of arguing at length over outworn concepts such as the virtues and failings of modern architecture. When an idea reaches maturity and is consciously questioned, it is no longer a motivating idea. For example, the theory and engineering artistry of medieval armour did not reach perfection until after the invention of gunpowder rendered armour all but useless.

Today, the motivating creative force of engineering seems to be that of optimization, in which labor and materials are constantly and compulsively minimized, sometimes disastrously; yet, this idea is unchallenged. It is a self-evident unquestioned axiom for user, client, and engineer.

Optimization was foreign to the engineers of antiquity. If it were not, evidences of their work would not have survived. The original sewer culverts of Rome are still operational. If two millenniums of use were divided by materials and labor cost, these would be the cheapest sewers ever engineered, although they were probably the world's most expensive at the time they were built.

The scientists of Yucatán had a firmer grasp of mathematics than the conquistadores. To the Maya, numbers were sacred. They were used as symbols for the days of the month, to foretell the seasons, and to predict eclipses. In the clash of the two cultures the simple calculation of the trajectory of an iron cannonball proved of more lasting significance than the calculation of the orbit of the moon.

The engineering of our physical surroundings today, although less dramatic, is no less vital to our well-being. In our urban world the impact of strange and unfamiliar building forms upon our sensibilities may not be so immediately detrimental as an iron cannonball but may prove nonetheless deadly to our perceptual well-being.

If we are to adjust to the forms of a rapidly emerging engineered world, it must be comprehensible. Optimization is a vital, unquestioned rationale not yet in good currency.

The purpose of this book is simply to explain some of these ideas through the work of one of today's foremost engineers.

Most dedicated architects and engineers have a very strong personal view of the world. This is a book describing such a view. Lev Zetlin sees the universe clearly as an unending succession of connected force and counterforce, stress and strain, holding its structural form together and susceptible to infinite manipulation and adjustment.

Zetlin changes the form of the world with the utmost assurance, and in the process has developed a unique philosophy. These ideas and their variations may well be responsible for the physical form of our cities for the next century.

As modern engineering tends to change our world, our perceptions based on traditional building form are jarred. This portrait of the work of an inspired engineer may or may not calm such perceptual disquiet but it will help the reader to understand the logic behind the strange and unfamiliar forms increasingly dominating our lives.

The objective of this book is not a biography of a man but the chronicling of his ideas.

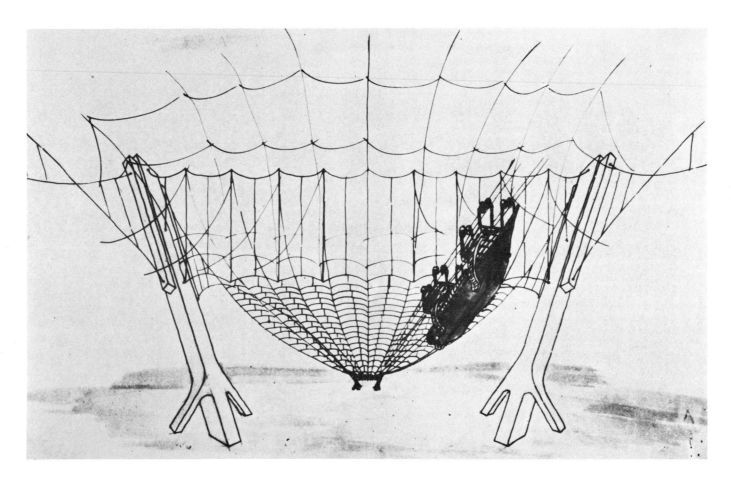

The Structural Engineering Of The Universe

Structural engineering is anything in nature that embodies the interaction of stress and strain. Wherever there is gravity there is stress and strain.

The earth's gravity affects everything on our planet. Structural engineering exists not only in the physical environment but in our mental attitudes as well. It exists in the structure of the universe and perhaps in other things beyond. Therefore, all things must concern the structural engineer.

The structural engineering of buildings is only part of the structural engineering of the universe. The involvement of the structural engineer can be limited to some part of the stress-and-strain problem such as building structure. But the design of buildings involves the study of all the earth's processes, such as wave motions, the stability of the earth's crust, the strength and denegration of materials, wind, sun, rain—our entire environment.

Engineering is only the redirection of energy which is never lost. When engineers design, they use that part of energy they are intelligent enough to redirect for their purposes. A measure of an engineer's skill is the amount of energy he can harness to solve the problem he has set himself.

From the beginning of time until the recent past structural engineers have manipulated intuitive systems. The Romans

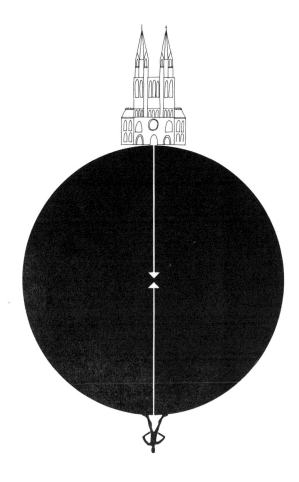

built stone arches wherever they went, yet it was almost two millenniums later that arch design theory was developed. Such historical intuitive empirical solutions have no place in today's engineering.

Structural engineering in our time is the result of thinking, not intuition. It joins values and analytical methods. The elements of a problem must be studied and the results of their application examined. This is a reversal of the historical procedure of building.

Unfortunately, the practice of engineering today does not often differ from its historic pattern. It is usually practiced like a bookkeeping system. The problem solution, that is, the building form, is given a set of rules prescribed by the various building codes and a solution sought in the engineering handbooks. This is a far cry from civil engineering.

The design of a building must embody a conception of it as a container in the world, integrating every aspect of this implication. If a functional form that embodies the plan, which is a diagram accommodating the human use of the space within the building, is combined with building services and the interplay of structural forces and a shell designed, which is in reality the most efficient form for the building, this process will approach civil engineering. The container must be conceived as a by-product of building techniques and construction skills. Then, and only then, does a basis for structural engineering exist.

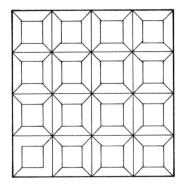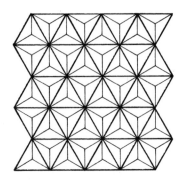

This is a difficult integration to achieve. The architect, engineer, and builder acquire their specialties and practice them separately, yet everything within the building must be interrelated. For example, an element of the mechanical system may influence the physical enclosure of space while the geometric form of the building will influence the interior climate within the building. In turn, structural systems that control physical forces generate spatial relationships; these, in turn, affect the perceptual reactions of the building users.

Design ideally is a synthesis. It is the solution of a multitude of simultaneous interrelated factors rather than a sequential succession of activities. Yet the professions that are responsible for building design perform in sequence. First a plan is devised, then the structural and mechanical diagrams are imposed upon it. A series of adjustments are made, none of them entirely successful. Each is a compromise among the parts. The end result is a combination of adjustments, none of which fulfill their potential individually or perform well as an assembly. Much of the difficulty arises from an abstract conviction that such a thing as "correct structure" exists. The structure is in reality a series of compromises between all the conditions the building must accommodate. Its correctness is derived from adjustment, not a preconceived aesthetic.

Structural engineering, although commonly termed "building science," is not science. Engineers sometimes call themselves scientists and scientists sometimes term themselves engineers. Both science and engineering observe natural phenomena, establish patterns of these natural phenomena, and extrapolate the relationships between them. Science supplies formulae for the interrelationships between the various natural factors involved in building. Engineering assembles these factors, establishes relationships, and applies them directly to an artifact for human use. Engineering deals with the applications of science.

If you know the result, it can be achieved. If you know the trajectory of a bullet, you can build a gun that will throw a projectile along that trajectory.

The variety of factors that account for natural behavior is infinite. Science starts with a statement concerning this behavior. It does not consider characteristics. The engineer cannot

avoid them. The engineer must make approximations to compensate for a lack of information. This is a primary reason for factors of safety in building design.

An example of the difference between science and engineering was illustrated by a scientist who worked out a thermal problem. The solution depended upon very specific conditions. Given these conditions and only these, the problem could be solved. Science considered this information useful, yet it proved of little engineering value. The engineer could not tell the building department that he would take into account a temperature transfer of only 10 degrees between two floors. The realities of physical conditions make it necessary for the temperature to be controlled within a variation of well over 100 degrees. In this instance the scientific answer was inadequate.

All technological progress originates with the military. The competition between nations has caused the tremendous jump in technological progress. Civil engineering is the result of military engineering. Cologne contributed so much to civil engineering because of Napoleon's need for military engineers. Technology during the Second World War developed because of radar. The competition in the flight to the moon has resulted in the technology and new materials of the aerospace industry being developed.

The Roman Empire marked the turning point in man's civilization. The Romans built under any and all circumstances. Yet why did the Romans, during the space of 100 years, devise thousands of innovations in military combat but not change their construction methods. Construction deals with large entities. It is not an independent phenomenon. The architect or en-

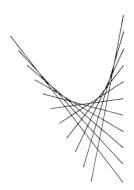

gineer is not building the project by himself. As a result of this, freedom of imagination is curtailed. The tendency is not to take risks. If the building is built in proven ways, then those who commission buildings feel secure.

If a Roman master builder did not use stones but proposed instead to use a more economic method, his ideas would not have been adopted.

For this reason the engineering of a single project did not and will not change the environment in Roman times or today. But patterns will be set by small improvements, which eventually will accomplish far-reaching results.

Engineers are beginning to think in a different way. They are not so concerned with the extension of mathematical ideas but instead are concerned with bringing innovations to the construction industry. We do not seek innovation by designing more accurately or in developing sophisticated computer techniques, but instead consider changing concepts.

Part of this change can be seen in the design of tall buildings. Engineers and architects all over the world are trying to establish construction criteria for tall buildings. Tall building construction originally evolved from smaller buildings and is often an arbitrary extrapolation. As a result, solutions do not apply to the problem. A tremendous penalty is paid for this practice. If we see tall buildings as problems in themsleves, we will then find innovative solutions.

We cannot afford to experiment in the field. When an idea is committed to paper, the engineer has to be 100 percent sure it will work. We cannot put a new structure on paper without creating a new theory. Yet we know that until it has been tried the new theory is only theoretical.

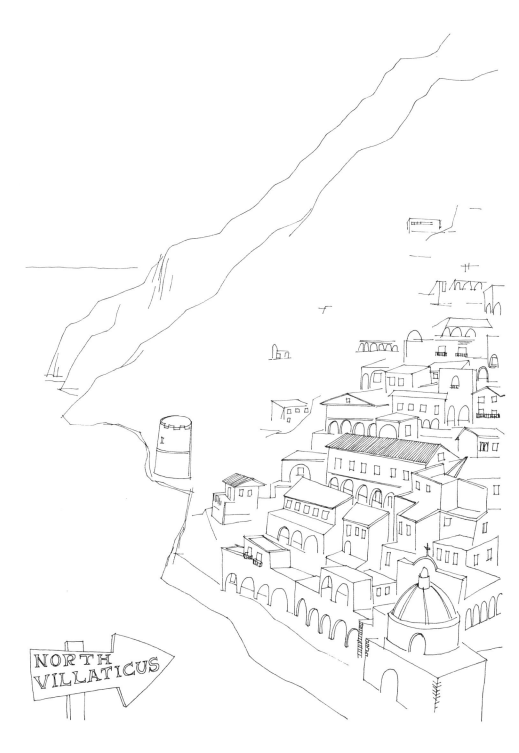

NORTH VILLATICUS

Underlying Principles

The search for engineering solutions must be directed toward underlying principles. We engineers must ask ourselves, what is homogenity? What is elastic deformation and what is not? Instead of asking these questions we all too often resort to intuition.

Intuition is not nearly enough; for example, it does not consider structural connections. When we think of connections, we should not look for the perfect single connection as we usually do, but instead the essential underlying principle of connecting. Once a principle is understood then the engineer can use his intuition.

The engineering profession fails to do many things it is capable of doing because of the necessity of taking shortcuts. If instead of a 97 percent solution, 30 percent more money must be spent to realize a solution that will be 100 percent perfect, the exchange is deemed too expensive. Therefore, the engineering profession seldom seeks perfect solutions.

Some of the engineering profession's attitudes are illustrated by the old story of the teacher reading to a class of children from the Old Testament. He read that Moses took a little stick, struck the Red Sea, and the water parted. A child asks, "How could it be that you can open the Red Sea with a stick?" and the teacher replies, "How can you question? The Book says so."

Many solutions in engineering are not questioned. For example, the code books say that every reinforced concrete slab must have a minimum amount of steel temperature reinforcement proportional to .02 percent of the slab thickness.

This ruling has dictated the provisions of every code in the world devised for concrete construction. It is obviously ridiculous. The same requirement cannot hold true for large and small, continuous and single spans. A garage slab obviously does not need the same amount of steel as an arch, and concrete over steel does not have to have the same reinforcing as concrete without a steel beam inside.

There is no reason for such uniformity of solution. It was discovered that the Americans copied this provision from a German building code and German officials did not know why it had been included. Further investigation disclosed that the idea began at around the turn of the century with an engineer

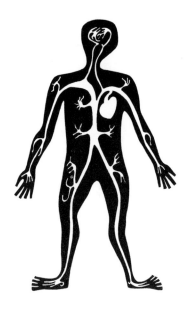

in Vienna. Experimenting in his basement, he determined that a concrete slab containing .02 percent of temperature steel resulted in the least amount of shrinkage cracks. This engineer published a paper and somehow his conclusions found their way into the Vienna building code. Today this code provision is accepted universally. A rational solution to this problem would save hundreds of millions of dollars.

There are a great number of similar nonsensical provisions in building codes and engineering books that presently have no basis in fact.

Engineering is not unique in this respect. The same condition applies to a number of other professions. The physical structure of a person, the wonderful wholeness that keeps flesh and bones together, is a wonderful example of structural engineering. Yet dentists employ primitive engineering and doctors repair bones empirically, not scientifically.

The inept repair work accorded the marvelously engineered human body is much less than the human body deserves. If doctors and dentists would analyze these problems in terms of stress concentrations and the remedial measures available to them through engineering, a revolutionary advance would occur in the medical professions.

Dental bridges are built by art and craft, not science. Engineering could devise better dental bridges and artificial limbs, and technology could develop a systematic approach. If dentists, doctors, and engineers could work together, they would find that, while none of their professions had the answers, they could discover them together.

We must rethink all of the theories we have taken for granted. We must, for example, rethink the concept of elastic strain. We have assumed that material is elastic. We retain an unchanging concept of the modulus of elasticity.

Thousands of books have been based on this idea, yet it is essentially false. What occurs if the beam is composed of little pieces and creates rigid body slippage? We do not have a theory for this beam yet we build precast concrete beams like it every day.

These beams are calculated as if they were elastic, yet no one has had the courage to say we are applying erroneous theory. We have theories that describe this condition but we do not use them. If we developed such theories, they would form the basis for new discoveries.

What is buckling? It has nothing to do with strength. Buckling is purely involved with the geometric properties of a structural member. Given two columns, one of butter and the other of steel with the same modulus of elasticity, identical in geometric characteristics, they will buckle at the same load. Elasticity has nothing to do with strength. It is concerned only with how a material elongates under load.

Buckling, like flutter, is instability. Flutter is dynamic instability, buckling static. It is surprising how few people comprehend buckling. My definition of buckling is a level of a state of energy. Buckling is incipient, concerned with a small delta of energy. Our building structures are in stable equilibrium. If you take a steel beam and bend it down, it will return to its original position. This is stable equilibrium. There is also the condition of unstable equilibrium. In this instance the object bent will not return to its original position. It will move away and collapse. For example, a retaining wall does not have to break. It may slide. Once it starts moving, the movement continues.

Finally, we have what is called neutral equilibrium. The object moves and stays, like a dead man.

With buckling, if you have a little movement, the movement continues. For some reason, any reason, it will continue. That is why buckling is referred to as elastic instability. Actually this is not true. Every column, before buckling, moves a little and stays. We do not like to consider this because we do not know where equilibrium stops. We know that neutral equilibrium can move over the precipice to unstable equilibrium. We know that even if there is no additional force to generate buckling the column will buckle. We know that there are always forces to generate buckling. We understand that all of this happens, but we do not understand why.

The problem is that we do not know how to measure eccentricity; it is not due to force times distance as we now explain the phenomenon. A good example is that of a telephone wire hung with icicles. A small bird lights on the wire and all of a sudden flies away. The wire gets excited. It begins to vibrate. It can excite itself into actually breaking. This is dynamic instability and is a characteristic of the geometry of the icicles and the wire. The energy put there by the bird increases into a much larger energy. The same phenomenon is even common with people. You may call someone a nasty word. He answers with a nastier word. Then he has a second thought and begins using more abusive language and jumps up

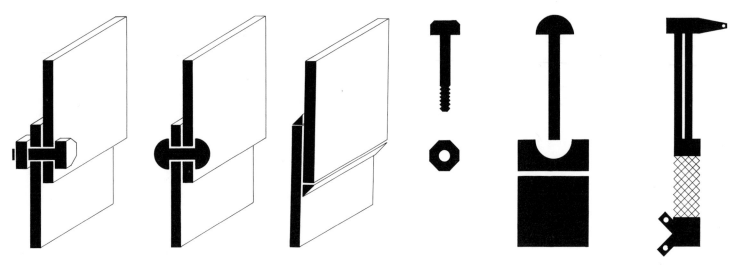

and down, getting more and more excited, and finally has a heart attack.

Buckling is an identical situation. The column bends more and more and collapses, but the increasing bending condition was not caused simply by the bending moment.

We accept a shape and create everything in that image. Precast concrete members were originally made in the form of steel I beams. Aluminum never realized its construction potential because it was designed in imitation of steel. Different materials require different form, and different theories. Someone must say, "Gentlemen, we are applying engineering theories to structures that do not apply to these structures."

Engineering books begin with conclusions. The knee brace used in industrial buildings will be described, with 55 pages devoted to how it is designed. The book will not explain why a knee brace is applicable to an industrial building.

A knee brace should be compared to a space frame and the logic of this comparison should be shown. The book should describe who plays what part in its design and who is responsible for its construction and should then go on to the engineering ramifications of these explanations. It is more important that the reader be provided with tools for judgment than that he labor over other's conclusions.

Another failing is the lack of engineering emphasis on how elements are connected. The average construction book will talk about elements 98 percent of the time. The other 1.8

percent of the book will be devoted to how to erect the structure, and the remaining 0.2 percent will describe the connections.

It may instruct the reader to grout all connections. But what is grout? They do not say grout is the key. During the Second World War the British started with precast concrete buildings. The problem then was grouted connections. It still is. When new companies emerged, they changed the elements but paid no attention to the connections.

When faced with a complicated structure 20 years ago, we found the analysis so complex that we changed the structure to simplify calculations. The engineer lacked analytical capability and tended to use structural systems that he knew. He would have had to calculate by longhand and compromise his calculations in the process.

With the new problem-solving technology the engineer can solve complex construction. That is one advantage; there is another. In the old days engineers simplified their analyses and in so doing committed innumerable structural crimes. We made construction inaccurate, expensive, and unsafe. Safety factors were not equally distributed. Today this is no longer necessary. We can analyze the structure accurately.

Felix Candella used hypars with no analysis. His analysis served merely as a yardstick for dimensioning, not as an indication of the hypar's behavior. He employed a simple beam theory and applied it to a shell. He could not solve the theory

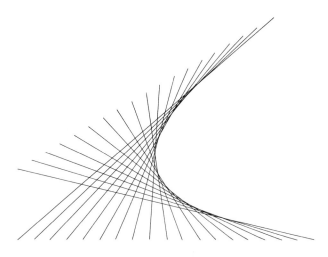

longhand because it involved a complex differential equation, so he simplified the theory.

Consequently, the only way that he could use a hypar was to test it. This he did by asking 100 peons to stand on its surface. From that point on he used intuition to extrapolate this questionable data. A great deal of creative flexibility is lost when the engineer is tied to an antiquated structural theory and applies this criteria to create new structures. To use such information for comparative judgment is permissable. To use it as a basis for design eliminates design flexibility.

There are no engineering miracles. Penalties must be paid for major innovation. The trick of good engineering is to save a lot and pay small penalties. If you save $100,000 at the cost of $100,000 there is no advantage. You must only pay a small percentage of what you save.

Creating any theory is only as good as its assumptions, and once you make an assumption your theory is not accurate because any theory is based on known data. Data must be fit to your assumptions.

The Theory of Intolerant Structures

During the past few years we have tended toward more precise building joinery. When rivets were used in steel construction, a tolerance of $\frac{1}{4}$ inch was permissable. With the introduction of welding, tolerances were reduced to $\frac{1}{16}$ inch.

Such close tolerances imply structural geometries other than crude columns and beams.

This is the wrong engineering direction. We should strive for an increase in the tolerance for error in present structural systems. Tolerances have become more demanding but building joinery techniques and skills have decreased. We will eventually realize this contradiction and develop building systems that make these allowances.

The methodology presently available to us must be utilized. This was once called "high-powered" engineering analysis. Sophisticated stress analysis, optimization, and mathematical simulation are part of this methodology today. For example, our analysis of the LaGuardia Pier did not develop new concepts. It required a tremendous use of methodology and interdisciplinary cooperation that eventually involved the spreading of the airplane wheel base as well as the design of the pier. The interface between the airplane and the landing deck were correlated involving aeronautic and civil engineering.

Factors of safety are used because engineers are inaccurate. The basic premise of structural design must be questioned. The solution to the American Airlines hangars utilized a light metal deck held together by random tack welds that could be bent by a workman's foot. The 10,000 tack welds did not demand precision. The average strength lay in the sum total of the welds. If 10 percent cracked, nothing would have happened to the structure.

The basic premise was changed in almost direct contrast to the present idea of increasing precise tolerances. Sophisticated engineering analysis made contractor errors foolproof.

Aerospace

The space industry opened new horizons by introducing new materials. It also introduced new methods of mathematical analysis, unique approaches, and other means of solving complex problems.

We can only benefit from this activity. Yet we cannot use the exact technology of the space industry. Their materials are much too expensive. A pound of steel in the space industry costs 5 dollars; in the construction industry it costs 50 cents.

Aerospace designers do not imitate the traditional solutions evolved by carpenters. They do not select details from a catalog as do architects.

They integrate systems and components because they enter the building industry without preconceived ideas. When carpenters think of a house, they consider each part assembled in sequence. The aerospace industry has the image of a house and does everything necessary to see that the final product resembles a house. The image rather than the components is their goal.

In construction the tendency is to begin with hand-assembled nuts and bolts. The aerospace industry does not think in this fashion. They invent differently from architects because they think differently.

A tremendous source of available technology has been evolved by aerospace. Its potential is barely realized. When the wheel was invented, it was used to do a thousand different things. We now have so many different wheels that we do not know what to do with them. It will require decades to realize the implications of the wheels invented by aerospace technology. The aerospace industry brings a different way of thinking about construction. This will force change.

Creativity—The Engineer

The function of the engineer is to build buildings that people can use and afford. He supplies data to be put in a system with little emphasis on emotion. The building is implemented by the architect's emotion.

Electric impulses in one's mind may have a great deal to do with creativity. Intuition is probably composed of such electric processes. Ten engineers with creative knowledge will all have electric impulses, yet, obviously, one will have different impulses from another. Each individual will be creative in his own way. Without knowledge these electronic impulses cannot be used profitably. Limited knowledge means limited intuition.

Intuition may not solve a bending-moment diagram for a complex structure but with it you can understand what a bending moment is.

The best stimulator of electric impulses is the desire to succeed. An engineer does not want to fail. He must evolve ideas that cause people to talk about him. He must prove that he is right. He must be ambitious and value his name more than material rewards, and value praise more than safety.

An engineer cannot tolerate being wrong. The motivation of proving a point is a prerequisite to success in proving it. There is no valuable intuition without knowledge, but you must have a motivation for that intuition. It is usually said that Emile Zola's interest in the Dreyfus case was justice. He did not take the case because of justice. He could not tolerate the image of the great Zola as one who had refused to participate. It would have damaged his ego.

When a husband is told he is a bad provider, he is ready to tear the world apart. He cannot let an image be created that he has failed to provide for his family. Any famous architect or engineer has the same attitude.

If a man makes a contribution to engineering in ten minutes, which is equivalent to that made by another man working a year, then the first should be paid as much as the second.

This is a principle little understood by engineers and architects. They think that payment should be proportional to their efforts and goodwill. When you think you are doing a great job, the tendency is to appreciate yourself. Self-appreciation is only that; it is not useful work.

The contribution of individual talent to engineering has not diminished. Design teams function around such talent, yet we no longer live in the world of the virtuoso engineer. A man with a special skill will make his contribution as part of a team. More and more people are beginning to know a lot more about less. The leader of an engineering office plays on various disciplines to make a larger melody than he would if he played by himself.

The engineer lives in a very clearly defined world. Construction technology is a tool; it is not a method of solving social problems. However, technology is needed to build more structures, at less cost, which will have social implications.

The engineer contributes to the solution of social problems as a citizen through his profession. He hopes that the leaders of the community will use the tools that he provides.

Idealism is futile. It is always motivated by personal interest or the interest of some group of individuals with their own interests. Man is what man is, a very inferior animal, full of greed and competition. He is also very generous. We live with these contradictions. Perhaps the imperfection of man is the perfection of life.

Engineers seem to lack concern about the large social pressures, although they seem conscious of the necessity of being active in their community and church. They can understand social turmoil and if there is such a thing as social aspiration, they comprehend it, but engineers seem little involved. They are given problems and they try to solve them. The engineer thinks it is appropriate to talk about human problems for five minutes while he eats dinner, but he can talk about a roof for eight hours. He believes that to solve the large problems he must first solve the small ones; that is, the problems closest at hand. For him this is not cynicism, but reality.

The engineer is a realist. If he got a job with a 7 percent fee and was forced to pay a 1 percent kickback, his attitude would be that he got the job at 6 percent with a 1 percent consultation fee.

Although engineers are involved in the design of separate items, people create in teams, not as individuals. Masses of people use the engineer's designs. His clients are usually groups of people. You cannot produce buildings or structures by living as an individual and creating in isolation.

Isolation deprives the designer of the experience upon which creation is based. The extrapolation of one's experience to the design problem is the basis of design. A student cannot, therefore, be equated with an experienced designer. A student can only be educated to seek experience. The function of a teacher is to educate students who will learn from experience. The teacher can train them to acquire experience. We can encourage a way of looking at problems that generates intelligence, that is, transforms the most possible experience into conscious thought.

A major failing of engineering is its lack of an interdisciplinary approach to design. For example, the automobile is not related to the highway, and rapid-transit vehicles are only marginally related to the railway. We are surrounded by designs, conceived individually, that must adjust to unrelated conditions as best they can. Little consideration is given to the interface. Interfaces require adjustment with mutually acceptable solutions.

When the engineer becomes involved with things outside of his profession, he broadens himself as an engineer. He acquires a greater working base on which to find solutions and stimulate his thinking.

The merger of an office into a larger multiprofessional combination allows the engineer to experiment with risky projects. For example, a large office can research rapid-transit problems, mass housing, or any current problem—giving the engineer a sense of freedom.

When an engineer has only his own office, he lives with the feeling that the next day he will go broke. If a client complains or a contract is lost, he feels he is finished. The principal of a small engineering office is usually the most humble member of its staff. He cannot afford to be a prima donna. A junior engineer might call a client stupid, but the principal would never do this.

The ordinary engineering office cannot hire all the specialists it needs. A conglomerate or large company can simultaneously engage in a number of fields. This is of great importance in interdisciplinary work and the significance of conglomerates to the engineering profession.

Optimization

Optimization means different things to different people. If a function such as weight depends on the parameters of minimum cost, labor, time, highest strength of materials—and I want to optimize a beam in relation to these parameters—then optimization would mean the following: There is a relationship between cost and the various parameters. For example, doubling materials means doubling cost. Double labor means triple cost. Double time in construction means quadruple cost. You now have a function. The cost depends on the relation between functions and each of the parameters. Minimization can be obtained in relation to any one of these factors. Mathematically one function can be made zero. However, in respect to another parameter—such as labor—the cost may be so high and time of construction so long that the cost would be so large that it would no longer be optimum.

The optimum is a compromise involving all parameters. Today's optimum may involve one emphasis, yesterday's another, and tomorrow's another.

In Roman times labor was so cheap and material so expensive that the optimum relationship was much different than it is today. The Romans used slaves, and had no labor parameters. Their only parameter was the number of rocks they were willing to cut and true. When Romans built arches, they did not consider how much labor was used. Today the problem is the opposite, the labor is important, the complexity of the design is unimportant. Optimization is taken at a point in time in respect to the values prevalent at that time.

Our time generates dominant factors within the equation of optimization. You have to be sensitive to these factors and adjust your thinking to the prevalent market.

Optimization is more easily realized using the capabilities inherent in the computer. What are the optimizing factors that have to be considered? Today's problems demand we bring all the elements into focus. Yet the human mind cannot consider a great number of variables. We are capable today of deriving form through the process of considering all the minute details influencing each of the parameters. We can calculate accurately the man-hours, as a factor, in the choice of a system. Ten years ago such decisions were derived by haphazard judgment.

Engineering design today derives form as the result of various inputs. It is not arbitrary or imaginary. Although designers say they develop form arbitrarily, their mind is a working computer. Form is the result of subconscious evaluation. The difference today is that the starting point of the building concept has shifted.

A generation ago the starting point was a formal aesthetic. Today, at one end of the spectrum, form is of almost no importance. Spaces, costs, building time, and the technique of building assembly are the essential elements. The degree of influence exercised on the design by the various factors changes with individual designers.

Some still design with formal prejudice. When an architect designed a library 20 years ago, only the form of the library counted. Today it is completely different. Even consciously formal architects such as Paul Rudolph recognize the mundane facts of construction.

Such changes are tantamount to a revolution in engineering.

The Emergence of a New Geometry

Our national objective is to build four times what already exists. Yet we cannot provide more, in the traditional way, with-

out straining our national resources to the breaking point. How can engineering do this at a fraction of today's cost?

It is obvious that present structural theories cannot solve a problem of such magnitude. At best present methods will reduce man-hours and material consumption by a fraction. The alternative is new methods, new theories of structure, and new materials, which will inevitably result in drastic new building geometries.

We will accept the new forms as we begin to live in spaces different from the cubes of traditional building, much the same as we changed from knickerbockers to long pants. With new living spaces, we will accept new materials.

This is part of the changing condition of building design. As the building process becomes interdisciplinary, the engineer is forced to consider architectural requirements, the construction sequence, the field conditions, the materials, and the economy of the enterprise. Building owners turn to construction managers, engineers, and system methodologists before architects because architects do not seem capable of considering all parameters.

Architects could exercise design alternatives. For example, Iron Curtain countries do not have design teams. Building components are numbered and ordered as if they were Erector Sets. Projects are controlled by coordinators who may or may not be architects.

Building components will eventually be industrialized in the U.S. A component catalog system is inevitable. It is doubtful that U.S. systems will be as inflexible as European systems with such little opportunity for architectural planning or expression. There will be a variety in U.S. systems but design will be very much different than it is today.

Innumerable standardized systems already exist within our construction process. But we use them in the wrong way. Instead of employing them for design flexibility we standardize them into uniform building shapes, often at great cost and effort.

The press of our needs will force us to devise new building geometries very quickly. There will be a period of readjustment. A form of brainwashing will take place similar to our adjustment to glass office buildings. Many people were originally opposed to metal curtain walls, but they represented the right dollar amount so we adjusted our thinking to accommodate their appearance.

What is building aesthetics? How much of aesthetics is due to impressions formed in our minds? When I was young, I thought Notre Dame was beautiful and the Panama Canal a triumph of engineering. When I grew up, I was given a tour of the Panama Canal. It was obviously no engineering triumph. Two hundred thousand coolies simply dug a ditch.

Later when I saw Notre Dame, with the clunky columns, and spaces that nobody could use, and that nonsensical roof, I was not impressed. I had the feeling that if I had seen Notre Dame uncolored by childhood admiration, I would have thought it ridiculous.

At one time Westminster Abbey impressed me. All I like now are the sculptured effects of some of the cornices. Are these buildings pretty or do we like them because of childhood impressions?

In the Soviet Union 77 percent of the women are fat. I am convinced that Russian men like sex as well as American men. When I first looked at Russian women, I had no desire for sex. But when I had been in Russia for about a week, I appreciated the new geometry.

Our present and future economic climate dictates optimization in the economy of construction and it can only be achieved with the employment of new forms.

There are basic criteria to be used in approaching this problem. Very simple constructions systems must be developed. The product itself can be complex but the assembly must be simple even though it is the result of sophisticated technology. I have always sought to use sophisticated engineering to optimize the flow of stress. It seems the more complex a structure is to design, the better the structure will be. I sometimes, therefore, seek out the most difficult structure that will satisfy the requirements. Very often it turns out to be the best structure in all of its other aspects.

The revolution in construction, as in other technical fields, will be in the hands of a limited number. For example, the computer has revolutionized almost every operation for which it is used, yet it is operated by pushing buttons.

During the past 20 years we have become increasingly accurate. Rivets in steel construction allow $\frac{1}{4}$ inch tolerance; welding reduced tolerances to $\frac{1}{16}$ inch.

A steel member 1 inch off dimension cannot be welded or riveted. We must, therefore, consider different systems other than spanniing steel beams between steel columns. For example, the light guage deck in metal buildings spans between steel beams and has a much greater tolerance than the steel beam—the folded plate sections simply overlap. Changes are possible utilizing available technology and methodology.

In the redesign of the LaGuardia Airport Pier we guessed that it could sustain an airplane three times as heavy as those specified. An extremely accurate analysis combined with certain adjustments to the airplane itself made the pier three times as effective. No new building methodology was developed.

Engineers are inaccurate because they calculate simply. The question is: how inaccurate are they? In the case of complex structures the answer is very inaccurate. Therefore, new methodologies must be evolved.

The geometry of the structure must be used in the engineer's thinking. The present practice is to design buildings to conform to preconceived geometries. A house is a box, an office building is a square tower. The engineer calculates structures with preconceived geometric forms in mind.

The construction process, techniques of building assembly, the air-conditioning system, and the plumbing system all influence the structural geometry. If the functional need, the planning of spaces, the aesthetics, and structural inputs are fit into the design simultaneously, the correct geometry will result.

This simultaneous combination might generate the living spaces we will eventually use. The result might mean we no longer build boxes or square spaces.

Social problems are created by the inadequacy of our physical environment. An improvement in the physical environment may improve the social environment. The physical environment, of course, is not everything, but it is a significant part.

We have to build more to solve social problems. If we build conventionally, economic limitations will force us to outstrip our resource capabilities.We can either not build or build with 5 percent of conventional material using new high-strength materials with 1 percent of the weight. To do this, new geometries are necessary.

2 Incremental Change

Incremental change marks a transition period in the form of the built environment as radical engineering innovation lies hidden behind the façades of conventional buildings. Subjecting past empirical solutions to exact analysis using sophisticated engineering techniques has improved the engineer's ability to optimize. But the implications are much greater than the simple immediate objective of reducing building costs. Minor economies often involve major changes in structural concepts.

A century and a half ago the simple wire nail and the milling of lumber to 2-inch thickness totally altered concepts of American house building. The need for skilled joiners required to fit heavy timbers together and the work force that had to be gathered together to erect the building was eliminated. A farmer, his wife, and their son could nail their house together.

These small, seemingly insignificant changes were the basis of a unique American building form, the balloon-frame house. In the short span of fifty years these houses covered the prairies and the gold fields of California and Alaska. The wire nail and the scantling helped to house a nation in flimsy houses, formed the basis of a prefabricated housing industry, and burned very satisfactorily in the Great Chicago Fire.

The manufacturers of the wire nail, the millowners who cut their logs into scantlings, or the carpenters who devised the framing system had in effect revolutionized the house-building techniques of a nation. Hidden in the incremental changes occurring today may be similar revolutionary building techniques.

There is one certainty about technical innovation. Its virtue is never questioned and its consequences cannot be predicted.

Evolution—Incremental Change

The age of great discoveries such as those made by Edison are over. Today the discovery of ideas could be compared to exploration for oil. In the old days it was only necessary to drill—oil was everywhere. Oil exploration today is difficult because most available fields have been exploited. We cannot invent anything new in construction. We can only formulate construction processes and promote team cooperation.

Several million steel beams have been used in New York City during the past 20 years, yet there were only about four hundred groups of beam sizes. All beams fell into one of these categories. The buildings on Twelfth Street had identical beams to those used on Seventy-second Street. Yet each of those 20 million beams required a sheet of computations for the beam's design.

The paradox is that each beam is custom-fitted yet all are mass-produced. They are used under similar circumstances demanded by the same building code. The immediate construction breakthrough may not involve a change in beam design, but the simpler use of beams in a more accurate and creative way. In the future, building components will offer much more flexibility in construction than the limited options offered by today's beam production.

A technological breakthrough requires new management techniques. Conventional construction has an established management pattern that has existed for hundreds of years. A new manager of any operation will try to streamline a few operations. He will work with given entities but will not invent. Creative management requires creative attitudes and creative tools, not simply streamlining. Technology may offer these tools.

The automobile manufacturing process and the building process are often compared; this is dangerous unless comparisons are clearly defined. There will be much more flexibility in building in the future, through the introduction of numerous factory-made components similar to those found in the auto industry. They will be unique components individually ordered but not individually manufactured. The factory may manufacture and store them. The problem is essentially the managerial problem of distribution.

The requirement for skilled labor will diminish in the near future. The engineering and construction industry will direct its efforts toward improving our existing means of construction. The Romans taught us that construction must evolve, it cannot be revolutionized. Progress is slow and daily undiscernable. Change is discernable over a period of years, yet will eventually be so extreme it will appear revolutionary.

We may anticipate a shift in the relationship between design and the types of materials and construction techniques used. In the beginning manufacturing techniques and construction will dominate and engineering will change of necessity.

This is why, for the time being, we will continue building buildings with columns and girders. We will improve the rigidity of the structure through bracing. Dynamic gadgets may be introduced to resist wind load, but even these will not drastically change our present concept of building structure.

We will still build concrete-frame apartment houses with flat plates and concrete core stairs. The difference will be in the introduction of new structural partition components offering more flexibility. Perhaps staircases that can be erected more quickly will follow. An improvement in concrete control could give us thinner floor slabs involving slightly different engineering approaches.

Once techniques to assure rigidity and continuity are accepted, the next step will be to use them to dispense with poured-in-place concrete floors. In their place an industrialized floor could be dropped into rigid connections.

Today there are a lot of conventional projects and, in each, engineers are trying to introduce something that will do a little bit more toward shortening construction time or improving those areas that require precise connections. Anything that requires precision on the part of contractors is dangerous. It is here that errors occur and contractors cannot predict the cost. Drastic change will be cumulative.

During the last ten years we have seen tremendous change in tall buildings. For example, bracing has been moved from the center of the building to its exterior face, and building cores eliminated. This is a major step that would not have been accepted 15 years ago.

We have improved factory-made continuity connections to replace riveted, bolted, and welded field connections. We find more and more shop rather than field welding and a different concept of erection techniques has resulted. There is a greater acceptance of lighter materials such as structural plastics. We have prestressed concrete, which is much different from post-tensioning concrete in the field.

Shells are beginning to be posttensioned as well as the exterior surfaces of buildings. There are better epoxies, which give more freedom in finishing concrete with less skilled labor. Different types of walls have been evolved in apartment buildings. As a consequence, different concepts of detailing emerge.

Building assembly is now the reverse of craftsmanship. It is no longer dependent upon skill. Builders are primarily assemblers. Their skills have passed from craft to technology. The process involves skilled factory technology but requires little or no feel to assemble.

We have seen steel grow in strength during the past 20 years. However, as the strength of the steel changed so did its weldability, and welding became more complex.

The award-winning steel projects during the past few years display a marked change of form because of workability and labor. As connections became more difficult, such forms as the arch had to be dispensed with.

Stress concentration and brittleness in steel has been overcome. Two kinds of connections are used—welding and high-

Connections must be carefully considered, but the more carefully elements are connected, the more expensive the cost of their workmanship. Systems building is, therefore, quite expensive. We must think of industrialization because the quality of labor is rapidly deteriorating. Labor cost 5 dollars an hour last year, 7 today, and probably 9 tomorrow. The work done in that hour is worse than a year ago and will be worse than it is now in another year. Less is demanded of laborers—they have less training and are less disciplined. Fewer skilled men on a project encourages the introduction of second-rate laborers. As a result, few tradesmen serve a full apprenticeship. The engineer must design around bad labor. It becomes a factor because of cost, which forces product design change.

We cannot imitate the work of engineers such as Nervi. What was successful in Italy with Italian labor and the Italian concept of building would not be correct in any other place. We utilize management and machinery and devise systems dependent on them. As builders, the Italians are watchmakers, we are not.

Although our workmen are primarily assemblers everything is not assembled. The state of the building industry is somewhere between hand craftsmanship and total assembly. Masonry is still masonry and welding is still welding.

The situation in building is analogous to the housewife working in her kitchen. She does not have to be an old-fashioned cook. She can get everything in cans but she still has to cook the spaghetti. In building we must still do certain things; there is ready-mixed mortar but you have to wet and lay the brick.

Structural design is often dictated by fashion. During the last few years the fashion has been to be enthusiastic over European building systems. Yet every European system transplanted to the U.S. has been unsuccessful. Millions of dollars have been wasted. We cannot imitate Europeans. We can only duplicate other systems using the same parameters that they employ, which are not possible for us to establish.

We must therefore follow our own path, using the peculiar conditions of our situation. When we do this, we will establish successful American building systems. The process is slow, change is incremental. We are in the midst of an evolution, not revolution. The process is moving inevitably toward new concepts of engineering.

strength bolts, depending on friction rather than bearing. Welding continues to generate problems but there are better electrodes and corrective means of relieving bad welds. Structural members are becoming more compact and as steel strength increases, thinner steel sections appear.

The spans in buildings have increased. Spans of 60 feet are quite common in industrial plants. A few years ago we used a frame or a truss and purlins on 20-foot centers. Today cross-members are centered at 40 or 60 feet; they are fewer and heavier. It is more economic to fabricate fewer pieces using less steel.

There is talk of systems building but this involves connections. Bad connections transfer weakness to other elements.

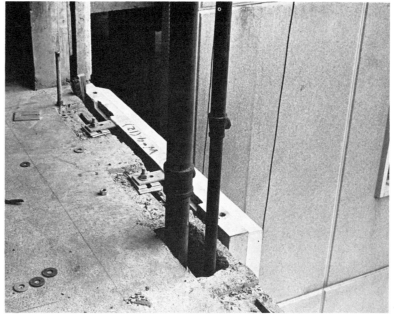

Slab Penetration

Mechanical installation is the major cost in building. The notion was that you could penetrate the slab only at the center of the slab, which is usually the center of the room, not next to the columns where it is the most efficient. The most convenient and economical approach is to penetrate the slab next to the column. It would save mechanical installation costs, but engineers did not want to follow this approach. The normal procedure was to pay the extra cost of the installation of mechanical equipment piping. The ACI limits the number of slab penetrations because the code is designed in a very simple fashion. They do not prevent you from penetrating the slab where you wish if you analyze it accurately. You can dispense with code requirements—if you can prove you are right, you can do what you want. If you cannot, stick with the code.

Slabs have very high torsion resistance. Torsion has not been a major factor in slab design because no one paid attention to it. Realizing that this characteristic can be used promotes design innovation and saves a lot of money.

43

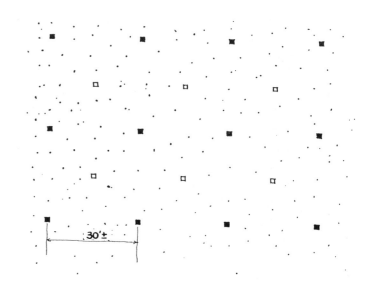

A New Look at Flat-Plate Construction

Excerpts from an article by Professor Seymour Howard of Pratt Institute, Architectural Record, *May, 1961.*

Flat plates in reinforced concrete consist only of columns and slabs, without drop panels and without capitals for the columns. The external form does not follow the distribution of forces as they vary through the slab and column.

Flat-plate design has been used with increasing frequency in the United States over the past ten years. Flat slabs with capitals and drop panels were developed for warehouses and factories. Flat plates have been found to have an advantage for lighter live loads in multistory apartment houses, offices, and hospitals.

The omission of beams and column capitals simplifies the formwork, permits ductwork and piping to be run without obstruction, and usually reduces floor-to-floor heights. Although flat-plate slabs are typically thicker than those supported on beams, usually about $\frac{1}{36}$ of the span,

the total quantity of concrete may be less than in beam-and-slab floor construction. The amount of reinforcing steel is usually greater.

One of the advantages of flat-plate construction is the freedom in column location, sometimes called "spatter column" design. Irregular column spacing requires more complicated and hence more expensive structural calculations than regular spacing. Irregular bays necessitate variations in sizes and lengths of reinforcing bars, increasing the cost of placing reinforcement.

A concrete flat slab acts differently than a steel plate of similar span because the stiffness and the strength of the concrete varies with the amount of reinforcement. When the spans, slab thickness, and column dimensions are given it is not impractical to accurately calculate the deflections and hence the moments at any point on a steel plate under a given loading condition because the material is uniform throughout. With concrete these conditions vary with the mix of the concrete, and the amount and distribution of reinforcement, the age of the concrete and the duration of loading.

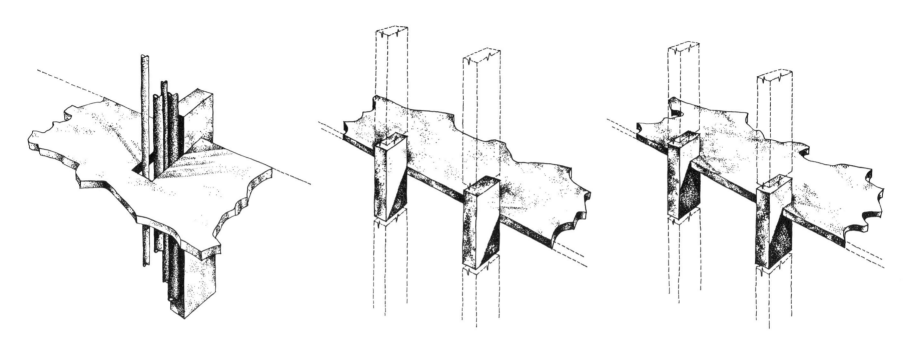

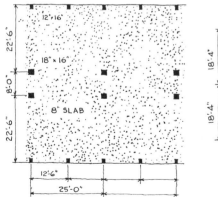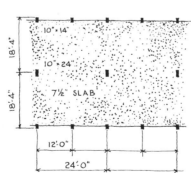

Although the most economical spans for flat plates are in the 16- to 24-foot range, Zetlin has designed 11-inch-thick flat plates spanning 36 feet for the East Branch Public Library in Yonkers, New York. He also developed an ingenious method of preventing excessive deflections in long spans without using such great thicknesses. For example, a thin slab with a span of 30 feet is calculated with the four corner columns providing necessary moment connections as well as support. Since this will give considerable deflection at the center, another column is introduced as a prop to remove the deflection. This center column can be more slender than the corner columns.

The total number of columns are only doubled, while with the conventional solution of cutting all the spans in half, the number of columns would be quadrupled.

Zetlin has used a similar device to reduce deflections along the outside edge of a slab and to reduce the torsional moments on the exterior columns. The spacing of the columns along the façade is half that of those on the interior, again minimizing obstructions to free planning flexibility.

45

Connection Between Slab and Column

Much more critical than the general reinforcement of the slab or the placement of columns is the connection between the slab and column, particularly if the columns are at the edge of the slab. There is a danger of failure if this connection is not adequately designed.

There has been a reluctance to use flat-plate design because some engineers do not believe sufficient stiffness can be provided in the column-slab connection to resist horizontal forces such as wind and earthquake.

This problem is generally overcome by using spandrel beams, which stiffen the edges of the slab as well as provide an increased area of contact between slab and column. Openings in the slab near the column have been generally avoided.

Under the pressure of mechanical engineers demanding pipe, duct, and conduit space and because of the money-saving advantages of simpler formwork, Zetlin has found that the spandrel beam can be omitted and that openings of considerable size can be provided next to the columns. To do this, advantage must be taken of the true shearing strength of concrete and of the great increase in stress resistance achieved by combining the concrete with additional reinforcing around the edges of the section.

The problem can be considered in terms of three possible failures, first imagining the concrete to be unreinforced. Taking the worst possible case, with a large opening next to the column, the first drawing indicates the familiar "diagonal tension" failure. Although concrete is strong in shear, about half as strong as in compression, it is weak in tension and cannot resist the tensile stresses which occur along a plane at 45 degrees to the planes of maximum shear. This is prevented by diagonal bars or by vertical stirrups.

The second drawing shows failure in tension due to negative bending. The top steel will prevent this. The region of negative bending will typically extend out about $\frac{1}{5}$ of the span from the column.

46

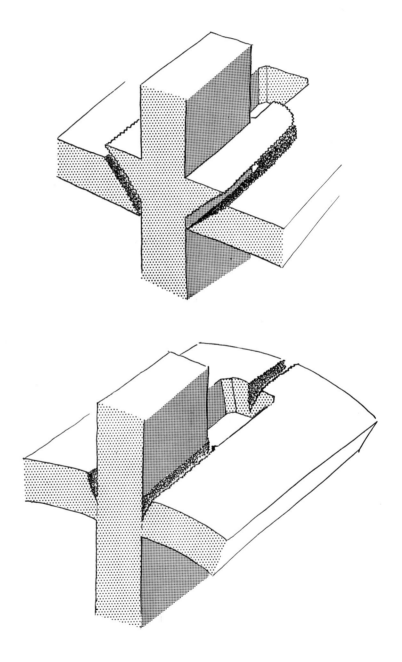

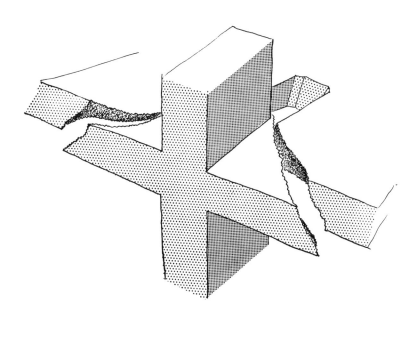

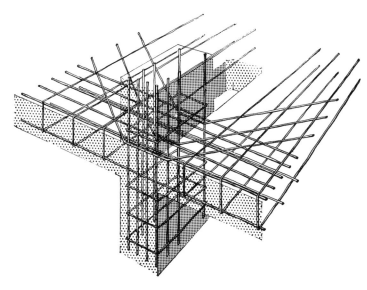

The third drawing shows the most dangerous possibility and the one most likely to occur. This is torsion of the slab, which is twisted away from its connection to the column. Just as vertical shear results in tension failure in concrete, so shearing stresses due to torsion cause tensile stresses to occur along a surface laying at 45 degrees to the surface of maximum shear.

Similar failure, with tension along a helicoid surface, can be seen by twisting a piece of ordinary chalk or a square eraser until it breaks. The source of the torsion of the slab is found in the rotation of the slab edge as the flat plate is bent, or in bending of the column as it resists the wind.

Analysis of stresses due to torsion arose chiefly in the design of machinery shafting. The French mathematician and physicist Barré de St. Venant published the first complete study of this in 1853. With a circular shaft, the maximum shearing stresses occur along the surface and diminish linearly along radial lines to zero at the center.

With noncircular sections, however, warping of the cross sections occurs. The maximum shearing stresses for a rectangular section will be found at the middle of the long sides, with no shearing stress at the corners.

The column-to-slab connection shown here is somewhat different because the warping cannot occur immediately adjacent to the face of the column and a greater resistance to torsion is provided. It can also be seen that the tensile stresses due to vertical shear and those due to torsion will tend to cancel out, except when torsion occurs in the opposite direction due to the bending of the column under wind loads.

The fourth drawing shows a schematic arrangement of the reinforcement as it might be placed to prevent all of these failures. To simplify the drawing, the general slab reinforcement is not shown. It is, of course, provided.

Analysis by Zetlin has shown theoretically that the stresses in the concrete in such a detail are within the capacities of the material, and experience with constructed buildings has proven the detail to be practical.

47

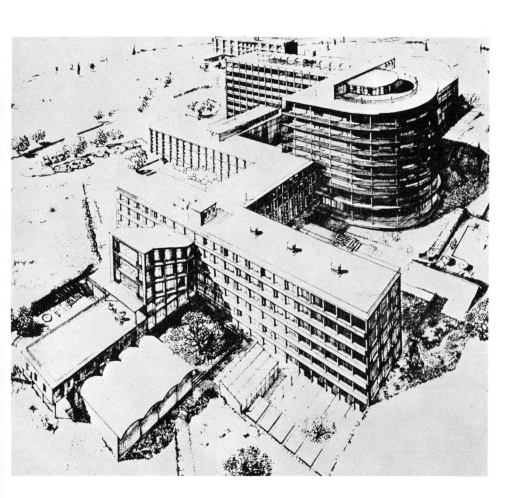

Hadassah Hospital

Hadassah Hebrew University Medical Center, Jerusalem, Israel
Joseph Neufeld, architect
Lev Zetlin, structural consultant

Shrinkage of Concrete

At a recent engineering congress I gave a paper on making concrete shrinkage your friend. The Romans used to unleash wild bulls toward their enemies, but sometimes the enemy would scare the bulls and the bulls would turn and destroy the Romans. Concrete shrinkage can be used as the Romans used bulls if you remain in control. Shrinkage can be used to prestress concrete without mechanically stressing cables.

The medical center was a large round concrete cantilevered building with radial reinforcement. I poured the concrete of the first exterior ring, then waited until it hardened and put other concrete in the middle of the ring. This concrete was designed for shrinkage. As the inner disk shrunk, it pulled on the radial reinforcing rods putting the exterior ring in compression. The slab will always be in compression and will not crack. This was prestressing without using mechanical means through the arrangement of a sequence of operations. Normally, this slab would have been poured in pie-shaped segments.

This same idea can be used in many ways. In a long building where you wish to eliminate expansion joints, flexible columns can be employed and alternate open strips. The strips will be poured after the main slabs have hardened.

For years it was thought that we have to install expansion joints every 200 feet. The reasoning was that concrete slabs

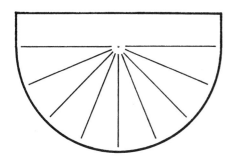
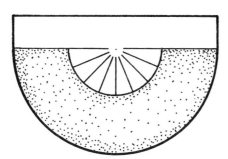
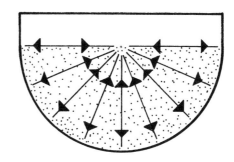

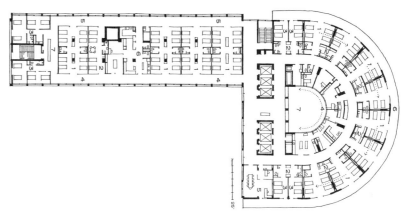

and columns increase by elogation as the temperature changes. The slab then tends to bend the columns. Thus column-bending resistance introduces compression into the slab. The danger is that the slab will buckle. If the columns want to bend and are too stiff, they exert a force that causes cracking in the slab. Double columns with expansion joints have been used to counteract this condition.

If a 300-foot slab wants to bend the columns 3 inches, a 100-foot slab wants to bend them 1 inch. A short slab of 100 feet wants to bend the columns less since the force is only one third. That was the theory. It was not a very comprehensive theory. The problem was not only temperature. Investigation showed cracks did not occur during temperature fluctuations but instead within the first six months to a year after the slab had been poured. Temperature variations had some effect but the reason for the cracks was concrete shrinkage.

Concrete shrinkage is equivalent to a drop in temperature. Shrinkage is not a linear problem. It is a complex mechanism akin to torsion that develops warping.

Shrinkage is a time-limited phenomenon. It is not cyclic. It occurs within the first year or two. Suppose we pour a long building slab in pieces and leave open strips. When the slab shrinks and bends the columns, the force is too small to cause cracks. One good thing about shrinkage is that 70 percent happens during the first 60 days after pouring. Wait, leave the formwork open for 60 days, then pour the concrete strips.

Kips Bay housing project in New York City by I. M. Pei was poured with shrinkage strips. Nervi did his UNESCO building in Paris without expansion joints. Buildings 1,000 and 1,500 feet long can be built using this method.

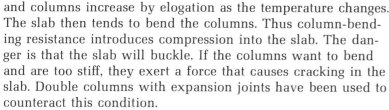

FLOOR SLAB —   SHRINKAGE STRIP

220'-0"

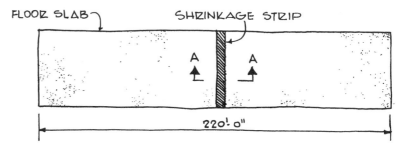

STRIP FILLED WITH CONCRETE AFTER SHRINKAGE

SECTION A-A

49

A New Look At Earthquake Design

It used to be said that an earthquake was a horizontal force. The ground had a horizontal acceleration of so many feet per second. Measured in gravity acceleration, if the ground accelerates at 3 feet per second at the rate of .01 G, and the building weighs 1,000 tons, the movement of the soil is equivalent to a moving force of one tenth of the weight of the building. If the building weighs 1,000 tons, it is assumed that the earthquake has a 100-ton force with the building acting as a cantilever.

We knew that this was inaccurate. When buildings failed under earthquake loads, we observed that there was little similarity between their failure and the horizontal forces we had designed them to combat.

If you are standing on your feet and are hit hard and resist the blow, it is going to hurt you. If you roll with the punch, it will be less painful. You absorb less energy because the punch is dissipated by your movement. Therefore, a building designed to withstand earthquakes should be flexible.

The principle is, simply, resiliance. An earthquake is equivalent to so much energy. If the building can absorb energy like a sponge, there are one set of conditions. On the other hand, if it can absorb only half the energy, the remainder will be used to break the building into pieces. Therefore, we have to design buildings so that they will absorb earthquake energy.

Thick sheer walls are unnecessary. This mistake is made frequently in Puerto Rico. Buildings are designed as rigid frames. You see the frames protruding through the rooms and corridors as you walk through them. There are other ways to control energy than brute strength.

An architect came to me. He had a commission to design a bank. "It will be the showpiece of San Juan," he said, "but I do not know what to do. When I design an office building or a bank, when the engineer finishes with his rigid frames, it is so clogged up interior design is difficult."

I told him the ideal situation is to build an absolutely symmetrical building, either round or square, and use prestressed concrete and no rigid frames. Use large, not short, spans and resiliant columns. I recommended channel columns spaced far apart. A large span will deflect more under load than a short one, which will absorb energy. Channel columns are less rigid and will deflect easily. He did exactly as I had advised and that was the way the building was built.

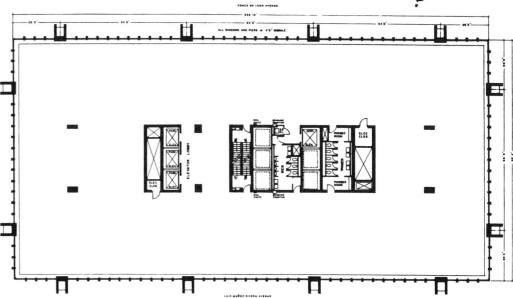

Banco Popular—Construction Notes

Banco Popular Center, San Juan, Puerto Rico
Architects Toro-Ferrer, of San Juan; Kahn and Jacobs of New York City
Dinos and Vafi of San Juan, structural engineers
Lev Zetlin and Associates of New York City, consultants

The 12-million-dollar building came in at 10 percent below the budget. It has flexibility of office space and meets the stringent earthquake and hurricane requirements of Puerto Rico. The shallow posttensioned floor joists kept the 20-story building 1 inch below the height limitation of 258 feet set by the Federal Aviation Agency.

The rectangular building is 210 by 104 feet with a central service core formed of concrete walls. The core walls contribute 75 percent of necessary lateral resistance to wind and earthquake forces.

There are 12 exterior columns, four on each long side of the building and two on each end. They are spaced 54 feet on centers, with the building corners cantilevered 24 feet from them. Because of the 54-foot column spacing, the spandrel beams are 5 feet deep and act as part of the building's curtain wall.

The columns are channel-shaped sections whose geometry serves to resist lateral loads. The space between the flanges is used as a chase for the perimeter air-conditioning system. The columns taper from a depth of 8 feet at ground level to 2 feet at top.

The column shape posed an obstacle to the posttensioning of the floor joists. If they had been cast monolithically with their full depth perpendicular to the building wall, they would have resisted the posttensioning forces applied to the joists. To avoid this condition webs were cast three stories in advance of the flanges.

The floors were posttensioned and the flanges added. Since the web is relatively weak in bending, the loss in prestressing force was negligible. The columns also resist vibration due to wind loads since the natural frequency of the exterior columns differs from that of the concrete core. Vibrations in the exterior columns are dampened by dissonant vibrations in the core.

The posttensioned concrete floors span 39 feet between the core and the long walls of the building. A pair of columns is located between the core and each end wall that supports a floor system of three continuous spans of 39, 26, and 39 feet on shallow beams and joists. Posttensioning reduced the maximum floor-joist depth to 17 inches and was the key factor in limiting floor height to 11 feet, 3 inches and finished ceiling height to 8 feet, 3 inches.

51

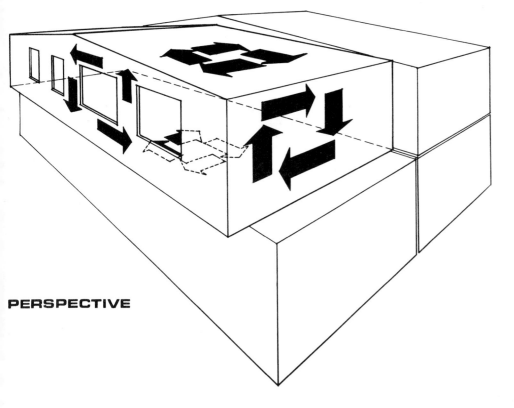

PERSPECTIVE

From Wood Frame to Stressed Skin

We developed a prototype wooden housing unit for Levitt Building Systems, Inc. to be mass-produced in factories. If we had had this project a decade ago, we would probably have ended by using a frame of 2 x 4's with a plywood skin.

Today we must consider production techniques and the dynamic behavior of transportation. We found that the solution was to forget the frame and use the 2 x 4's as spacers. The plywood exterior skin became the structure. We reversed the traditional procedure of fabrication of wooden houses. There was not only the structural engineering problem of materials to consider but the production technique, the way people work, and the way they communicate.

Traditional thinking is not always right. Levitt wanted wooden houses because that's what is going to sell. But he wanted them factory-produced. There were two problems: the first was how to streamline production operations, and the second was how to make the building strong enough to withstand racking, lifting, dropping, and other transportation hazards.

This is a new idea in wooden structures. Past experience suggested that wooden houses are always built with 2 x 4's, so the solution would be to reinforce the 2 x 4 frame, making it strong enough to withstand lifting and transportation stresses. But if you consider that strengthening the frame would make it three times more expensive and you must improve mass-production techniques as part of the problem, this was not the answer.

You will find that a house on an assembly line is very difficult to build as first a frame, then adding the exterior plywood skin. We decided to reverse the procedure. The plywood became the structure and the 2 x 4's were used as spreaders or spacers. When we did this, we got everything we wanted and improved construction techniques.

All we had to do was induce continuity to the plywood sheets. This was very important. We had to have a complete mummylike envelope. So we developed a method of bevels with U.S. Plywood Co. The sheets of plywood contact each other and are glued in a way that provides continuity and saves a lot of money. The design is a reversal of thinking about wood-frame construction.

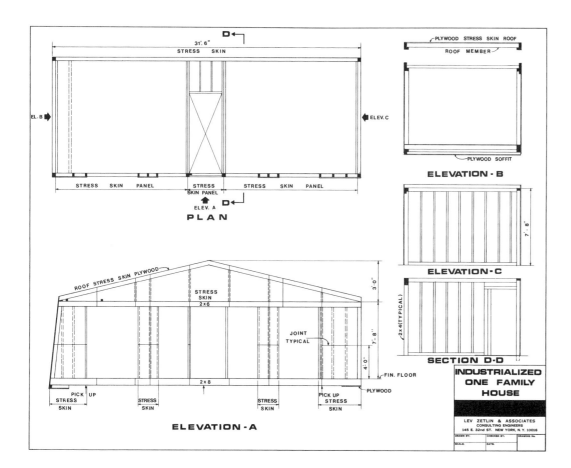

INDUSTRIALIZED ONE FAMILY HOUSE

LEV ZETLIN & ASSOCIATES
CONSULTING ENGINEERS
145 E. 32nd ST. NEW YORK, N.Y. 10016

Industrial Wood Townhouse Modules Engineered as Stressed-Skin Enclosures
Levitt Building Systems, Inc.

A structural envelope for townhouse modules to overcome constraints to industrialized production of a wood building system was designed for Levitt Building Systems, Incorporated by Lev Zetlin Associates.

The manufactured system is designed to be preassembled into townhouse modules to act as stressed-skin enclosures. The units were to be complete with kitchen cabinets and appliances, bathrooms, mechanical services, and carpeting. The modules were to be transported from the plant by truck for installation at various regional housing sites.

The structural solution was based on a modular box, 34 feet long maximum, 12 feet wide, and 11 feet, 9 inches high, to meet highway transportation requirements. Four modules, with two placed side by side on foundations and two stacked on top, were to form a single-family, two-story-high townhouse unit. Each four-module townhouse was designed to be attached to adjacent units on either side to permit optimum use of land and creation of garden-type communities.

The key to the system is the structural interrelationship of the module's stressed-skin side walls with front and rear walls, floor. ceiling, and interior partitions. The side walls of the module are designed as deep stressed-skin girders, using plywood braced by 2 x 4 studs, to carry primary loads to the foundations. When the module is assembled the interconnection of floor, ceiling, front and back walls, and interior partitions to the stressed-skin, side-wall girders results in a box that acts as a unit.

53

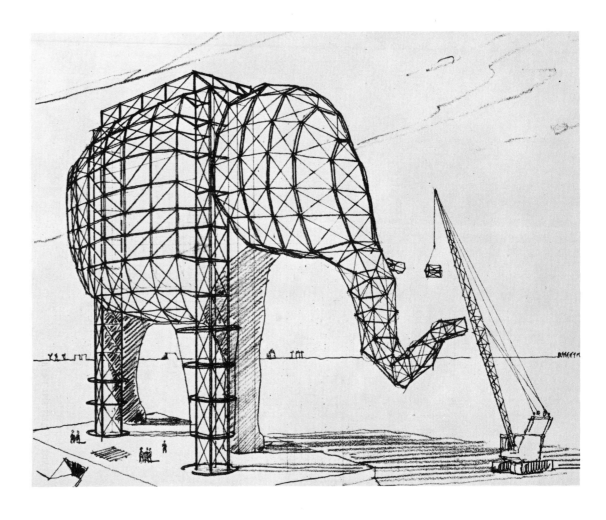

An Elephant Built Like an Elephant

An amusement park called "Circus World" commissioned the Lev Zetlin office to design a giant elephant measuring 120 feet from trunk to tail and 350 feet from toenail to pagoda. It was to be the largest "animal" in the world and the main feature of the park located in Barnum City, Florida.

The Zetlin engineers studied the bones now stored at the Museum of Natural History in New York City. They took exact measurements and photographs and projected them onto a large screen for an accurate sense of scale.

Instead of devising a frame like a building, our solution was to study the bone and muscle structure of the elephant. We came up with a space frame that created the envelope of the elephant. The strength of the space frame is distributed in the same way that the strength of the elephant is distributed.

We could have taken the center of gravity and distributed the weight and built it as we would have a tall building. The legs would have been framed towers. We would, or somebody would have devised an exterior skin. This would not have been honest. What we did instead was tremendously exciting and economical.

54

Barrel Pyramid

"Christo," the world-famous artist, had designed a very simple pyramid made out of a million barrels.

My idea was to restrain the barrels by tying them together with cables. The pressure on the barrels would be the same as that on a footing resting on granular soil. It is divided by the area that distributes the load. As you go deeper, the pressure reduces. By the time the pressure reaches 300 feet the load of the entire pyramid may be only a few pounds per square foot. The reason for this is obvious. When you compress soil, the grains are pulled together because of cohesion. The same thing would happen with the barrels if one would grab the other—the load would then be distributed.

The cables can be placed as much as 50 feet apart in all directions. The problem is to eliminate distortions. My idea was to build an interesting structure. Christo did not want that. His idea is pure sculpture. He piles barrels for the sake of piling barrels.

The idea is now the property of a famous advertising agency that represents a famous oil company. Not only is it sculpture, but the structure would serve a very useful purpose. They do not know now what to do with the barrels.

Sailing Mountains

Valley Curtain: Grand Hogback, Rifle, Colorado. Span 1,250 feet; height 185 to 365 feet; 200,000 sq. ft. of Nylon Polyamide; 110,000 lbs. of steel cables

It was to be a curtain 400 feet high and 3,000 long. I presume that if Archimedes could have created a valley curtain that he would have proven that the earth could fly.

Large gunboats had sails as large as 40 by 80 feet, but this was a proposal for a curtain almost 400 times that area. It was to be red and black, and stretch from the top of the two hills to the bottom with holes for animals to go through. It was to be a sail that could move mountains.

I proposed using a big plastic pipe at the bottom of the curtain and filling it full of water to stretch the cloth and using air-inflated tubes between the bottom and the top. Air and water are very cheap.

It was to be a screen like a hanging skirt, not a screen in the sense of a sail and Christo wanted it to flap.

When it came to actually designing the curtain, we told Christo that the first problem was to make certain that the material would be strong enough. The materials manufacturer assured him that it would, so all we designed were the cables.

In a curtain of that size a small ripple of wind is equivalent to a hurricane. Since the manufacturer said there would be no problem with the material, it was excluded from our calculations. We designed the cables and the connections.

The cloth tore apart in one hour. Christo was satisfied. This was art. All he needed were some photographs.

LaGuardia Pier

LaGuardia Airport, New York, N.Y.
Client: McDonnell-Douglas Corporation
R&D Directors and Consulting Engineers: Lev Zetlin Associates, Inc.

Structural investigation was performed for American Airlines and McDonnell-Douglas Corporation to determine the adequacy of the pier to accept the DC-10 Airbus aircraft. The study included yield line analysis of plates, lateral load analysis of piles, and effect of shrinkage stresses on load carrying capacity of a structure.

The reengineering of the LaGuardia Airport Pier in the late 1960s was an interesting program that proved a cornerstone in engineering development. It is a prestressed concrete pier in Jamaica Bay [New York] set on 200-foot-deep piles. It was originally designed to accommodate the 727. The engineering principles of the time assumed it should be designed as the roof of a warehouse. Such conditions as lateral loading and vibration to combat the localized effect of aircraft landing were considered. This may not have been the exact concept, but it was the starting point.

Live loads were assumed to be the equivalent of static loads. The old approach to wind design was to assume a 100-mile-an-hour wind is the equivalent of 30 pounds of horizontal pressure. This is not true. A horizontal wind of 100 miles an hour is equivalent to a 100-mile-an-hour wind, and 30 pounds of horizontal pressure is 30 pounds of horizontal pressure.

A 100-mile-an-hour wind, for certain kinds of buildings, could be equivalent to 30 pounds of horizontal pressure. But for another type it would be 20 pounds and for another it might be 200. It depends on the dynamic response of the building to winds of certain velocities, certain temperature, and certain frequency.

When the DC10 and the 747 were evolved, the entire issue of whether those two airplanes would be manufactured and put into service or not depended on whether they could take off from LaGuardia Airport, which meant landing and takeoff from the pier. If they were not able to take off from LaGuardia, they would not have been ordered. This represented a 2- or 3-billion-dollar market.

At the time, the notion existed that a DC10 that weighed ten times as much as a 727 would require a new pier. This represented 100 million dollars in new investment plus the political machinery that had to be put into motion by the airlines to convince the government to finance the pier.

We were asked unofficially by the airlines whether we thought that the pier could be strengthened. Our preliminary approach was to examine the pier as it was subjected to airplane loads, not to visualize it as the roof of a warehouse. By using the sophisticated methodology we had available as a by-product of the aerospace industry, we sought to identify loads accurately. It was our opinion that the pier could take these additional heavy loads without much reinforcement. We were awarded a contract to analyze the pier. We indicated that by combining an exact understanding of the construction and behavior of the pier with the unrecognized structural dividends that actually existed, the pier would support the loads as constructed.

One of the reasons was that concrete had been poured on top of precast concrete. The shrinkage of the poured-in-place concrete had posttensioned the entire pier. Shrinkage had contributed strength.

The bonus of this additional strength had not been considered in the original design. Sophisticated methodology, a year and a half of work, and 600 hours of computer time were required to make an accurate analysis. We showed that the pier did not need reinforcement. Conventional design is often three times overdesigned. If accurate methodology is used in the beginning, a great deal of money can be saved. We saved at least 100 million dollars and made the manufacture of these larger planes feasible.

This is what I term the science of engineering. It was not very creative, but you develop a fantastic sixth sense from such analysis. We used this sixth sense later, on our design proposals for offshore airports.

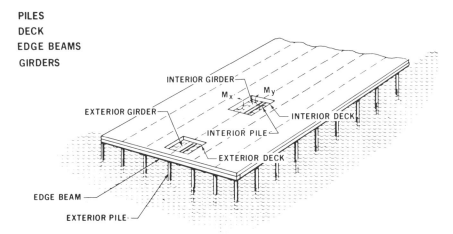

PILES
DECK
EDGE BEAMS
GIRDERS

INTERIOR GIRDER

M_x M_y

EXTERIOR GIRDER

INTERIOR DECK

INTERIOR PILE

EXTERIOR DECK

EDGE BEAM

EXTERIOR PILE

Munson-Williams-Proctor Institute Art Gallery, Utica, New York

Philip Johnson, architect
Lev Zetlin Associates, structural engineers

Concrete control was the key to building an ingenious two-way lattice-roof girder system for the Munson-Williams-Proctor gallery. Four intersecting girders afforded a columnfree interior above the main floor. Cast-in-place and posttensioned, they carry not only the 177-square-foot roof, but also a 30-foot-wide balcony hung 18 feet below.

Exterior concrete wall girders, 31 feet deep and 11 inches thick, cantilever 30 feet supported on eight exterior columns.

Roof girders are inverted tees, 129 inches deep, with 22-inch webs and 34-inch flanges. Two girders span east-west, and two north-south between the eight exterior columns. They form nine rectangular roof areas: four corner bays 30 feet square, four side bays 30 by 57 feet, and a central bay 57 feet square.

Precast double-tee roof sections span the 30-foot dimension of the eight exterior bays, bearing on exterior walls and on 60-inch flange lugs at the bottom of the girders. Twelve cast-in-place tapered ribs, 50 inches deep, span each direction in the central bay, forming a coffer. Plexiglass

domes cover the 45-inch-square openings, admitting natural light to the gallery floor below.

Balcony framing consists of 10-inch one-way slabs spanning 30 feet between the exterior walls and four shallow beams framing a 57-foot-square interior opening. Sixteen 2½-inch-in-diameter steel rods, hung from the prestressed girders above, support these balcony floor beams.

Zetlin specified a monolithic pour for the roof-framing to avoid construction joints, which might reduce compressive strength of the prestressed girders.

Some 350 cubic yards of concrete—the four girders and the central coffered section—had to be cast in one day. Under this condition, concrete for the prestressed girders had to meet these requirements:

• Ultimate strength of 5,000 psi at 28 days.
• Slow initial set, to avoid cold joints in the long casting operation.
• Good workability, to prevent honeycombing and voids in the deep girders crowded with reinforcement, sleeves, and cable conduit.
• Rapid development of creep, to obtain full girder deflection as soon as possible.

The admixture selected for the mix reduced water-cement ratio, increased workability, and entrained air for protection against damage from freezing and thawing.

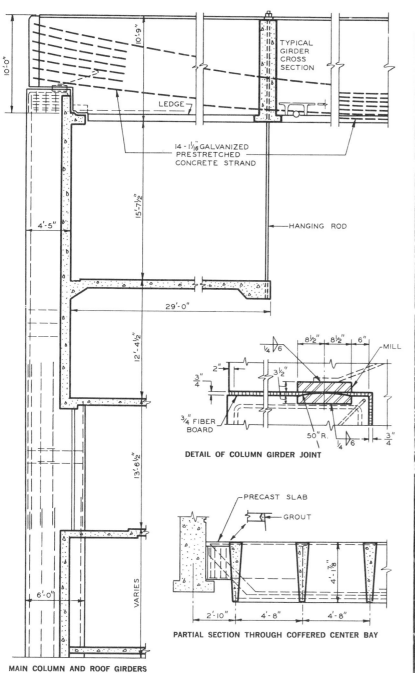

10'-0"

10'-9"

LEDGE

TYPICAL
GIRDER
CROSS
SECTION

14 - 1 1/16" GALVANIZED
PRESTRETCHED
CONCRETE STRAND

15'-7 1/2"

4'-5"

HANGING ROD

29'-0"

12'-4 1/2"

8 1/2" | 8 1/2" | 6"

1/4 6

MILL

2"

3 1/2"

3/4"

3/4 FIBER
BOARD

50" R.

1/4 6

3/4"

DETAIL OF COLUMN GIRDER JOINT

13'-6 1/2"

PRECAST SLAB

GROUT

4'-1 7/8"

VARIES

6'-0"

2'-10" | 4'-8" | 4'-8"

PARTIAL SECTION THROUGH COFFERED CENTER BAY

MAIN COLUMN AND ROOF GIRDERS

Concreting the roof required 16 hours from 8 A.M. until midnight. Two crews, each handling concrete from a 1-yard crane bucket worked from adjacent corners across the building. A third crane and another crew joined in at 5 P.M. and stayed to the finish.

Workers eased concrete into the deep girders through elephant trunks to prevent segregation. They had to vibrate thoroughly to work concrete into the 6-inch flange lugs that support the precast roof-framing at the bottom of the girders. Extreme care was necessary to avoid damaging the conduit for the prestressing tendons.

Concrete slump varied from $3\frac{1}{2}$ inches at the start to $2\frac{1}{2}$ inches during later stages of the operation to assure a uniform setting rate.

Crews posttensioned the girders two weeks after casting when the concrete had attained a strength of 4,000 psi. (Actual average strength of test cylinders at 14 days was 4,985 psi.)

Workmen threaded prestressing tendons through 14 2-inch-diameter flexible steel conduits arranged in two rows of seven each and draped in parabolic curves.

Tendons consisted of $25\frac{1}{4}$-inch-diameter wires banded together. Threading them through the conduit was delayed until after concreting. This averted the danger of kinks or bends hampering movement of the tendons in the conduit. Workmen lubricated them with liquid detergent to ease them through the conduit. Tendons were pressure-grouted inside the conduits after posttensioning.

Tendon anchorage works on the bearing principle. Two upsets at each end of the individual wires bear against anchorage hardware. This hardware consists mainly of a split-holding ring at the interior upset and a split-cone fitting inside a stressing adapter at the extreme-end upset. Threaded to a pulling rod inside a hydraulic ram, the adapter transmits the jacking force to the tendon and tensions it.

Zetlin specified an initial jacking force of 218 kips for each tendon to offset losses from steel creep and cable friction resulting from curvature of the conduit. This is 25 percent over total design tension, which is 175 kips at a working stress of 140,000 psi. Creep losses over the years should reduce the initial prestress to the design stress.

Prestressing added $\frac{1}{2}$-inch upward deflection to the 2-inch camber built into the formwork. It also shortened each girder $\frac{1}{8}$ inch. To prevent this $\frac{1}{2}$-inch movement from cracking exterior walls and columns, Zetlin designed a curve-surfaced cap plate for the column and a plane-surfaced bearing plate for the girder. Both plates were highly polished and lubricated. Measurements after prestressing showed zero deflection in the columns. The plates were then welded together.

Girder deflection under dead load was $\frac{3}{4}$ inches. Under sustained creep over the years the framing will approach a horizontal position.

Zetlin provided control of shrinkage cracks in the superstructure by leaving a 3 by 30-foot diagonal strip at the corner of each floor unpoured for a two-month period. After this period, during which almost all shrinkage occurred, the contractor concreted the open areas.

This same method of controlling shrinkage cracks was applied to the walls. The contractor left 3-foot-wide corner sections open full height and poured them two months after the original concreting operation.

Lightweight concrete, weighing 110 pounds per cubic foot, was used in all parts of the superstructure except the prestressed girders.

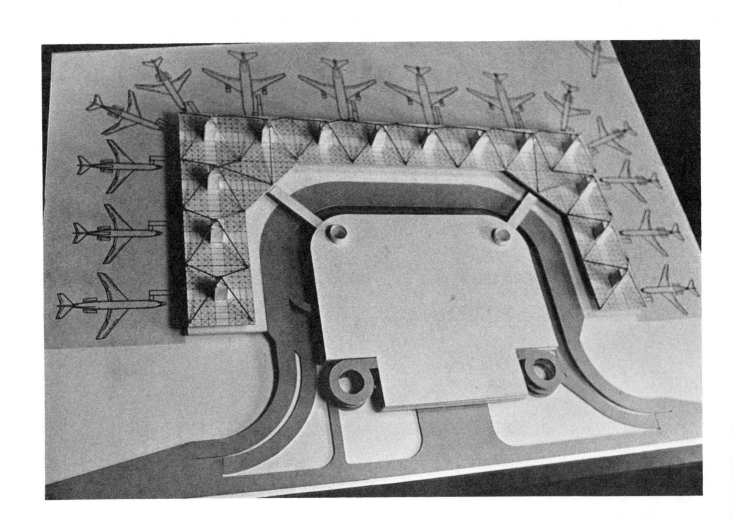

East End Terminal

LaGuardia Airport, New York, New York
Architect: William Pereira and Associates
Lev Zetlin Associates, structural engineering, grading, drainage
and soils analysis

Ideas materialize as the product of various thoughts and situations due to the necessities of a particular time. I have exposed myself to many problems in the past. My background is a fertile field of ideas that can be called upon to apply to a particular situation. Past thoughts and situations can be called experience. As new situations arise, experience stored in the subconscious mind can be used to cope with them. One idea generates another. All projects have problems, constraints, and requirements to be solved. A solution to a particular project is a compromise between the various factors inherent in that particular project. Optimization means that a perfect solution is not devised for any one part of the project but accommodates instead all the constraints and requirements, but none perfectly. The optimum is a compromise with equal emphasis on all the factors—cost, space, aesthetics, location, and available labor. The mentality of the world can be considered a major constraint. Once all the factors are stated, the problem is brought into focus.

For example, Eastern Airlines wanted to enlarge their shuttle terminal on the site of their present facilities. Usually the architect decides what the building will be in terms of his aesthetic requirements, such as the function of the building and the nature of the surrounding buildings. I started with another idea. The idea was that of "X" dollars, which was a very large number. I wanted to reduce it. The entire LaGuardia Airport is sited on garbage fill. The foundations of this terminal were to be set in the worst garbage dump in the entire area. The site was the biggest constraint. Piles would have been numerous, difficult to drive, and expensive.

If the thousands of piles required were reduced to a system of eight supports, the building would be much cheaper. This is not typical of engineers' thinking. Customarily they begin with the simplest solution, in this case numerous piles and grade beams. This is what I mean by imagination. You decide the best structural system by examining the constraints. One constraint was that we did not want 100-foot cantilevers. The problem became, how do you assemble molecules to create a 200 by 200-foot building in one unit? The answer seemed to be to build a mushroom cluster of modules around a stem and wrap a wire around them to hold them together.

The mushroom stem would be the caisson with the buildings attached to the top. This design would have required a lot of concrete. How the support of the entire structure could be solved without employing excessive concrete became the next constraint to consider. We developed a system that was a combination of mass-produced steel suspenders attached to the tower and thus reduced the amount of concrete.

The idea evolved was the result of considering the various aspects of the project in their entirety. We will never do another building in this way without the peculiarities of this particular site and program.

Niagara Falls Convention Center

The fact is becoming increasingly clear that instead of the engineer waiting until the architect finishes the building and then sizing the beams as the architect shows them, it is much better for the engineer to familiarize himself with the architect's problems at the outset. He should discuss the mechanics and conditions of the project and aid the architect in developing his first general ideas.

This was the method followed with Philip Johnson in the design of his convention center at Niagara Falls. The architect and engineer lunched together and talked about a building. Johnson had the preconceived idea of using concrete. The labor conditions for the use of concrete at Niagara Falls were very poor. Familiarity with good concrete technology was al-

most nonexistent in the area. The easiest solution was to bring in Canadian steel. Canadian labor has different characteristics than American labor. Analysis showed that it would be better to use welded connections than bolted, and transportation problems seemed to indicate that space frames were preferable to rigid frames. Under these conditions the architect and engineer undertook preliminary sketches to find the optimum form to suit these conditions.

The questions they both sought to answer were, What was the optimum space desired, and the optimum in transportation facilities that permitted a certain length of member to be transported? They found they could use a longer length member if the building was skewed, that is, turned on its side. The finished building is, therefore, skewed in plan. The concept was developed simultaneously by the architect and engineer without prior prejudice on either side.

NEWS Cahners Books

A Division of Cahners Publishing Company, Inc. • 89 Franklin St., Boston, Mass. 02110 • Tel. 617-423-4310 • Telex: 94-6314

*CR 081804

For Release: immediately

Contact: Dave Dunton

Review copies available on request

New Book Chronicles the Ideas of a Great and Original Mind

Some years ago, Forrest Wilson -- then an editor of Progressive Architecture -- was assigned to work with Dr. Lev Zetlin in preparing an article for the magazine. This started a personal project of intermittently-spaced interviews, conversations, and question-and-answer sessions with the noted design engineer. Mr. Wilson has now shaped this material into a new book, Emerging Form in Architecture: Conversations with Lev Zetlin (Cahners Books, Boston, 222 pp., $25.00).

Available in September, the book is written for practicing architects and engineers as well as for students. It reveals both how and why a gifted engineer works: his approach to an engineering problem, and the values that guide his thought. It also explores the results of Zetlin's thinking in a text liberally illustrated with drawings, diagrams and photographs. These show his ideas applied first in a traditional way and later in new contexts wherein innovation plays a major role.

The total thrust of the book -- its description of the framework within which a talented engineer solves problems -- is intended to offer inspiration to architects, engineers, builders, construction managers, teachers and students.

The author is currently Assistant Dean for Architecture and Chairman of the Department of Architecture and Planning at the Catholic University of America, in Washington, D.C. Formerly he was Director of the School of Architecture, Design and Planning at Ohio University, and before that Assistant Professor of Architecture at Pratt Institute. Former Editor of Progressive Architecture, he has served as designer and construction superintendent on numerous building projects. Mr. Wilson has written ten books and more than 200 articles on various architectural topics.

####

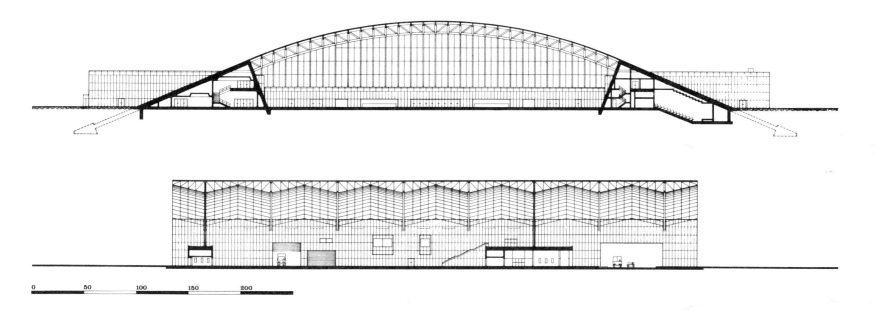

0   50   100   150   200

Niagara Falls Convention Center, Niagara Falls, New York

Architects: Philip Johnson and John Burgee

The 4,000-seat Niagara Falls Convention Center features eight steel arch-rib space trusses spanning 355 feet with a 70-foot rise. During the design, attention was paid to the detailing of the steel arches to assure ease and economy of fabrication and erection and to eliminate cross-bracing.

The facility's abutments are also framed of structural steel to allow fullest possible use of the space within. Since both end walls of the approximately 550-foot-square building are of glass, close attention was given to the effect on the glass walls of the structure's expansion, contraction, and deflections.

The resulting lightweight, modular structure contains butterfly trusses, spaced 10 feet center to center and spanning 60 feet between the arches. Crossbracing of the butterfly trusses was eliminated by designing the building's light-gauge metal roof deck to act compositely with the trusses. In addition to taking vertical loads, the deck provides lateral resistance to horizontal loads.

Tower of Light

Charles Center, Baltimore, Maryland
Architect: Rogers, Taliaferro, Kostritsky and Lamb
Lev Zetlin Associates, structural engineers

A 23-story office tower designed to rise in Baltimore's Charles Center, but never built, would have had a six-sided shaft sheeted entirely with glass with no visible spandrel or mullions. The 5 by 11-foot glass sheets of $\frac{1}{2}$-inch-thick tempered solar gray glass were to be fastened to the structure through stainless steel buttons and clips. The prime design considerations of the structure were a façade entirely of glass, requiring minimization of structural deflections and distortions, elimination of interior columns, and economy of construction. The structure chosen—to meet these criteria—was a slip-formed reinforced-concrete core, steel columns at the exterior, and a composite steel and concrete slab. The mezzanine, the plaza, and the commercial space were to be below grade and the 76-car garage was to be constructed entirely of reinforced concrete.

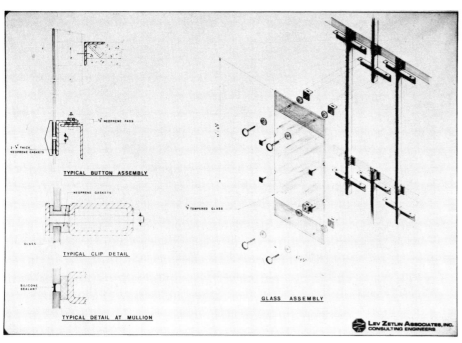

TYPICAL BUTTON ASSEMBLY

TYPICAL CLIP DETAIL

TYPICAL DETAIL AT MULLION

GLASS ASSEMBLY

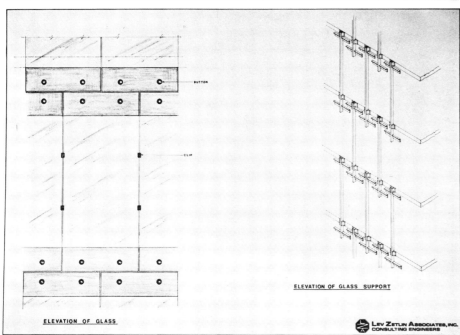

ELEVATION OF GLASS

ELEVATION OF GLASS SUPPORT

3 New Forms

As engineering sloughs off the egocentric pretentions of aesthetic form, new configurations emerge in our built environment as prototypes of things to come.

The phenomenon is not new. For a few years, from the early 1960s to the 1970s, the architectural and engineering professions were seduced by the idea of omnibuildings or megastructures. Their names indicate the inability to conceive them as entirely new entities of the built environment. We insisted on calling them all-encompassing or large buildings. The fact that such multiples of buildings had caused a qualitative change and were no longer buildings in the usual sense of the definition did not occur to their proponents or detractors. The new forms could only be conceived and identified in terms of buildings as we knew them.

Megastructures or omnibuildings did not have to be invented; they existed long before they were identified. The city megastructure or omnibuilding designed itself. The process is obvious in the form of building and settlement patterns generated by train stops, bus stops, and subway stations. The point at which transportation terminals punch their way through the earth, or are located on rails or highways, first spawns houses, then businesses, and eventually minor city satellites.

Buildings are also nodes on a network of connected mechanical arteries of life-support services: light, heat, water, sewage removal, and food supply. They are individually designed warts on the cities' life-support systems, as part of its organic growth. Yet we insist on calling attention to their individual significance. The new forms emerging in engineering are similarly the result of an unplanned, linked, and compelling process.

What follows in this section of Zetlin's work are the isolated forms emerging that result from a process that will shape the future of our built environment whether we recognize them as part of a system or continue to view them as individual phenomena. As Zetlin says, they represent "the right dollar amount." We will adjust to them as we did to miniskirts from Dior's "new look."

American Airlines Prototype Hangar
Maintenance Hangars for American Airlines
Constructed at Los Angeles International and San Francisco International Airports, 1970–1971
Designer: Lev Zetlin Associates, Inc. and Conklin & Rossant

The solution for the American Airlines hangar came to me at the opera. It was a boring classic opera and I could not fall asleep as I mused over the problem and how to solve it. I asked myself, What is a simple element that can be erected by simple people with a large margin for error? I needed an element that would not burn, sink, or twist, and if connected to a number of similar elements, would be very strong. Such a structure had not yet been built. There was, therefore, no design methodology. I was convinced that the idea was sound and once convinced of this, I knew the last act would be the design.

Connections were essential. I could assume these to be either elastic or rigid, but what they actually would be, I did not know. The task was to develop a mathematical design from which I could derive theoretical data from a number of assumptions.

Then the validity of the various assumptions must be tested against static, dynamic, wind, earthquake, and moving crane loads. I knew the structure would be lighter than the wind suction exerted on it. I could visualize that this particular roof would have a tendency to fly up rather than to fall down even under relatively mild wind conditions.

This is why in the end, in addition to theoretical design calculations, we resorted to exhaustive model testing. Models were made for all aspects of the design and the test data proved to be very close to our theoretical assumptions. We observed the structure after it was built and it confirmed our the-

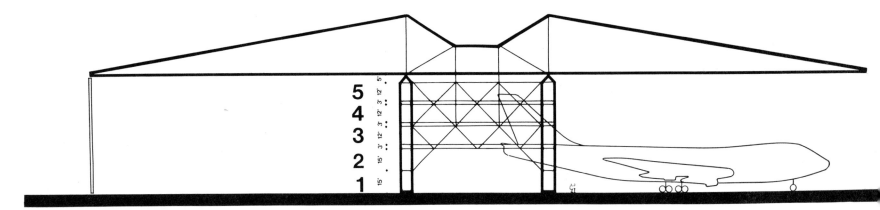

oretical data and model tests. The structure, in fact, proved more rigid than we had calculated.

But to return to the problem, how do you combine efficient workmanship, efficient time, simplicity of elements, speed of erection, and function? When you combine all of these in an optimum design, you arrive at a suitable form. But within this formal range there are a number of variations. If you look at the hangar as it was finally built, you will find a valley over the core that cut through the "T" form of the cantilevered arms. This angle was dictated by the tension force exerted by the cables extending from the ridges of the cantilevers. A certain angle proved the most efficient form. The form was the result of optimization. We had to cover a volume with the least material—that is how the form emerged. An architect might have determined that slope. It could have been built at a number of angles. But the depth of the cantilever at the core was dictated by construction requirements.

The angle could be played with because it was not important, only aesthetic. It was the only thing the architect could

have contributed aesthetically. We were the prime contractor and hired an architect. The building had suspended floors, staircases, and almost a 40-story office building in the core. It had 40,000 square feet of space. Computer, office, and service spaces had to be designed. This is the task that involved the architect.

American Airlines risked $50 million on a construction principle never used before. I told them it would cost $50 million instead of $58 million, the cost of a traditional hangar. If it did not work, they would have lost $50 million and four years' time. This would have finished them because the 747s were coming off the assembly line, and if the hangars were not ready, American Airlines would have lost another $100 million.

The Chairman of the Board had to make a decision. Under normal circumstances he would have had the hangars in three years and spent $58 million for each of them.

I realized his dilemma and that my first problem was to secure the Chairman's confidence. In war and in business mental attitudes are more important than anything else. To design

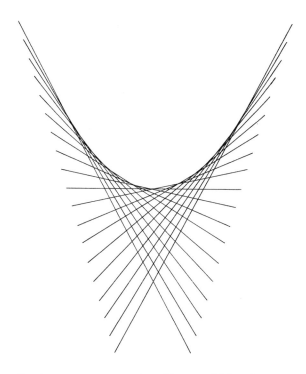

the hangars conventionally would be the easy way out. I also stuck my neck out and that is where I succeeded.

I tried to instill confidence in a simple elementary way. I brought them many extrapolated and interpolated examples; I showed them my "safety pins." I told them why. However, this was all just talk. A building such as this had never been built before. I let them know I had built many impressive buildings. That was part of getting their confidence. In itself it was not enough. They had to decide to take a chance.

We used hypars for roof covers to resist both vertical and lateral loads. This design was possible because of the continuing chronological development of these forms. Torejo worked over a span of 30 years, but in that time his work and the conditions of his work did not change. Today changes occur daily.

Since all steels have the same modulus of elasticity, it was necessary to devise a structural form that would make a strong steel stiffer. How to make the form stiffer in a 230-foot cantilever was the problem. My hypar has a depth of 40 feet at the core. If you look at the cross section, you will see that the

amount of steel in it is only 9 pounds a square foot and it has deflected only 1 inch or $\frac{1}{900}$th of the span.

A regular truss as a cantilever would have had a 40-foot depth, a weight of 35 pounds per square foot, and a deflection of 6 to 8 inches.

"I," the moment of inertia, times "E," the modulus of elasticity, is a measure of deflection. With two cantilevers of the same span, and the same loading made of different materials, if the EI of one is twice that of the other, there would be half the deflection.

The hypar shell has the same E but the deflection is $\frac{1}{6}$th of a steel truss. Why? The "I" is not important anymore.

EI is the measure of deflection when deflection is due to bending. We have thought for generations that the deflection of structures depended only on the bending moment. That is not true. A shell has different stresses than a beam. If you look at the steel hypar of the American Airlines hangars, you might say that it is merely a cantilever with a triangular cross section, but it is not, because its stress distribution is different.

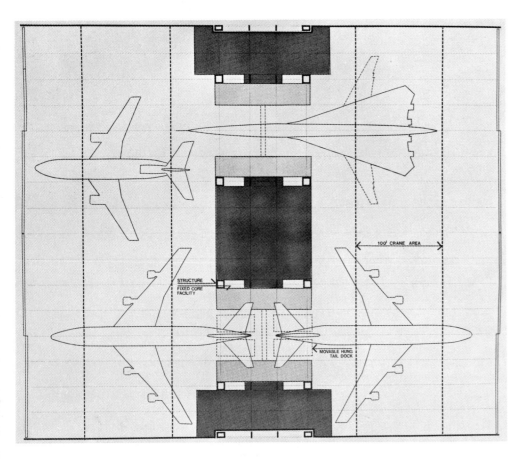

STRUCTURE
FIXED CORE
FACILITY

100' CRANE AREA

MOVABLE HUNG
TAIL DOCK

Napier and Verneuli told us that when a beam bends, the beam section becomes plane and the stresses are distributed in a certain manner. In a shell the sections do not remain plane and the stresses are distributed differently. Deflection is the result of cumulative strain. Even though the hypar looks like a beam, it has a different deflection.

For example, if you twist a round rod, you will observe that the round cross section rotates with the section. We know that this form of torsion creates shear stresses. It can only rotate by developing shear stress and shear strain.

Everything has a measure. The measure of that rotation is a property termed the polar moment of inertia. If a rectangular rod in the ratio of 1 to 2 had the same polar measure and were twisted, each cross section would rotate less than a circular section. It would develop axial stresses parallel to the axis of the rod, but these stresses would tend to turn the section back, thus reducing the tendency to twist.

The moral of this example is that we would have thought that the two rods would have twisted the same because the polar inertia was the same. Yet one rotates less because deflections do not take place. Its sections do not stay plane and they develop additional stresses that are actually helpful. The same thing happens with the hypar. The stress distribution is helpful. It tends to decrease bending. The modulus of elasticity and the moment of inertia have changed. In a shell it is not the product of EI that determines bending, but other properties. We are quite familiar with the example of two beams, both of steel, one rectangular and the other I-shaped, and both with the same amount of material. We know the I section will deflect less than the rectangular.

This is the advantage of skin construction; the cumulative strain is the result of a different kind of deflection. Shells have different shear and stress distribution. Therefore, high-strength materials dictate the use of different geometries.

Skin structures are skin structures because the forces are resisted by skin instead of bending stresses. Members that resist load only by skin stresses within the plane of their surface are very efficient because all the material is stressed. There is no neutral axis.

American Airlines Hangars

Extracted from "Hangar Features Stressed-Skin Hypars," by Charles H. Thornton and Richard L. Tomasetti, Civil Engineering, November, 1970

Two giant maintenance hangars for sheltering large jets, featuring a major advance in structural design, were built by American Airlines at the Los Angeles International and San Francisco International Airports. Their most significant feature is the innovative design of the hangar roofs: each is made up of 16 hypar modules, with each module roof, a hyperbolic-paraboloid surface fashioned from standard light-gage steel decking, and providing the primary structural support for the module, marking the first time that standard metal roof-decking has been used as the primary support material in a large structure.

The result was a 40 percent reduction in hangar roof weight and, therefore, substantial reductions in structure costs. Indeed, the prime motive for developing this lightweight roof system was to reduce the cost of such structures. This is an important goal when one considers the tremendous size of a typical hangar. Economy was achieved by developing a roof system that could be put together by mass-production methods using a conventional, readily available, light-gage steel decking. These hangar designs will serve as the prototypes for other hangars that American Airlines has programmed for construction at Chicago's O'Hare Airport, New York's Kennedy International Airport, Boston's Logan International Airport, and Newark Airport.

The secret to the structure's success is that normally used steel trusses that support the entire weight of the roof were not used. Roof purlins and steel deck, which furnish about 20 percent of the total steel roof tonnage, in a normal hangar contribute nothing to the primary structural support. In the hypar system, the deck serves both as primary support structure and roof surface: the heavy steel trusses are eliminated and the thin steel deck acts as a "stressed-skin" membrane to carry the roof loads.

The lightweight steel decking, twisted into a hyperbolic-paraboloid surface, is able to support the entire weight of the module because this hypar geometry carries applied loads primarily by means of shear forces

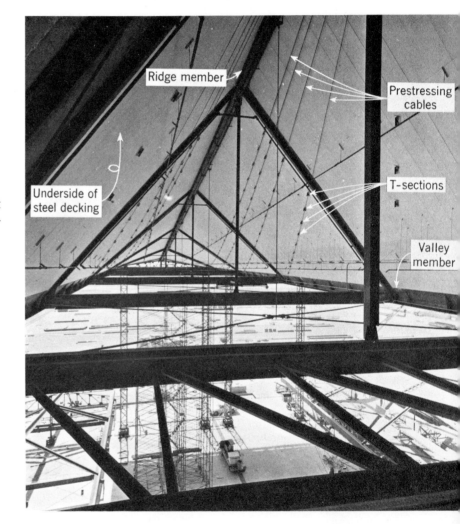

Central core

Hypar module

Ridge member

Valley members

Temporary towers

Hyperbolic paraboloid surface made of light-gage steel decking

acting in the plane of the hyperbolic-paraboloid surface; shear forces normal to hypar surface and bending and twisting effects are negligible. Since light-gage steel decking has a high shear strength-to-weight ratio, it carries applied loads with ease. Also, in a hypar surface, a uniformly distributed load produces a uniform state of stress at all points on the shell surface. Accordingly, the shell can have the same cross section for the entire surface, thus enormously simplifying mass production of hypars.

Since the superbay hangar design is a prototype, it must be sufficiently flexible to be used anywhere in the world. Specifically, the loadings on the hangar roof vary with geographical location due to weather, winds, snow, and other factors. To provide such flexibility, the module design incorporates a series of cables that run from a single point on the hangar core to various points along the valley members of each module. Tightening up on these cables or prestressing them tends to counteract the loads on the module, thereby relieving the shear resultant in the deck by as much as 20 percent. For example, in colder climates where snow-loading is important, the same deck configuration as in the California hangars would be used, only the load carried by the cables would be increased. Also, the cables provide a means for making minor alignment adjustments during erection or for controlling the natural frequency and flutter of the structure.

Another interesting structural feature is found in the way that adjacent deck elements are joined. A male-female joint between these deck elements acts as a bellows when tensile or compressive forces act perpendicularly to it. If no release were present, as in the case of a lap joint, the deck stresses near the ridge and valley members would become very high because of strain compatibility. Indeed, computer studies indicated that without these stress-relief bellows, the uniform distribution of shear forces throughout the shell would have been upset making the uniform cross-section roofing system unfeasible.

The structural ideas embodied in the American Airlines superbay system trace their birth to the 1966 study conducted by Lev Zetlin Associates for six U.S. airlines. The purpose of the study which has now become a reality was to define the maintenance environments that would be required by the advent of advanced aircraft.

Place Des Jardins
Modular Hypar Roof

La Société La Haye-Ovellet, architect

A unique use of prefabricated lightweight shell structures was employed to construct the new Place Des Jardins' Mall Roof in Montreal, Canada. The entire roof, spanning 180 feet in both directions, utilizes a series of repetitive 3-foot-square stressed-skin modules. The advantage is a highly efficient shell geometry that promotes repetitive construction operations minimizing field labor.

Each prefabricated module in the form of a hyperbolic paraboloid was fabricated with straight steel-edge members. Strips of prefabricated light-gage metal decking were placed along the hypars' straight-line generators, forming the shell. The decking, in the form of a hypar shell, has a high shear strength to weight ratio.

The decking forming the shell is composed of flat 13-gage sections; 18-gage stiffeners are spot-welded to it. The flat section is the main structural element of the shell, which develops the shear stresses. The stiffeners prevent local buckling and increase the shells' bending rigidity. The combination of the shells' bending rigidity and curvature prevents overall buckling.

A finite-element computer program was used to assist in analyzing the roof structure. The individual behavior of a single prefabricated module is predictable by classical methods of analysis for roof loading; however, special attention had to be given to the interaction between the modules. The computer program analyzed both the loads transferred between modules and the behavior of the individual module due to unsymmetrical loading conditions caused by interface loads.

Tension rings at various elevations and cables strung from four towers support the roof. The result is a clear uninterrupted space below the structure.

The shell geometry utilizes readily available prefabricated deck components formed into large prefabricated shell modules, taking advantage of industrialized mass production and thus reducing construction cost.

Cable Roof Structures

The justification for a cable structure is best understood in comparison to the structural methods usually employed to span long distances: the plate girder, truss, and arch. Shear, buckling, and bending instability are involved with an increase in span in the plate girder. The truss suffers from connection costs and depth of construction as spans increase. As the arch increases in span, it is increasingly liable to compression buckling. Cable limitations are only in dead weight and anchorage.

In a cable suspension roof, the cables themselves and their erection usually represent the smallest portion of the cost. The largest cost is in fittings, their connections, and the anchorage of members. Because of this cost relationship, suspension roofs are most economical in spans in excess of 150 feet, in contrast to the girder, truss, and arch.

When a continuous cable is used to traverse a span several times and an erection method is adopted that dispenses with fittings and anchorages at the end of each cable, short spans are economically feasible. With large spans, cables are extremely economical since the proportional cost of fittings to the area covered is greatly reduced.

Cables used in buildings can be classified into four groups: suspended roofs, vertical hangars or suspenders of horizontal floors from towers or abutments, auxiliary structural components of main load-carrying structural components, and, last, cables used as the main structural system of a building—including the structure below the roof.

A cable employed as a structural member is always under tension with uniform stress distribution through its cross section. The interest of the engineering profession in using high-strength cables, particularly in long-span roofs, is because of one salient advantage. High-strength cable is a material that is approximately four times as strong as structural steel, and is obtainable at a proportionately smaller cost per pound than its increase in strength. Thus, its use results in less weight of structural material, and, therefore, lightens the dead load. It is almost as easy to string a 400-foot-long cable into a structure as one 50 feet long. All of these factors are conducive to economy of construction.

Design of cables in structures differs from design of conventional structural components mainly in two respects: anchorage forces and dynamic behavior.

Since cables are always in tension, that tension must be resisted. This resistance can be achieved by various means. The cable ends can be anchored into foundation abutments, or into continuous structural members such as a ring or a similarly continuous, closed structural shape capable of resisting anchorage loads within itself, or the geometry of the structure could be such that it offers the necessary resistance to the tension anchorage forces. In this instance the stability of the structure requires external forces coinciding in magnitude and direction with the anchorage tension forces created by the cables.

Of these methods, the first one is usually the more expensive. The latter is not only the more economical but, in many cases, can reduce construction cost below that of a conventional frame.

For decades the structural frames of most buildings were designed to meet only the laws of statics, strength of materials, and elastic stability. To whatever dynamic loads a frame is actually subjected, and whatever its response to them, they were normally treated as equivalent static loads in engineering calculations. Suspension structures are quite different in that they demand consideration of their dynamic behavior.

An individual suspended cable or a grid of cables are susceptible to motion, usually referred to as "flutter," occurring under the influence of such exterior dynamic forces as wind, mobile and seismic loads. In extreme cases flutter is due to sound waves or vibrations in the ground set up by vehicular traffic.

Prior to the early 1950s cables were only used to a limited extent in the construction of buildings. Although cables had been used for centuries in temporary buildings such as tents, their application in permanent buildings was rare. However, with the completion of the North Carolina State Fair Building at Raleigh, North Carolina in 1953, a new era in cable construction began.

The Raleigh arena was the first major cable-roof structure built in the U.S. Its design departed radically from conventional practice.

For centuries space has been spanned by the beam, the truss, and the arch. The major loads of the building were born by structural members in compression. The variety of suspension-roof structures that began to be built in the U.S. and abroad following the building of the Raleigh arena was part of the search for new architectural forms that characterized the goals of the architectural and engineering professions during the mid-1950s to the late 1960s.

Yet, the new forms of the cable that began with the suspension bridge and transferred the suspension principle to building was not new at all. Isolated attempts had been made in the past, such as the locomotive roundhouse pavilion at the Chicago World's Fair in 1933, and tent forms such as the circus tent have been used since the beginning of time.

Although part of the interest in cable structures was the prevailing, almost perverse, desire on the part of virtuoso architects and engineers to create novel shapes and abstract forms, the hard, simple, engineering fact remains that the most economical means known for spanning large spaces is the cable.

The great strength factor of steel in tension works to enormously reduce the dead load of structure and provides ample strength to support the live loads. Economy, although it is often violated, is the major drive and passion of engineering and it is this that motivated the trend toward cable structures in the 1950s.

Conventional methods of building not only fail to use all the strength of their materials, but waste those materials in an excessive way to meet "margins of safety" for which no real need exists. In the 1950s dynamic new concepts and analyses of building structures began to emerge. Structures were conceived as organic wholes with one force leaning and acting upon another. The point of collapse in such structures is reached only when the structure fails as a whole, rather than the failure of any single structural member such as a column or a beam.

There began to emerge the concept of ultimate strength design in steel and concrete, the use of new materials and joinery, space frames, and shell forms. A revolution in architectural structure occurred led by a group of creative engineers. Suspension structures emerged as part of this revolution.

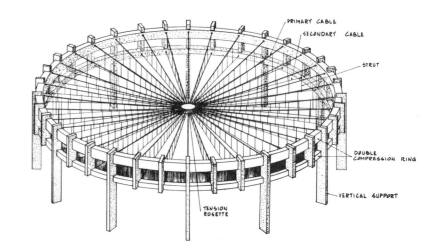

PRIMARY CABLE
SECONDARY CABLE
STRUT
DOUBLE COMPRESSION RING
VERTICAL SUPPORT
TENSION ROSETTE

SPAN: 200'-400'

ROOF DECK IS SUPPORTED ON CABLES. SECONDARY CABLES HAVE DIFFERENT TENSION FORCE THAN PRIMARY CABLES. THIS DAMPENING EFFECT ELIMINATES FLUTTER.
TYPICAL SAG/SPAN RATIO: $\frac{1}{12}$ TO $\frac{1}{15}$

ROOFS WITH SINGLE OR DOUBLE SET OF CABLES DOUBLE CURVATURE (+)

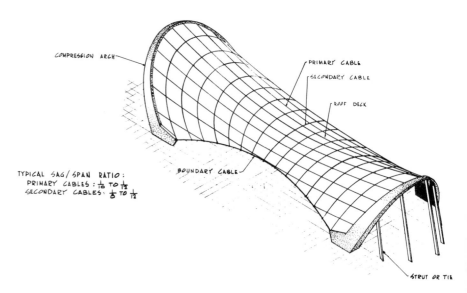

COMPRESSION ARCH
PRIMARY CABLE
SECONDARY CABLE
ROOF DECK
BOUNDARY CABLE
STRUT OR TIE

TYPICAL SAG/SPAN RATIO:
PRIMARY CABLES: $\frac{1}{10}$ TO $\frac{1}{12}$
SECONDARY CABLES: $\frac{1}{6}$ TO $\frac{1}{12}$

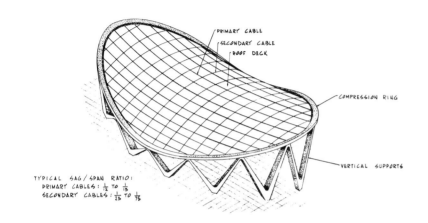

PRIMARY CABLE
SECONDARY CABLE
ROOF DECK
COMPRESSION RING
VERTICAL SUPPORTS

TYPICAL SAG / SPAN RATIO:
PRIMARY CABLES: $\frac{1}{2}$ TO $\frac{1}{15}$
SECONDARY CABLES: $\frac{1}{25}$ TO $\frac{1}{75}$

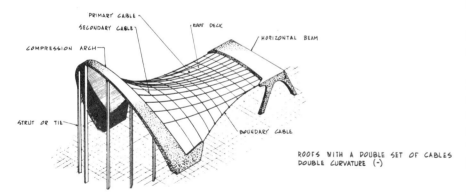

PRIMARY CABLE
SECONDARY CABLE
ROOF DECK
HORIZONTAL BEAM
COMPRESSION ARCH
STRUT OR TIE
BOUNDARY CABLE

ROOFS WITH A DOUBLE SET OF CABLES
DOUBLE CURVATURE (-)

In transferring suspension principles to buildings, all the basic rules of bridge building applied, but many additional problems and possibilities of failure emerged.

Every form of building has its limitations and breaking points. In the beam, which resists loads by bending, it takes the form of cracking or shearing. In the arch it is buckling. In the high-tension cable, which resists loads by tension, the most feared destructive force is vibration, particularly flutter. This is a complex and, until very recent times, highly mysterious phenomenon.

It was nearly a century and a half after James Finley built his bridge of 70 foot span over Jacobs Creek, Pennsylvania before engineers were conscious of the vibrational effects and flutter in suspension structures. The primary reason for this was that the span length from 1889 to 1929 was comparatively modest, increasing only 150 feet in 40 years. The growth of knowledge was slow. However, in the ensuing eight years the span was more than doubled. The George Washington Bridge has a span of 3,500 feet and the Golden Gate 4,200.

On November 7, 1940, the most spectacular bridge disaster of all time took place. The Tacoma Narrows Bridge, a conventional suspension span of 2,800 feet, was racked to pieces by a comparatively mild gale.

David B. Steinman, an American engineer, had identified the phenomenon only two years earlier. He found that all materials have a natural molecular vibration or frequency range. If an outside force acting upon a material comes within that frequency range, it causes the material to vibrate internally or to flutter. A vibrational state may be reached where the outer and inner forces are in tune, called resonance, and the material flies apart.

Even without reaching resonance, the uneven loading of outside forces, such as wind, may cause a material to vibrate visibly up and down, which builds up rhythmically to destruction. These forces, plus faults in design, destroyed the Tacoma Bridge. In heavy compressive structures sheer weight has the effect of checking vibrations. The natural frequencies are so low that few external forces can induce resonance.

In light cable structures composed of exceedingly strong materials in tension, the members are extremely sensitive to uneven loading. Vibration and flutter become major design problems.

These are basic considerations for suspension bridges. But bridges are open and serve comparatively simple human functions. A bridge can allow for a certain flexibility and sway. Buildings are much more complex and must provide weathertight enclosure. The problems of stability and flutter are much more critical. A building of any permanence can tolerate very little movement.

Despite all of the engineering investigation in applying cable principles to buildings, the central problem of vibrational effects had not yet been solved by the mid-1950s.

The Raleigh arena as originally conceived was to consist of a juxtaposition of two canted catenary arcs with cables strung between them forming a saddle-shaped cable roof. The arc ends crossed and were embedded in the earth. Metal sheathing was hung between the cables, which were to be restrained solely by opposing forces in equilibrium.

The design was seen to be essentially unstable on its two-point foundation, even before construction. It was modified by the introduction of support columns under the arcs, and multiple guy wires with strong earth anchorages to insure stability were added. The problem of flutter was controlled by inserting damping springs at cable connections. Even then the roof deflected up to 10 inches in a high wind. A fair breeze caused the whole structure to "sing." This was corrected by graphiting the cable springs and adding acoustical treatment.

The arena has withstood several hurricanes and marks one of the first and most original attempts toward cable structures. However, the additional measures required defeated the potential economy of the new form without solving the problem of vibration and flutter.

Until the invention of Lev Zetlin's self-dampening cable system used at Utica, New York in 1956, all attempts to solve the problem of cables had been "brute-strength" solutions of adding weight and multiplying anchorages.

The significance of Zetlin's Utica Auditorium is that it is the first suspension-roof structure that solves the vibration-and-flutter problem with finesse.

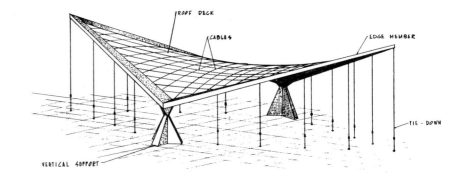

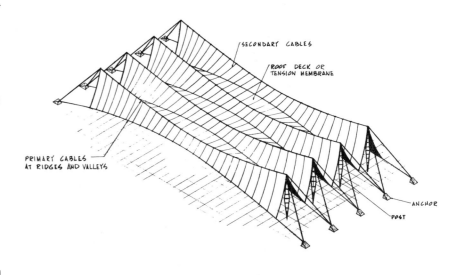

ROOFS WITH A DOUBLE SET OF CABLES
DOUBLE CURVATURE (-)

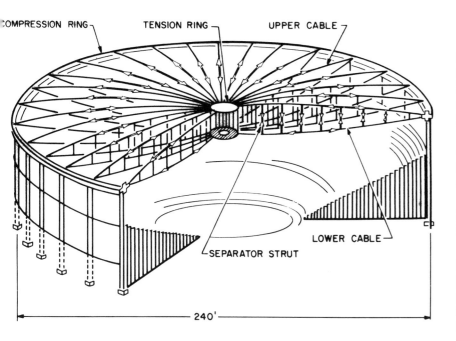

COMPRESSION RING — TENSION RING — UPPER CABLE —

LOWER CABLE —

SEPARATOR STRUT

240'

The City Auditorium at Utica

The commission for the design of the City Auditorium at Utica, New York, was one of the first projects to be awarded my newly opened engineering office. The most important factor in the solution was my desire to succeed.

Soil conditions on the site were extremely bad. A conventional structure would have resulted in a very heavy structure. The lightest available structure in 1955 capable of eliminating weight on the foundations was cables. Yet, cable structures were comparatively untried. The cable structures that had been designed up until this time did not seem to provide a satisfactory answer. I had an intuitive feeling, not a scientific answer, about working with two systems of cables, one restraining the other.

I asked myself, What is flutter? and investigated the Tacoma Narrows Bridge failure. The Tacoma Bridge had collapsed in a wind of 24 miles an hour although previously it had withstood 100-mile-an-hour gales.

The problem of flutter had always fascinated me. At Cornell my research had been in buckling, flutter, vibrations, and related problems. I concluded that buckling and noise were related. Flutter is simply a movement of energy and all that was necessary to solve the problem was to remove excess energy from the cables.

Energy takes many forms although it is all the same, whether chemical, heat, or potential. The proof of this is that it can be converted from one form to another. One means of converting energy is shock absorbers.

The shock-absorber concept of dampening energy was the basis of the solution eventually devised for the roof of the Utica Auditorium.

Kinetic energy such as flutter is easily converted. For example, a flying body has energy during flight. A piece of glass placed in the path of a flying rock will break the glass. The glass is shattered by the energy of the rock and the rock loses its energy and falls. The energy of the rock was converted to breaking the glass. The energy of the flying rock could also be changed by plunging it into oil. As it passed through the oil, the stone's energy would cause friction and kinetic energy would be converted to heat. In an automobile a box full of oil is attached to a disc on a rod called a shock absorber. The car's vibrations are converted into heat in the oil and the car does not jump up and down.

Real shock absorbers attached to a cable structure such as that at Utica would have been prohibitively expensive. Their size would have had to be as large as the auditorium itself.

This did not make sense. I considered using truck shock absorbers. Four thousand would have been required, so the idea of shock absorbers was discarded. Why must the energy of flutter be converted to heat?, I asked myself. Why not transfer the oscillation to another cable? This would dampen the first cable but then it would have to deal with another "culprit," the second cable.

I then arrived at the conclusion eventually used. I reasoned that if I used two cables with different natural frequencies working against each other through connections, and both oscillated at different harmonics, neither would vibrate.

The result was total shock absorption. The answer seemed so clear and simple that it could not help working. It did.

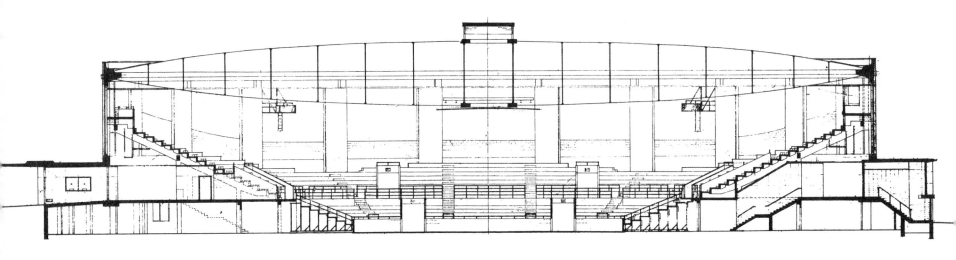

Municipal Auditorium, City of Utica, New York
Gehron & Seltzer, architects; Frank Delle Cese, associate architect

The Utica Municipal Auditorium is modest and undramatic, designed by Architects Gehron and Seltzer in probably the simplest of all suspension building forms. It is a circular arena with roof cables strung from a central metal tension ring in midair to an exterior reinforced-concrete compression ring supported by perimeter wall columns in the form of a huge bicycle wheel.

Self-dampening is built into the cable system by using two sets of cables, stretched apart by means of spreaders prestressed by forces of 135,000 pounds or more per cable.

Upper cables always have a different tension than the lower. The prestressing forces are applied against cables of different sizes; any applied load will increase the tension in one set of cables and reduce it in the other. Thus the two sets of cables always have different natural frequencies. No matter what frequency the wind imposes on the roof, even if it happens to correspond to that of one set of cables, the other set will be out of phase and quash the vibration.

The cables are anchored to a 240-foot-diameter concrete compression ring, and two steel tension rings and are kept apart by pipe spreaders. The compression ring is supported by 24 rectangular concrete columns spaced 15 degrees apart, making 72 pairs in all. The distance between upper and lower tension rings is about 20 feet, so the depth-to-span ratio is $\frac{1}{12}$.

How the Utica Auditorium Was Built

After the concrete columns were completed, the entire compression ring was poured using 5000 psi concrete. Pipe sleeves were cast into the ring to allow cables to pass through. In the meantime the upper and lower welded steel tension rings were fabricated and hoisted to a wooden tower in the center, approximately halfway between the final vertical positions of the two rings.

The placing of the cables was the most critical moment in the erection procedure because the edge compression ring was designed for forces evenly distributed at 5 degrees around the circumference, and

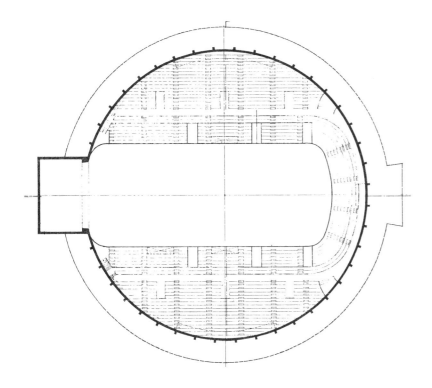

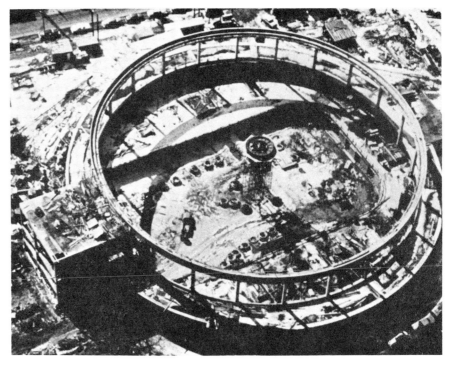

not for the force of one pair of cables acting alone. Thus, a carefully planned sequence for placing cables and pulling them into place was necessary to avoid excessive bending of the ring.

When all of the cables had been fastened, the initial prestressing forces were developed by forcing the upper tension ring and lowering the bottom ring apart by using jacks. The spreaders or stanchions were then placed, further increasing the amount of force built into the cable system. Introducing prestress by jacking approximately at right angles to the cable is much easier than applying an axial force using turnbuckles or tightening screws at the end.

Once the initial forces had been achieved, the delicate stage of the construction was passed. Installation of formed metal roof decking, insulation, and roofing was then completed. The space between the upper and lower cables is used for air-conditioning equipment, ducts, lighting, and other equipment. Sound-absorbing material was installed in the center and around the edge, leaving a wide circular area in between.

For an idea of the relative magnitude of forces, a 20-pound per-square-foot dead load would produce 12.6 kips vertical load at each fastening, yet horizontal forces are much greater because of prestressing.

No change occurs in horizontal pull on the compression ring when loads are added; horizontal components cancel out. Roof decking, equipment, snow, and other pressures decrease the tension in the upper cable and increase the tension in the lower. By creating a sufficiently large initial force in the upper cable, it will never be reduced to zero. Wind loads acting upward will produce the opposite situation.

Tension in the cables was predicted by geometry by anticipating the original length of cables and length of spreaders. Final tension was checked by installing a jack on the end of the cables, adjusting the nuts on the fittings, and reading a pressure gage.

Curves of the upper and lower cables follow the funicular curve for loadings. Since the loading is complicated, the true shape of the funicular curve is not a simple mathematical function.

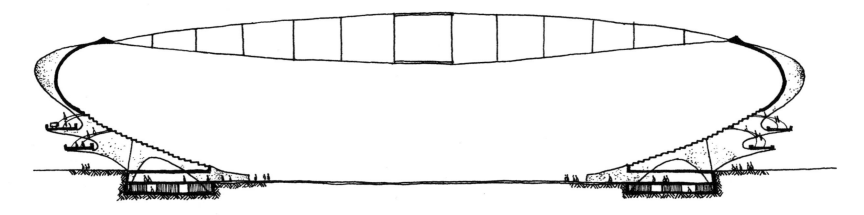

Stadium Proposals

The suspension principle involved in the Utica Auditorium was not particularly appropriate for "small" spans. Zetlin predicted the lower limits of economic applicability to be about 200 feet. The cost per square foot would actually reduce with span increase. The upper limit would be about 1,800 feet.

By increasing the number of cables, their size and initial tension could be kept constant. The spreaders would become heavier to prevent buckling as their length increases. But the cost of fittings and erection would remain more or less constant.

Architect Helge Westermann and Zetlin drew plans for larger buildings shortly after the completion of the Utica Auditorium. They took advantage of the constant horizontal force generated by the double cable system to balance cantilevered "C"-shaped frames to support grandstands. Two of the plans are shown here. One is a square building with rounded corners with a projected 800-foot span roof. The other is an irregular canopy over the seats for a baseball diamond. In this "C"-shaped grandstand design, the horizontal forces are distributed in elevation in such a way that they resist the tendency of the cantilevers to push back. This is especially important for the compression member at the top of the cantilevers, which looks like a giant "C" clamp in plan. The cantilevers try to pull it apart; the cables hold it together.

In the Utica Auditorium, the cable system is inert. That is, cables and rings merely sit on top of the columns. In these two examples, the cables actively support outside cantilevers, keeping them from tipping and permitting their span to be larger and their cross section smaller.

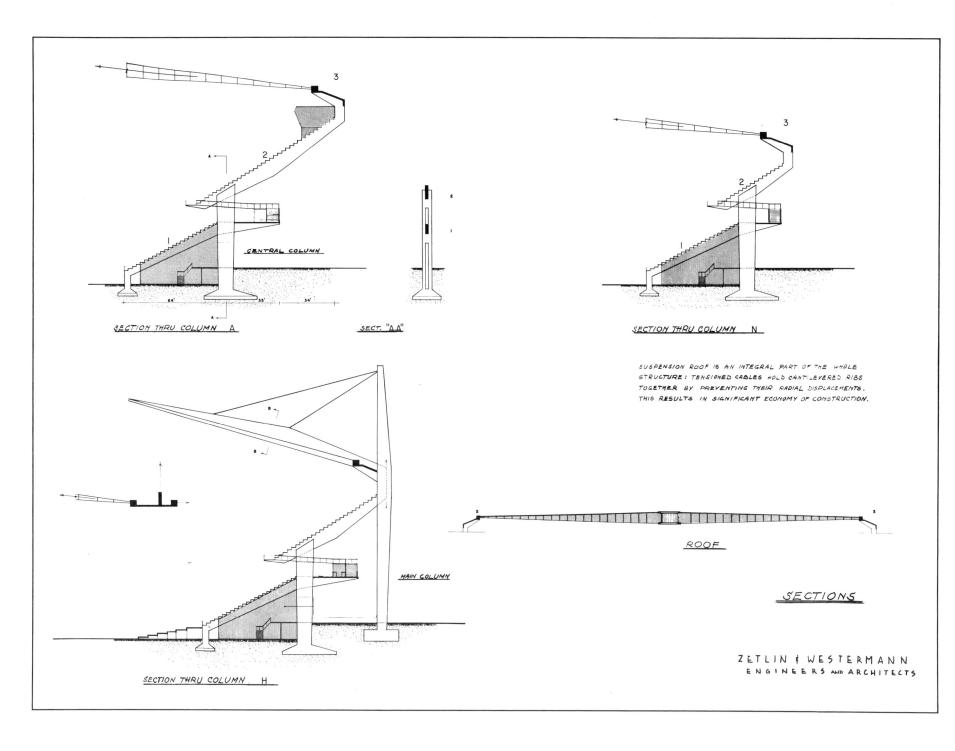

SECTION THRU COLUMN A

SECT. "AA"

CENTRAL COLUMN

SECTION THRU COLUMN N

SUSPENSION ROOF IS AN INTEGRAL PART OF THE WHOLE
STRUCTURE: TENSIONED CABLES HOLD CANTILEVERED RIBS
TOGETHER BY PREVENTING THEIR RADIAL DISPLACEMENTS.
THIS RESULTS IN SIGNIFICANT ECONOMY OF CONSTRUCTION.

SECTION THRU COLUMN H

MAIN COLUMN

ROOF

SECTIONS

ZETLIN & WESTERMANN
ENGINEERS AND ARCHITECTS

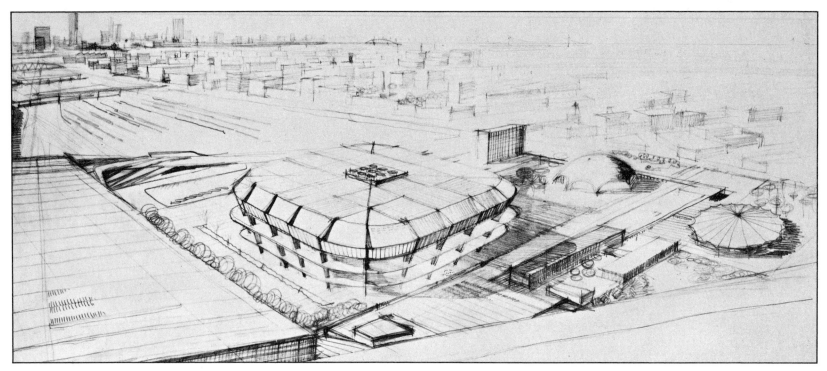

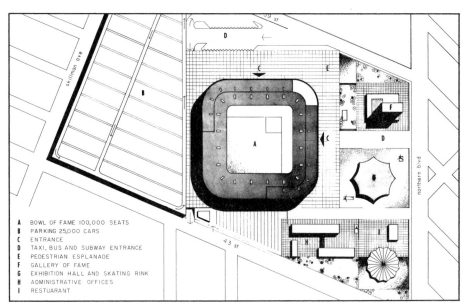

A BOWL OF FAME 100,000 SEATS
B PARKING 25,000 CARS
C ENTRANCE
D TAXI, BUS AND SUBWAY ENTRANCE
E PEDESTRIAN ESPLANADE
F GALLERY OF FAME
G EXHIBITION HALL AND SKATING RINK
H ADMINISTRATIVE OFFICES
I RESTUARANT

94

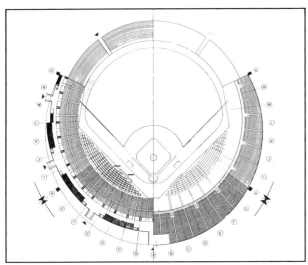

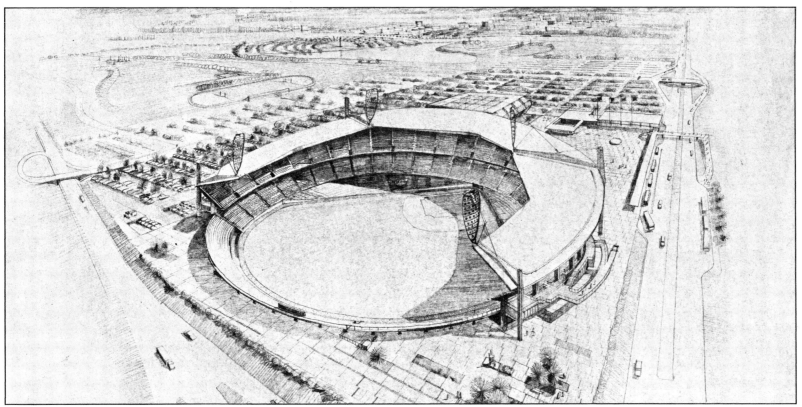

95

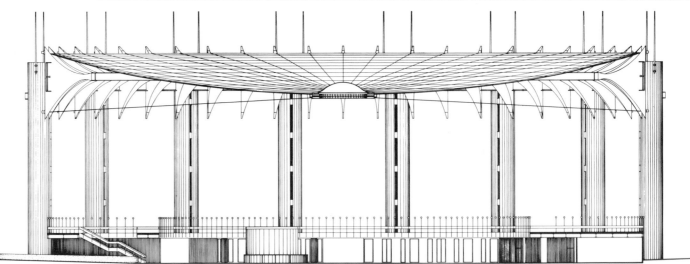

New York State Pavilion, 1964 New York World's Fair

Philip Johnson Associates, Architects
Lev Zetlin and Associates, Structural Engineers
New York State Department of Public Works
Division of Architecture
Nelson A. Rockefeller—Governor
Carl W. Larson—State Architect

An imaginative solution to roofing an exhibit area was designed for the New York State Pavilion. Called the Tent of Tomorrow, it was, according to architect Philip Johnson, "an unengaged free space as an example of the greatness of New York, rather than as a warehouse full of exhibit material."

The project consisted of three main components: the main pavilion, featuring a 350-foot-span, cable-hung roof; three observation towers rising 90, 185, and 250 feet and having 64-foot-diameter observation platforms; and the Circarama.

Suspension Roof

Covering an area larger than that of a football field, the main pavilion featured an oval-shaped prestressed cable suspension roof supported by 16 periphery columns, some 100 feet high. The hollow concrete columns, 12 feet in diameter, support the ring girder, which in turn carries the double layer of cables. These cables are anchored into the ring girder which floats on lubrite plates resting on brackets projecting from the inside face of the columns. The ring, actually a giant truss, consists of a U-section inner chord 4 feet deep, joined to a 14-foot-deep box-section outer chord having 48-web-plate truss members. These web

97

plates, 35 feet high, project above and below the outer chords. Suspension cables are attached to these webs, thereby locating them above and below the girder.

The outer ring is joined to the columns by a heavy steel carrier beam passing through vertical slots in the column faces, and anchored to a structural platform inside the columns.

The unusual feature of the roof measuring 250 feet in the minor axis is that it imparts no horizontal or bending moment forces to the columns due to the arrangement of 96 cables, which results in a rigid construction, avoids vibrations under wind, and behaves in much the same way as heavier steel construction.

The 52,000-square-foot roof was covered by 1,400 translucent plastic panels. The panels are attached to the upper cable of the suspension system with a weathertight batten system joining each panel to the next.

Observation Towers

The observation platforms are suspended from the tops of three 12-feet, 4-inch-diameter concrete cylinders having a 16-inch-thick wall. Faced with the problem of keeping sway to a minimum, the towers were designed using prestressed steel. This vertical prestressing, which reduces sway and helps reduce the amount of concrete necessary, uses 30, 1-inch-diameter, high-strength steel rods embedded in the walls.

To permit rapid construction, the towers were poured using 3-foot-high slipforms which moved at a rate of about 1 foot per hour. Pouring and prestressing operations were first carried out after the three towers had been formed to the height of the lowest tower. After this, forming continued on both towers to the top of the intermediate tower where prestressing was applied. The highest tower was then formed and prestressed.

The two lower towers have single-story platforms; the highest tower has a two-story platform. Cantilevered steel girders bearing directly on the tower walls support the platforms while suspension cables attached to these girders are also attached to the interior and exterior edge of the platform.

However, the two-story platform's inner edge is connected by spokes to the wall of the concrete tower to prevent torsional rotation. Two elevators riding on the outside of the highest tower also serve the two lower towers.

Baltimore Inner Harbor Crossing

Client: The City of Baltimore
R & D Directors and Consulting Engineers: Lev Zetlin Associates,
Inc. Submitted 1967

When cables were introduced to buildings in the mid-1950s, it was generally accepted that the principles used were to be borrowed from the engineering of suspension bridges.

When Lev Zetlin received the commission to propose a conceptual design for a bridge at the Inner Harbor at Baltimore, Maryland in 1965, he used the principles of self-dampening cables that he had perfected and patented for buildings. A building roof, that of the Utica Auditorium, where Zetlin had solved the problem of cable flutter, evolved principles that could revolutionize the design of suspension bridges.

There have been no innovations in structural bridge systems during the past four decades. Improvements have been limited to field construction or in the details of conventional structural systems.

Numerous schemes were studied for the Inner Harbor Bridge. They included concrete, prestressed concrete, and structural steel and entailed varied structural systems such as horizontal girders, arches, rigid frames, shells, and cable suspension. Because of the significant depth of structural members, most schemes did not offer the desired clearance under the bridge or clear sight lines from the bridge. The only scheme, other than cable suspension, that would meet the two requirements would be a thin concrete shell above the bridge, from which the decks are supported by vertical hangers. Although the shell is structurally unique and could prove aesthetically exciting, its cost was estimated as much higher than the cable system finally proposed by Zetlin's report.

In suspension bridges, structural-steel cables are assigned to carry all the gravity loads, that is, the moving loads as well as the weight of the bridge. However, suspension cables have no resistance to lateral loads such as wind or upward loads such as suction, and are unstable dynamically since they have a tendency to vibrate under wind and moving loads. To resist the secondary loads, so-called "stiffening trusses" are usually introduced. These trusses are extremely heavy, weighing as much as six times the weight of the cables, or four times the bridge deck itself and are, therefore, quite expensive.

The structural system proposed by Zetlin consisted of a basket of interconnecting high-strength cables, resulting in a rigid structure. Because of its rigidity, it would not require stiffening trusses. A light deck, sufficiently strong to span the width of the roadway, would be supported directly by cables. It would be a thin orthotropic steel deck whose weight would be a fraction of deck and trusses in conventional suspension bridges. This solution would eliminate over 10 feet in depth of the bridge deck, compared to other structural systems. A 65-foot bridge clearance would result.

The site surrounding the bridge is such that most of the approach ramps turn away from the bridge at the bulkheads. This feature would prevent continuation and tying of suspension cables in a vertical plane as is customary in conventional suspension bridges. The proposed structural system solves this problem by providing an abutment that can efficiently resist tension forces from the cables.

The gravity load is carried by four main lines of concave cables. Convex cables are anchored to the foundation in the two outer inclined planes and in four vertical planes between the decks. The function of these convex cables is to eliminate flutter and to resist upward loads such as suction. The inclined plane of cables stiffens the bridge laterally and is attached to the outer decks only. The middle deck would be connected to the outer decks through the 16-foot space between them with shallow struts approximately 36 feet on centers.

The approaches and ramps to the bridge would consist of precast-concrete elements in the deck and poured-in-place columns, as shown. Precast elements of the deck over the supports are hollow hyperbolic-paraboloid boxes.

The geometry of the abutments of the bridge is such that it resists the imposed cable loads in compression. The structural system for the bridge, although not used in this detail in bridges to date, is composed of components which commonly have been employed in construction during the past years.

The proposed bridge would employ 75 pounds of structural steel and 20 pounds of cables, or about 95 pounds of steel, per square foot. Any other presently used structural system for the same span of bridge would employ between 300 and 600 pounds of steel per square foot. This fact could contribute to both the feasibility and economy of the bridge.

The bridge was designed to carry Interstate Highway 95 and Key Highway across the entrance to Inner Harbor from a proposed interchange between Interstate Highway 95 and Interstate Highway 83. It consists of three decks at approximately the same level: two carrying Interstate Highway 95 each with five lanes, eastbound and westbound, respectively. The third deck carries a four-lane (two eastbound and two westbound) Key Highway, with a sidewalk offering pedestrian access to Federal Hill. The three decks at the same level offer convenient driving and an open view of the city of Baltimore.

101

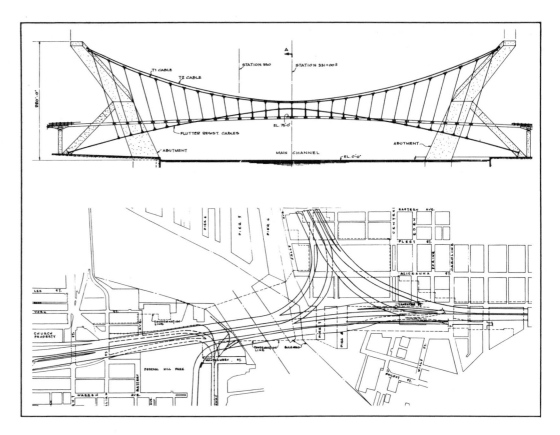

The Y-shaped abutments are designed to be built in either steel or concrete. They straddle the middle deck only. They are not only more economical to construct than usual vertical towers, but are less bulky. They do not obstruct the view of the bridge at its entrance, and the approach to the bridge becomes more convenient.

The concept for this bridge solves two difficult problems inherent in the traffic conditions and the grades of the terrain in the Inner Harbor: extreme width of the bridge and a 65-foot clearance under the bridge. Most of the world's bridges are narrow and long. The difficult aesthetic problem posed by the 14-lane width of the bridge was solved by using a three-dimensional structural system, which unifies the entire bridge into one form.

A conventional concrete or steel girder bridge would be over 15 feet deep. If connections to local streets were not to be overly remote from the bridge and have convenient approach grades, the maximum clearance under the bridge would be only 45 or 50 feet. One way to realize a minimum 65-foot clearance under the bridge using conventional bridge construction would be to increase the grade at the approaches. This would slow down traffic and inconvenience drivers.

The "tension bridge" could fill an important gap in the range of possibilities for large bridges. Suspension bridges have limitations because of the effect of dynamic instability inherent in hung-cable structures. Normally the necessary stiffener truss in the roadbed is about four times the weight of the total cable system. The economical span of the suspension-type bridge is a minimum of about 1,000 feet (305 m).

Compression bridges (including prestressed and posttensioned) spans become progressively less economical beyond 300 feet (91 m) in length. Between 300- and 1,000-foot, truss-combination tension-and-compression member bridges are usually used.

This tension-bridge structure is freed from reliance on the weight of the roadbed and stiffener trusses for stability. It would, therefore, seem to fulfill the spanning possibilities between 300 and 1,000 feet.

Shells

Structural engineering can make an immense contribution to the economy of construction and the flexibility of architectural planning. The contribution lies principally in providing a choice of structural systems. Although a very limited number of conventional systems are presently employed in the bulk of our national construction, innumerable other novel structural systems could be evolved through an imaginative structural-engineering approach. Such structural systems would offer new forms for buildings and open new horizons to architectural planning.

Effort spent in the search for alternative structural systems during the conceptual stage of a project might prove more rewarding than the extra effort spent on the refinement of the design of a conventional structural system to adapt it to the peculiar conditions of the project. The machinery and aircraft industries expend constant effort toward innovations of systems even though innovation means scrapping accepted practices, conventional components, and standard shapes. Certainly, such an approach would be justified in the construction industry, the largest industry in the nation, if it resulted in more economical and better construction.

An economically successful structural system has to meet three simultaneous requirements: minimum amount of material, minimum labor in fabrication, and maximum speed and ease of erection.

The first requirement is invariably met if the structural geometry assures that superimposed loads are resisted through internal axial forces. Such structures are commonly referred to as three-dimensional or space structures. They differ from conventional structural systems of plane frames whose resistance to superimposed loads is essentially through bending. Engineering ingenuity must devise space structures that satisfy the requirements of minimum fabrication and erection costs.

The purpose of innovation in structural systems is to create more economic, better buildings, irrespective of spans. Such innovations could result in large-span buildings at a cost equivalent to conventional smaller spans. Columnfree space offers flexibility for future expansion, and subsequent relocation of partitioned spaces as new demands are made upon a building years after its construction.

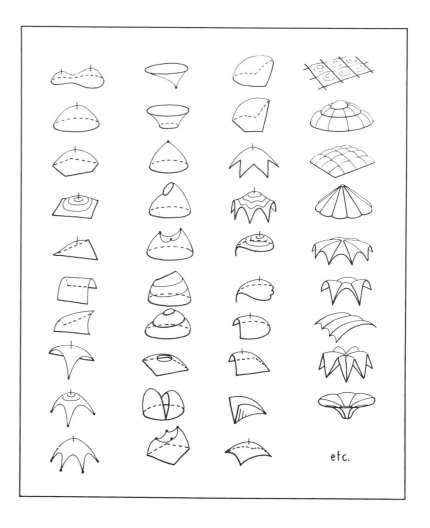

To facilitate innovation in structural systems, the engineer should draw more upon the scientific aspects of structural engineering than on standard structural-design handbooks. Mathematics and theoretical mechanics should feature more prominently in the engineering design of a construction project. More interest should be taken in current research in structural engineering conducted on a very large scale outside of the construction field—for example, the aircraft, nuclear, and missile industries.

Standard design handbooks deal, of necessity, with conventional structural systems. On the other hand, thorough knowledge of basic engineering theories and their frequent use is conducive to developing a designer's vital sixth sense of imagination and innovation.

The scientific aspects of structural engineering should become an important ingredient of structural-engineering design. But an awareness of the limitations inherent in most engineering theories should always be present. Knowledge of the limitations of the scientific tools available to structural engineering would help us to make more and better use of the tools available.

The powerful theory of shells offers the potential of innumerable structural forms and shapes. But the most important feature of a shell structure is that the amount of structural material in it is but a fraction of the conventional plane frame or truss of identical span.

Of all structural systems, shells present possibly the best example of intertwining mathematics and field realities.

Inherently, the solution to shell theory results in structures capable of resisting stresses and deflections in any continuous surface. The solution indicates a long-span structure with a smaller amount of structural material than a conventional frame.

A thorough knowledge of this type of theory used by design engineers would result in new shapes and new structural systems.

However powerful and promising this theory appears, it cannot be left to mathematicians to actually construct buildings. There are too many inconsistencies between theory and construction realities and too many unknowns in the structural materials with which we are working. It is up to the engineer to modify the theories for application to construction, and to close the gap between theory and practice.

Let us look into the limitations of the shell theory. First, as the equation stands, we do not have the mathematical ability to derive a general solution for any arbitrary shell surface. Before the advent of computers, extreme simplifications were necessary to make this equation solvable. These involved using only a few terms of the equation and simplifications of the remaining.

Another, and probably the greater, limitation is that this differential equation is based on the theory of elasticity. Immediately, therefore, during the design stage, one has to realize to what extent the structural material, or the structure as a whole, for that matter, possesses the characteristics on which this equation is premised. If the material and the structure as a whole do not possess the elastic properties around which the differential equation was developed, obviously the stresses and the deflections in the actual structure will be different from those predicted by this equation.

Due to these restraints shells of only limited geometrical shape, such as cylinders and hyperbolic paraboloids, have been designed and built. Even ventures into these simple shapes, by the engineering profession, have been slow and cautious. Designs have been extremely conservative.

In spite of these limitations, the theories should not be shelved, nor should engineers retreat to the security of their handbooks. It was the creative drive of the engineers that evolved our present efficient beam-and-post structures by extending the theoretical principles of beam bending and of column buckling, developed by Bernoulli and Euler, into practical applications.

Theories such as those for shells should become the working tools of an everyday structural engineering practitioner. With the aid of computers and such tools as model testing, the gap between theories and practice could become smaller—and even disappear.

Eastman Kodak Pavilion, 1964
New York World's Fair, Flushing, N.Y.

Kahn and Jacobs, architects
Will Burtin, designer
Lev Zetlin and Associates, structural engineers

I received the commission for the Kodak Pavilion at the time that several shells, including the Sydney Opera House, were being constructed.

It had taken more time to construct the shells than predicted. There were several elastic shell theories at the time, which were used by the designers of these structures. Obviously, they had to make guesses and assumptions even though it is wrong to force approximate theories. A shell theory is workable if the shell form has been built numerous times. The theory itself is only a symbolic representation and all that it indicates is that if you follow it, the shell will perform satisfactorily. If you follow the theory for a barrel shell, you will design a sound barrel shell. If you extrapolate the same theory to develop the design of a new form, you will have to allow for numerous trials and errors in the design development. The Sydney Opera House is a classic example of a forcing of theories.

It has been claimed that it was wrong to design an arbitrary shell form that did not correspond to known theory and that the forms should comply with some known geometric formation. I do not agree.

The Kodak shell could have been falsified using conventional construction to appear as a shell form. It would have been extremely costly. I chose not to use plastic theory, which would have been a disaster, like using the wrong medicine for the wrong disease.

My approach was to use the collapse theory. This theory is used more and more in practical application in place of the elastic theory. It presupposes a state of stress in the design load and has a certain factor of safety. I used this theory, which was much easier to develop, and combined it with model testing.

Eastman Kodak Pavilion, 1964
New York World's Fair, Destroyed

The two-level pavilion, 394 feet long and 220 feet wide, covered an area of 52,000 square feet. The basically self-supporting reinforced concrete shell achieved clear spans of 117 feet. Four main, tapered concrete columns, integral shell parts, provided support on one side and also served as drains for surface water accumulation. On another side of the pavilion the shell sloped to the ground to form an arcade of eight closely spaced portal arches. In addition to these supports, six freestanding steel columns met the concrete ceiling without capitals. Topping the pavilion was an 80-foot-high pentagon, which held five 30-by-36-foot color prints. Ten steel columns provided the tower support.

The pavilion's varied curves and angles could not be readily translated into specifications and drawings, nor could it be engineered using traditional methods of analysis.

To ascertain stress and deflection at critical points a sculptured model of acrylic plastic was constructed at 1:64 scale and used to plot 70,000 points on the shell surface.

The model was loaded to determine deflection and strain patterns and a precision theodolite and 500 strain gauges were attached to the plastic. Working drawings were completed from readings from these gauges.

After the drawing had been completed the construction method was considered. The use of wood trusses and heavy traditional concrete construction was discarded. Zetlin calculated that as much as $500,000 would be saved if a thin-shell approach were used. Savings in structure more than compensated for additional engineering design.

The irregular shape of the roof structure precluded the use of general shell equations. To define the structure into geometric shapes that could be calculated mathematically would have increased the time required for design and added to the total cost.

The solution involved a combination of mathematics and model testing. The model testing was the most productive approach used to determine the placing of reinforcement since stress patterns and values were easily plotted across the model's surface. To utilize the reinforcement in the shell to its maximum efficiency, reinforcing bars were laid out to conform with the lines of stress. Wherever possible, high-strength steel was used to reduce weight. To assure that no strain or tension would be added to the bars they were allowed to drape naturally, conforming to the shape of the shell at any section.

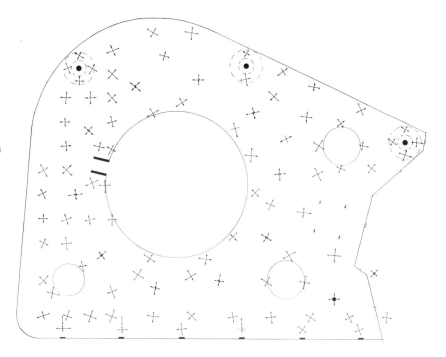

The Theory of Statistical Average Strength

The construction industry is facing an increased demand to create more structures faster at less cost at a time when the skilled labor force is declining and the cost of labor increasing rapidly.

The result has been a change in the traditional optimization-cost relationship between labor time and materials in the construction process. Established value relationships must be revised.

The present-day challenge of construction is an optimum relation between the altered cost of labor and material. The engineering profession is forced to examine new materials, new technologies, and new structural and geometric concepts. Fabricated shells and stress-skin elements satisfy these prerequisites and hence constitute important engineering elements for the construction industry.

Where used, these forms have considerably reduced construction time and the construction cost of projects. Three major factors must be considered in the development of any present-day structural system. They apply particularly to prefabricated shells: 1) increase in the permissible tolerance of error in the field, 2) reliance on the statistical average strength of connections rather than on the strength of individual connections, 3) simplicity of erection.

Engineering design methodology has improved considerably in recent years and structural members have become thinner. Engineers tend to specify smaller and tighter tolerances in the field, demanding greater accuracy of field construction. This is contrary to labor capabilities, which suffer from a continuing decline of precise skill. As a result, field problems and cost have rapidly increased. Paradoxically the use of more economic structural components has resulted in higher final construction costs. To achieve economy and avoid such field problems the contractor must be allowed larger margins for error than those required by conventional structural systems.

Connections must also be rethought. In the traditional engineering approach, the strength of a structure with a given number of connections theoretically depends on the strength of

each connection. If one connection collapses, the entire structure is considered inadequate. For example, if a welded truss with 50 welded connections has one broken weld, the truss would, and should be condemned. However, if the number of connections in a truss could be divided into localized groups, the strength of the truss would thus depend on the "statistical average" strength of these localized connections in each group rather than on the individual strength of each connection. Such dependence would permit a greater margin of field error.

Consideration of permissable tolerance in the field and reliance on statistical average strength would result in more complex structural analysis. Such analysis would have to consider plastic deformation and slippage of joints, as well as relative rigid body movements of components.

Using today's available methodology, such a complex and sophisticated structural design should not prove a great impediment in time or cost. The higher cost of engineering design is only a fraction compared to cost savings in field labor due to the increased margin for permissible error. It is also obvious this would result in a structure that could be erected easily and simply. For the purpose of this discussion we define the term "simple" as a process that does not require stringent tolerances, extremely high labor skills, or thorough planning.

A simple erected structure does not have to consist of a simple structural system or of simple components. It could be a very complex structural system, requiring an extremely sophisticated structural analysis, as long as the result is a simple erection procedure.

The importance of continuity and, hence, homogenity of prefabricated structures has not been stressed in existing engineering literature. Lack of continuity between prefabricated components was the cause of many poorly behaved and unsuccessful prefabricated structures in the past. Particular attention should be paid to connection details, their elasticity, slippage, and plastic deformations.

Theories of static and elastic bodies will not result in adequate solutions. Design theories have to be developed that take the behavior of joints into account. Such engineering theories, if pursued, will result in novel concepts of structure and form. Modern engineering analysis should enable us to solve these complex problems of connection behavior and aid us in the development of new theories.

The Paper Bridge

The paper bridge was an experimental design developed for International Paper Company in 1970. The bridge is now housed in the Smithsonian Institution, Washington, D.C.

The objective was not to build a paper bridge, which would be toymaking. The important element is the concept of the bridge, which is a concept usually not associated with bridges. The paper bridge consisted of molecules—not beams and girders. These molecules are a series of identical, joined geometrical forms.

The connections differ from the very precise joinery required of normal bridge structures which, because they are very expensive, necessitate a great deal of care in assembly. The paper bridge is connected haphazardly.

The theory is that of statistical average strength rather than specific strength at every point. Using this molecular concept the bridge was built weighing only 7 percent of the weight of a conventional bridge. A helicopter picked it up easily. Now that this idea has proved workable, it can be used with aluminum, concrete, or any other material.

When we accepted the challenge of the paper bridge, we had to throw away everything we knew about conventional bridge design. No one had ever built a paper bridge before. There were no guidelines.

The solution is based on the unique tensile properties of paper tiself. It is the stressed-skin principle in which the bridge flexes with the texture of the paper as pressure is applied. It is a different type of innovation that includes more factors than before.

Paper Bridge of "Shell Molecules"

The paper bridge was designed, analyzed, tested, and constructed entirely of paper and glue. The bridge, weighing 9,000 pounds, was shipped to Nevada where it spanned 32 feet across a gorge in the Valley of Fire National Park. A 12,000-pound truck was successfully driven back and forth over the bridge more than 40 times.

The bridge is 32 feet long, 10 feet wide, and 4 feet deep. The "shell molecules," with approximately 4-foot lateral dimensions, are made of paper. The molecules, pyramidical in shape, interconnect to form the bridge. They were formed by folding thin membrane sheets of approximately 1-inch-thick solid paper fiber (cardboard). The deck on top of the "molecules" consisted of thin-walled tubes sandwiched between two flat membrane sheets. The tubular deck assembly distributed stresses under the concentrated loads of the truck wheels.

On the average, paper is not lighter than concrete in the same proportion as it is weaker in strength. A bridge constructed out of solid paper beams, girders, and deck would have weighed almost as much as a concrete bridge. Under such conditions its dead weight would have been several times the design live load. Because of the "molecular" shell structure, the bridge weighed 9,000 pounds for a designed concentrated load of 18,000 pounds. The bridge was lifted by helicopter and dropped into place. It safely carried a 12,000-pound truck and was subjected to tests and to service loads for long periods of time, exhibiting excellent performance both in durability and deflections.

During load tests, the bridge deflected only $\frac{1}{2}$ inch in a 32-foot span subjected to 12,000 pounds of superimposed load. It was calculated that the bridge could carry six times this load or span $2\frac{1}{2}$ times farther under the same loading.

The strength and stiffness properties of paper differ greatly in compression and tension. Paper is also anisotropic (displaying varying struc-

114

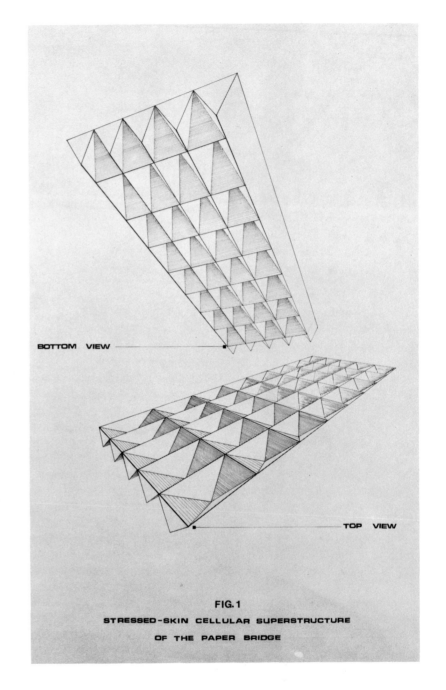

BOTTOM VIEW

TOP VIEW

FIG. 1

STRESSED-SKIN CELLULAR SUPERSTRUCTURE

OF THE PAPER BRIDGE

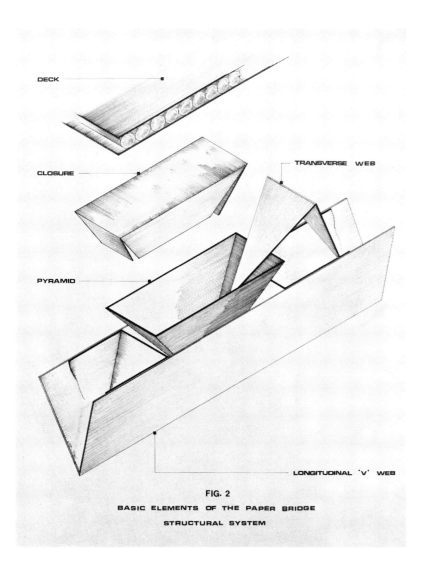

DECK

CLOSURE

TRANSVERSE WEB

PYRAMID

LONGITUDINAL 'V' WEB

FIG. 2

BASIC ELEMENTS OF THE PAPER BRIDGE
STRUCTURAL SYSTEM

tural properties along different axes). Satisfactory connections can be made only by bonding large surfaces.

These problems were overcome by developing a unique system of geometric folded shapes. The entire structure was constructed by simply gluing the various folded shapes together along adjoining surfaces.

The key to the rigid, highly reliable strength of the structural system is the design of the paper pyramids that interconnect the structure's longitudinal and transverse webs to form an integral, three-dimensional stressed skin that behaves like an orthotropic bridge structure.

Each face of the pyramidal "molecule" had a large surface area and faces of adjacent molecules were always in contact with each other. Since the contact surfaces were large, they permitted a "statistical averaging" of connection strength. In this case, the faces of adjacent pyramids were connected to each other by glue. It was not the strength per square inch of the glued surfaces that was important, but the average strength throughout the whole contact surface.

The bridge represents an example of simplicity of erection, a large permissible margin of error in the field, and a statistical averaging of the strength of connections. Its structure is nonconventional and, therefore, complex. Its analysis went beyond elastic deformations and required sophisticated design methodology.

This concept could be applied to other materials such as plastic, gunited mortar, or light-gauge metal sheet.

The entire bridge was built using a common household-type glue and standard-stock-size sheets of paper. The large surface areas available for bonding resulted in exceptionally strong and reliable connections. The system of assembly allowed points of discontinuity between standard-size sheets of paper not to affect the structural strength of the bridge.

Each element of the superstructure was formed by cutting out a flat, geometric shape and folding it. To maintain the strength of the paper at the various fold lines throughout the structure, the paper was scored before folding. The scored folds were then filled with glue to provide a strong structural joint.

Yeshivat Parat Josep

Moshe Safdie wanted to design little houses. There are many ways of solving such a problem. To do it the way Safdie wanted would have been a tragedy, like Habitat. The tragedy of Habitat was that engineering attempted to conform exactly to what the architect provided. It was not a creative engineering solution. It raped itself to make the design possible. The architectural concept could have been retained and creative engineering employed instead.

Safdie wanted to stack spaces. Four ways to do this were devised. The member sizes, the curves engineering provided, were different than Safdie conceived. Safdie usually starts with curves to arrive at spaces. Engineering did not devise Safdie's forms; it is incapable of originating building form; forms are evolved by conditions. Engineering merely helped Safdie's creativity. It is not important to know if engineering or architecture created the form.

Yeshivat Parat Josep

A religious complex in old Jerusalem, Israel
Moshe Safdie, architect

The Zetlin office was commissioned as structural engineers for the Yeshivat Parat Josep designed by architect Moshe Safdie. The project is sited in the old city of Jerusalem, facing the historic Wailing Wall. The structural system, inspired by the domed and arched buildings of the ancient city, is composed of modular, prefabricated concrete components.

The 100,000-square-foot complex's major spaces include classrooms, dormitories, two synagogues, an auditorium, meeting halls, and a swimming pool.

The project's unique structural system consists primarily of two-dimensional precast arch segments for wall and floor structure. When joined together, the arch sections form a building system of three-dimensional space frames that provide a high degree of architectural flexibility. Walls and floors are left open or accommodate circular flat plates, concrete, or glass-fiber domes.

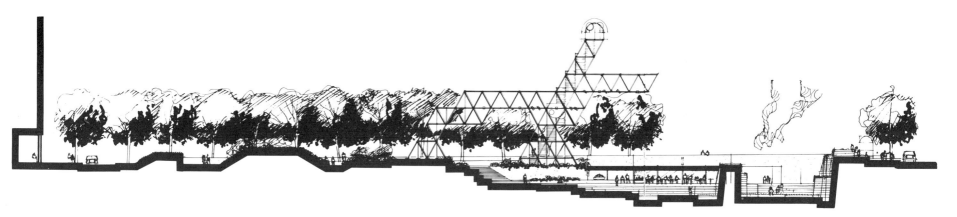

Space Frame and Observation Tower

Southeast Loop Park, Rochester, New York
Lawrence Halprin & Associates, landscape architects.
Lev Zetlin Associates, structural engineers for observation tower.

The Southeast Loop Park is a year-round recreation space located in the urban renewal area close to the heart of downtown Rochester. It has a plaza, fountain, gaming courts, gardens, tree-lined promenade, and a large meadow. In the winter, the gaming courts can be converted to a skating rink and the fountain to an amphitheater.

The plaza of the park is partially covered by an aluminum space frame approximately 100 feet by 100 feet by 50 feet high. It functions as a spatial enclosure and sunscreen as well as the support for theatrical lighting and plaza lighting, with sound equipment and radiant heaters for year-round use.

With water the sunken space becomes a fountain; drained, it becomes an amphitheater for concerts, plays, and other productions.

The space frame can be altered for seasonal events with decorative effects and special lighting. An observation tower rises from one of the supports to a height of 100 feet above the plaza. There is an observation platform at the top accessible by stairs.

119

Kennedy Memorial
Philip Johnson and John Burgee, architects
Lev Zetlin, structural engineer

The structural system developed for the John F. Kennedy Memorial in Dallas, Texas, visibly expresses the design principles of prestressed concrete construction. The structure's individually precast wall elements act as a monolithic element.

In plan the memorial is a 50-foot-square area containing one opening in the center of each of two opposite walls. The other two walls are solid.

The four walls are formed by 72, 30-inch-square, 30-foot-high prestressed panel elements placed side by side like a row of books. This entire roofless enclosure is supported approximately 2 feet above the ground by extension of four panels on each of the two walls containing the memorial's openings. These extended panels act as columns to support the 50-foot spans of the side walls, acting as deep girders. The four walls each are assembled of 18 panels.

To support these vertically pretensioned series of wall elements, the designers first assembled the two side-wall girders by clamping each set of 18 panels together with a horizontal series of posttensioned tendons. These elevated walls, in turn, are clamped with posttensioning tendons to the two walls containing the column elements. In adition, the five panel elements that cantilever from each of the panel columns to the memorial's openings are clamped together with the same posttensioning tendons that support the solid girder walls.

The structural proportions balance the weight of panels equally supported on all columns. The tendency of the solid walls to rotate outward is counteracted by the weight of the series of panel openings. The friction forces, developed at the panel joints through the posttensioning operation, transfer loads from one joint to another and are equal to the shear forces developed in a monolithic structure.

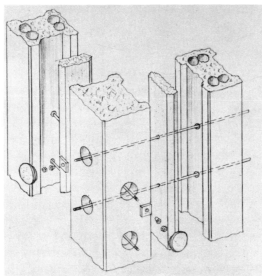

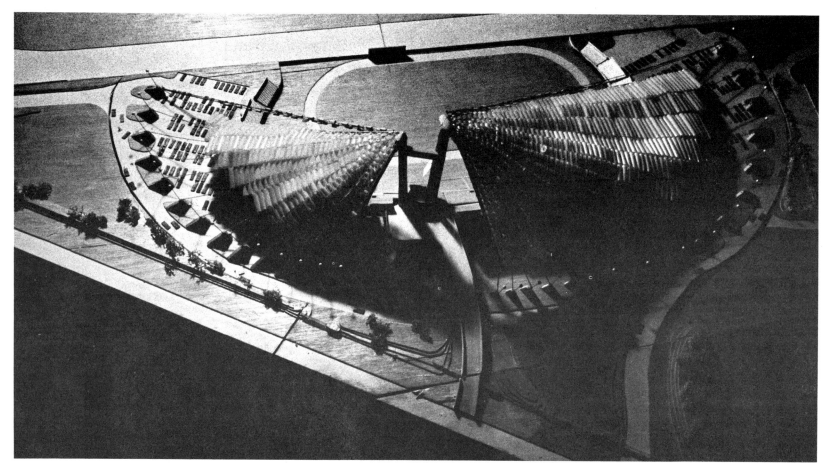

Saudi Arabia Stadium

Damman, Saudi Arabia
Owner: Saudi Arabian Government
Architect: Paul Rudolph
Lev Zetlin Associates, Consulting Engineers

This giant tent-like sports stadium was designed using the most contemporary design techniques, those of tension and inflation, to achieve a symbolic structure reflecting ancient royal traditions.

The roof was designed to be constructed of a series of 38 suspension cables supporting an infill of impregnated nylon. The nylon was to be fabricated in two layers and would be air-inflated to give the roof rigidity and to provide insulation from the sun's intensity. To eliminate flutter caused by high desert winds, additional cables tie the roof to the outside perimeter of the stadium. The stadium itself acts as a mooring. The roof was planned to be fabricated and assembled at the site.

The two concrete pylons would provide the central mast for the roof structure. The pylons fan out at the top and suspension cables are secured to the ribs of the fan. The cables then radiate downward and are secured at ground level to concrete guy anchors.

The stadium was designed for a capacity of 25,000 spectators to watch soccer, football, and a variety of track events. Tucked below the seating at the first two levels are health facilities, administrative offices, shops, galleries, and first-, second-, and third-class restaurants. The upper level will house a promenade.

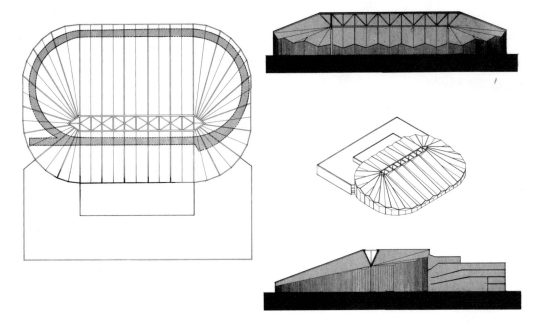

HYPAR SYSTEM

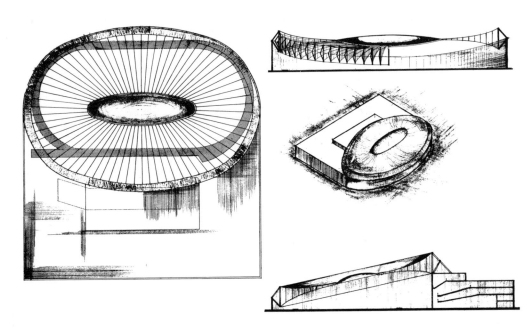

122   CABLE RING SYSTEM

Hallandale Race Track

Hallandale, Florida
Owner, Castleton Industries
Lev Zetlin Associates, designers

An Investigation into Novel Long-Span Structures

The design problem was to provide an economical enclosure for a 400 by 600-foot race track for the Hallandale Dog Race Track in Florida. The owner's decision to enclose the $\frac{1}{4}$-mile, 6-acre track was prompted by the loss of revenue during rainy days, high winds that reduced attendance, and a desire to use the facility for other activities during the racing off-season.

The goal of the enclosure was economy of construction. Zetlin based his solutions on his experience in synthesizing the results of his firm's latest investigations of the use of new materials, building components, technology, and efficient geometrical configurations that could be easily and economically built.

The result of the design analysis was the generation of twelve alternative roof enclosures four of which are shown here that ranged in estimated cost from $1.5 million to $3.3 million placing the structure in the cost range of 6 dollars per square foot. Five of the designs were selected for detailed investigation based on their ability to satisfy program requirements other than budget, and were further investigated.

The economy of the designs was based on the following key requirements: a geometrical configuration that encapsulated the minimum amount of cubic foot enclosure in terms of the desired sight lines; a material that could be easily fabricated in large components that could be factory assembled; and a simplification of detail and joint connections with a minimum use of field labor.

In these designs the grandstands are existing. The solutions had to provide for future removal of the existing stands and constructing new ones. In several cases, this requirement was satisfied by cantilevering half of the enclosure structure to the stands, thus eliminating foundations and structural supports in all areas slated for future construction.

The structures shown have a number of other possible applications with the ever-increasing need to cover large, traditionally open areas in order to provide daily, year-round, income-generating use of existing facilities. These include tennis courts, swimming pools, race tracks, open-air music centers, ice hockey and roller skating rinks, general sports arenas, and athletic fields in which traditional structural techniques and construction procedures are not economically feasible.

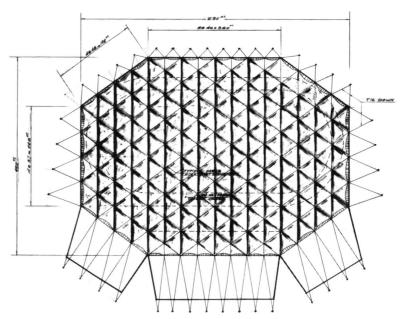

AIR - STRESSED CABLE SYSTEM - PLAN

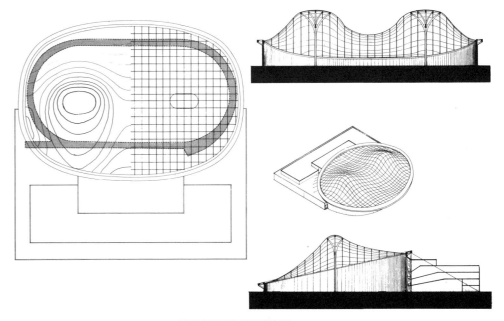

FORM-STRESSED CABLE SYSTEM

Travelers Insurance Pavilion

Donald Desky, a famous Madison Avenue designer, was responsible for the original form of the building. He designed it like an umbrella—a clam shell with the bottom sitting in a pod with water spurting up. The shell was about 200 feet in diameter. The contractor estimated the cost of the building, as best he could, as a 50-foot-round, six-story tower with truss cantilevers sticking out all around.

It was a reasonable system. I was called in as an engineer. The first question was, "What kind of fee do you want?" The usual question. When I looked at the drawings the thing that struck me immediately was the amount of material. There were thousands of pieces, and they wanted to build the building in three months. Obviously, something had to be done.

I was hurt by the question about my fee. They had assumed I would take a slide rule and figure the size of the members. I told them, "Let me consider the preliminaries and I will call you." I was hurt; my personality was involved. No one intended to offend me. As an engineer, I looked at the problem and thought instinctively, there is something wrong.

But aside from this I was driven to prove something. Looking at the design, the idea occurred to me that everything was in compression. If we could put some of the structure in tension, there would be fewer members.

I tried to support the cantilevers they had indicated with cables. This did not seem to work so I bent the cantilevers around like boomerangs. The idea then hit me of using six-story-high pieces of steel. These would be mass-produced, brought to the site in pieces, and put together. Instead of innumerable cantilevered trusses there would be 24 boomerangs.

Once I conceived the boomerangs everything fell into place. I then thought, is there any way to avoid the vertical force on the boomerangs? The only way that that could be done was to counteract this vertical force with hoop tension.

The theoretical principles governing the system take into consideration the following premises: Flexural members are avoided as far as possible. An attempt was made to utilize the material in either direct tension or compression. The geometry of the structure was utilized in resisting the loads. The structure as a whole resists the loads. The characteristic of the entire structure as an entity was considered in the structural analysis rather than the stresses in the individual members, leaving to chance the interaction between the members.

125

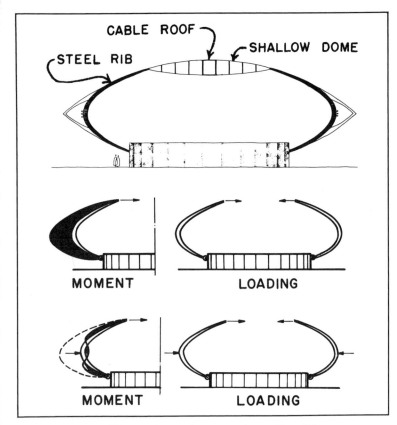

CABLE ROOF

STEEL RIB

SHALLOW DOME

MOMENT   LOADING

MOMENT   LOADING

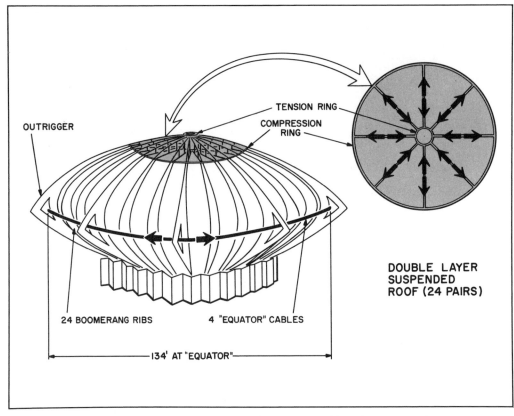

OUTRIGGER

TENSION RING

COMPRESSION RING

DOUBLE LAYER SUSPENDED ROOF (24 PAIRS)

24 BOOMERANG RIBS   4 "EQUATOR" CABLES

134' AT "EQUATOR"

Travelers Insurance Pavilion

1964–1965 New York World's Fair
Kahn & Jacobs, architects
Donald Deskey Associates Inc., exhibit design
Lev Zetlin Associates, structural engineers

Planned and executed for the 1964–1965 New York World's Fair, and subsequently dismantled, this building was designed as an abstraction of the famous Travelers Life Insurance Company's umbrella, mirrored by another form below it. The effect achieved was a scallop-edged saucer that seemed to hover over a wall of water showered up from a pool surrounding the base.

To build the structure using conventional techniques—cantilevered trusses, topped by a dome—would have required cantilevers approximately 6 feet deep at the base and a dome whose depth at the apex would approach 5 feet. The dome would be in compression accompanied by bending, while a bending moment would predominate in the cantilevers. And, if this system were to be built in steel, it would have been necessary for scaffolding to be erected, raising labor costs.

The tension-space structure that was substituted has a stress pattern reversed from that expected in the conventional structural system, resulting in thinner members. Weight of steel used in this system is approximately 9 psf.

The structural frame of the main structure, which is an oblate spheroid, consists of 24 "boomerang-shaped" prefabricated steel ribs with light outriggers establishing the umbrella points. It springs from abutments appended to a 23-foot-high masonry wall that encloses the ground floor of the exhibit building. From here, the ribs curve up and out, then inward, leaving a 60-foot-diameter opening in the apex. Diameter of the spheroid at the equator is 132 feet; total height above grade is 63 feet.

Erection Methods

To erect the exhibit the ribs were assembled in place using a single temporary support at the boomerang edge. The tops of the ribs were then connected by a double layer of cables to a tension hub of steel plates. This hub absorbed the outward thrust of the ribs transmitted by the cables.

Each length of cable extended from sockets on one rib, through the saddle, and back to a neighboring rib and was again socketed. The cables were spaced vertically with 3-inch diameter pipe, the upper connection of which received wide-flange purlins for supporting of roofing material.

The steel ribs had $\frac{3}{4}$ inch webs and 12 inch flanges to the height of a welded field splice. Here, the plate was reduced to $\frac{3}{4}$ inch. The rib depth of 36 inches at the neck of the base connection increased to a maximum of 42 inches and then tapered to 16 inches at the top. Purlins are mostly placed 6 feet on centers except for five courses of 8-inch pipe purlins at the equator, and edge purlins, which form the sweeping curves for the "fringe" of the umbrella. Bays were braced with diagonal, $1\frac{1}{8}$-inch-diameter tie rods.

The tension required to keep the cables dynamically stable was equal to that required to lift the ribs off their exterior supports. To effect further economies and stiffness, equatorial cables were wrapped about the ribs. Posttensioned, the final result avoids nonuniform distortions that might come about due to unsymmetrical loads.

The final structural system might sometime prove to be of tremendous potential for arenas and auditoriums. It results in a stable, sound structure, having an advantageous distribution of material throughout. The shallow space frame at the apex allows ample headroom and a maximum of usable interior space.

However, the superstadium concept preceded the Travelers Pavilion. The Travelers Pavilion was a smaller prototype structural variation of a structure Zetlin had previously conceived as a baseball stadium after designing the Utica Auditorium in 1956.

Super Stadium

Cable structures and their seemingly endless application in the form of huge structures fitted in very well with the dawning megastructure fad.

The Super Stadium shown here was a Zetlin dream and the forerunner of the Traveler's boomerangs. The design was hailed by Ford Frick, the then baseball commissioner, as a possible salvation for housing baseball in large economical structures.

The commissioner, quoted in *This Week* magazine May 15, 1958, claimed that baseball could no longer afford the cost of an open seasonal stadium. A roofed structure would permit year round spectacles and revitalize the baseball industry.

Zetlin happily obliged the baseball fans by proposing a mammoth stadium suitably exploiting the possibilities of cables in megastructures. He was able to realize this idea six years later in the Travelers Insurance Pavilion at the New York World's Fair.

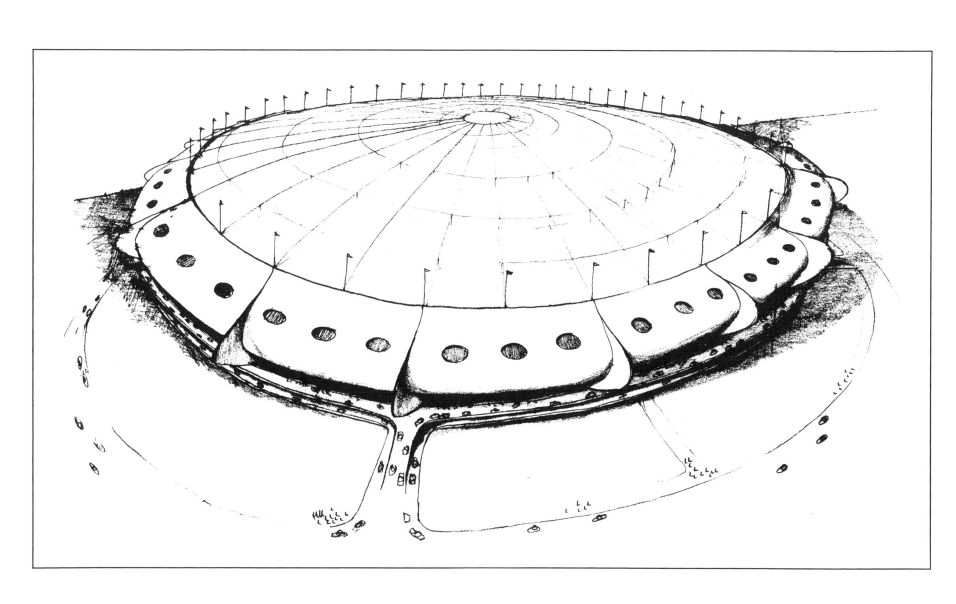

4 The Future

The shock of the future to our designed and built environment was anticipated by Jan Rowan, editor of *Progressive Architecture* magazine four years before Alvin Toffler published his famous book, *Future Shock.*

The magazine devoted its entire issue of December 1966 to the world we might anticipate at the end of the century. The issue was composed exclusively of research conducted by the magazine's editors with one exception: Lev Zetlin was an invited contributor. He wrote a short article titled ''The Engineer's Third Millennium,'' which proved to be a preface to his present predictions of the future.

We can distinguish more clearly the forms of his predictions today as we move toward the year 2000. The changes he anticipated almost a decade earlier in the organization of architectural and engineering offices is occurring as larger offices involve themselves in interdisciplinary approaches to problems. Only they are equipped, as Zetlin anticipated, to pursue the large contracts that will make the use of sophisticated engineering analysis feasible.

Architects become increasingly involved with developers and in the practical construction and financial facets of their profession. As Zetlin predicted, labor has become more expensive and inefficient. There is an increasing emphasis on factory manufacture and sophisticated design solutions to overcome field problems.

Flexure is increasingly circumvented as materials become stronger and buildings lighter. New geometries are emerging and with them the beginnings of another architectural aesthetic.

The architects of the modern movement adopted the clean, efficient lines of machines for their building forms although modern buildings continued to be the products of inefficient, antiquated hand operations. In the same vein we find that buildings now tend to ape the aesthetic of efficient forms of engineering. Yet this is only true in smaller buildings. When buildings grow beyond a certain size, the forms of engineering dominate those of architecture.

Zetlin's predictions of the future were primarily the result of his working with problems of the present. The American Airlines superbay hangars were an offshoot of the theoretical studies he described in 1966. The atomic reactor he designed for architect Philip Johnson in 1964 is related to the airline hangars of 1972 through the geniality of the hypar.

Each idea is enriched by its predecessor as they cross-fertilize each other. Although we can see emerging the outlines of the future as we view Zetlin's work in retrospect, we cannot predict with certainty the means we are going to use to arrive there.

The Role of Industrialization

System and industrialization are household words today. Industrialization is making inroads into construction; it has been introduced to a certain degree in Europe and in Russia. There is almost a universal agreement that it will stay with us and that in the future it will become an integral part of any building and, therefore, of any planning and design.

Logically, industrialization is inevitable. The need for living space is increasing; skilled labor is decreasing. Since the Industrial Revolution, experience has shown, industrialization is the answer to supplying any product which is in demand in large quantities without the availability of skilled labor to produce it.

It is also almost universally agreed that industrialization should be the result of interdisciplinary preplanning and design. These two factors, industrialization and interdisciplinarity, will cause change not only in the final product, namely the buildings, but in each of the present-day professions connected with construction, as well as in the relationship between the various members of the design team as we know them today.

I don't think that at the present stage the problem is whether or not the professions welcome industrialization or agree to it. It is no longer a debatable subject. We cannot deny the fact that in those areas of construction where engineers, architects, and contractors have failed to take the initiative, other industries—such as those connected with chemical and space products which hitherto had nothing to do with the construction field, or at most were merely suppliers of minor components to buildings—have moved into the construction field.

Not only are they suppliers but they organize entire construction projects offering to both manufacture and erect the buildings. We are in the midst of a change in the entire construction profession. In the past, industrialization has been a game. Now it is a serious business.

Attempts at industrialization have been directed toward *conventional* housing units, usually a box made out of steel, concrete, or wood, where some of the components of the box, usually panels, are produced in a factory. Sometimes electrical conduits, plumbing, and other outlets are incorporated within these components. Most of these elements—produced in factories, although termed industrialized—require a significant amount of hand labor. When those components are brought to the site to form a building, they are erected and connected in the same way as we erect conventional buildings. A completed housing project resembles any other conventionally built housing, except that the parts are larger.

Opinions on aesthetics obviously vary. But everybody will agree that the difference between industrialized buildings today and conventional buildings of 20 years ago is not the same as between a car today and the horse in the "preindustrialized" age. This applies not only within one city but from one country to another. There is a distinctive similarity between industrial housing in Moscow, Vienna, and Copenhagen.

In visits to projects erected by the "industrialized" process, my impressions have varied from relatively positive to negative, in respect to quality control of the finished product and in comparison to a traditionally built building. In countries such as Russia, quality control is poor. Concrete panels in concrete buildings are chipped and connections are difficult to fit. There is a lot of field patching.

Despite these negative observations there are two distinct, undisputable advantages achieved through present industrialization: building components can be produced year-round, and the proportion of unskilled labor that can be employed is higher than in conventional construction. It should be remembered, however, that presently only portions of buildings are industrialized. It is probable that even the industrialization of a portion of buildings has encouraged better organization of the labor than in the entire building.

One of the stated purposes of industrialization is economy.

As one traces why industrialized construction has been adopted in various countries, it is found that economics is not always the reason. In Russia, for example, there was a need to produce a quantity of housing in a limited time, irrespective of cost and quality. Surprisingly enough, the same situation existed in many other countries of Europe. Industrialized buildings were undertaken and financed by governments.

In some countries savings of 10 to 20 percent are claimed. In others there seems to be no cost saving achieved. If there are, the reasons given for them vary. In a certain housing complex in Europe consisting of a few thousand units, there were industrialized wall panels while the floors were cast in place. Most of the finishes were applied at the site. A 20 percent saving was claimed. One wonders if such a limited industrialization achieves any saving at all. Questioning disclosed that savings were not due to economies in industrialized production but because of the organization of field-construction operations. The fact that some parts were industrialized opened avenues to a better organization of construction operations. It should be noted that in each case of industrialized projects there are hundreds and often thousands of housing units in a single project. Because of the size of the project, a better construction organization is made possible.

After ten years of playing with industrialization, we should expect a much higher level of achievement in cost, concept, and number of industrialized components in a housing unit. Why has the industrialization that has taken place during the last ten years not resulted in greater economies, variety of components, and more flexibility in planning? The answer is obvious. Present industrialization attempts to imitate conventional construction. Perhaps it is wrong to industrialize conventional housing units with today's technology, new materials, and techniques of production. We should think more in terms of the concepts of buildings, space, and geometry rather than the mass production of components of conventional buildings.

Should a housing unit be a box? Perhaps new materials and new fabrication techniques will evolve a housing form different from a box. It may prove to be more economical to mass-produce complete housing units rather than mere components. We may end with a community that looks like *Alice in Wonderland,* with all manner of shapes for buildings. Having these new forms and new shapes may achieve the real economy and speed in construction that we seek. It may also result in a new environment.

The major effort of the last ten years has been expended toward industrialization of housing. This has imposed a limitation in developing building components. We should attempt to think in terms of new concepts for industrialization not only for housing but for a wider spectrum of building—and not of buildings as we know them today but rather of systems to enclose space against the elements. The purpose of the engineering professions is to create and build new space for people to live and work in. It is not to perpetuate traditional buildings. Conceivably the development of new industrialized systems for a wider range of buildings than housing alone would solve the housing problem as well. My own experience has been that the innovation and development of an airport pier contributed later to a better design of an electric generating plant. Similarly, a successfully completed research and development program for a portable theater for the State Department proved of immense help in developing a building system for a modular housing project.

My final comment is on interdisciplinarity. We agree that real innovations will not be achieved by hunches and intuition. With the complex state of technology today, innovations

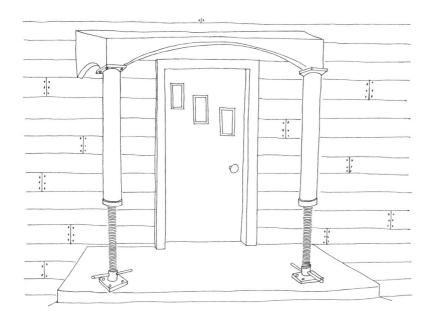

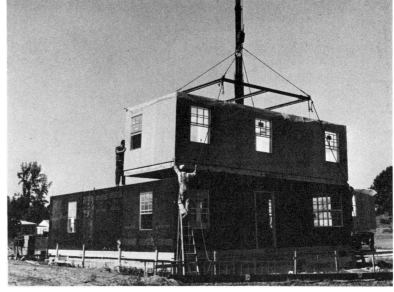

in industrialized construction should involve scientific input based on a thorough technological background. It is unfortunate that many projects sponsored by state and federal authorities for development of industrialized buildings have been given to individuals, often experienced designers of famous buildings. Not all of these men have the necessary preparation for development of industrialized buildings. These individuals, though able and talented, are quite limited in utilizing the technical alternatives now at their disposal.

Even if they engage technically trained consultants, the potential of the resulting vertical team is not nearly so great as that of a horizontal team. I suggest that research and development teams engaged by the governmental and industrial agencies should be interdisciplinary, and not led by one member of the team. Within such a team structure the contribution of each member will be pronounced.

In conclusion, industrialization of building construction will play an important role in the construction industry in the foreseeable future. Industrialization techniques in the U.S. will not be purely those imported from abroad. We shall modify those techniques and develop our own industrialization methods and building concepts properly suited to our market, mentality, standards, and production ability. To get the utmost

out of industrialization, there must be an interdisciplinary cooperation on equal level between the industry and all the professions that are presently involved with construction, or with those professionals in the field of technology and the humanities with a potential to contribute to the breakthrough in this field. This also includes close cooperation with academic interdisciplinary centers.

In spite of the availability of a whole range of new materials, concrete, steel, wood, and aluminum will be widely used for the forthcoming industrialized buildings in the foreseeable future. Emphasis will be placed on production techniques. If we concentrate our studies and investigations on these production techniques, we might find that the present concept of heavy bearing-wall panels or a grid of beams and columns is not the most efficient for industrialization and easy field erection. These systems are not required structurally or for planning. There are many other concepts that are able to create living spaces. It is toward this kind of building concept, which utilizes industrial techniques, rather than imitating conventional building concepts, that our efforts should be turned next. This route will bring us to our goal of economical and better housing more quickly.

Housing

The solution for housing will arrive in a generation or two and will involve a drastic reorientation of the concept of living.

If standardization is applied, people will have to get used to it. The reorganization of technology is required, which will mean companies going bankrupt. This has already happened in housing and will probably continue. This is a painful but healthy process, much healthier than the Russian approach. The Russians adopted a system of industrialized housing and worked themselves into a corner where there is no way out. Systems improve through use. The minute you change an element the final result is redefined. We expect certain things in housing, which makes us conservative. This is why housing construction changes so slowly.

It is not a negative attitude and is not due to stupidity but,

rather, human nature. Military innovation always keeps the old with the new. If a new tank is invented, the old tanks are retained. A new airplane might be designed but the old is kept. The military depends on the old as they take the bugs out of the new.

A means of getting to communities must be devised before houses are built. Manufacturing more cars is not a solution. You cannot create more energy by burning energy and ruining the air in the process. There has to be a solution that will supply our energy needs without retrogressing. I think there is one.

There must be a way to go short distances without using the automobile. I do not know how, but perhaps it is a system of rails above the sidewalks of existing buildings. Instead of being two horizontal rails, the rails might be vertical with the train riding between them.

I don't say this is the best idea but it does not require land use and it does not obstruct the street. It would actually

clear the street. I don't see why cars cannot be prohibited from coming into the city. Housing is only a small part of the major city problem.

Operation Breakthrough never got off the ground. Instead of $300 million only $60 or $80 million was spent. Instead of 25 projects there were only six.

They did not pay for themselves. Breakthough was not intended to solve any single project. It was to have served as encouragement for companies to enter into construction and to encourage novel ideas by sharing their costs. As soon as the government did not spend as much money as it had proclaimed, only a few companies were willing to take the risk. As a result, the number of experiments performed was relatively small. The failure was quantitative, not qualitative. If there had been more projects and more experiments, there would have been more Breakthroughs.

Innovation varied—on the big projects there was very little, and some of them only changed their management. Construction management is very complex. This could have been important. Some introduced innovation in the construction sequence, but usually only in small components.

Eventually each unit would become a component of something else. All of this will be put together to form an American system.

The feasibility of a Sears Roebuck–type house, where the owner could buy the component parts and assemble them himself, presents no technical problem. But how many people will be willing and capable? When a person undertakes to build his own sidewalk, it represents a limited effort. To build housing takes a tremendous, continuous effort. Very few have the patience and the tenacity.

Why do so few people install their own siding? Why do they go to a little contractor? Why not give that contractor something better than siding? But the minute it is better it creates a demand and becomes a large operation. The contractor becomes a tycoon and the system is back where it started.

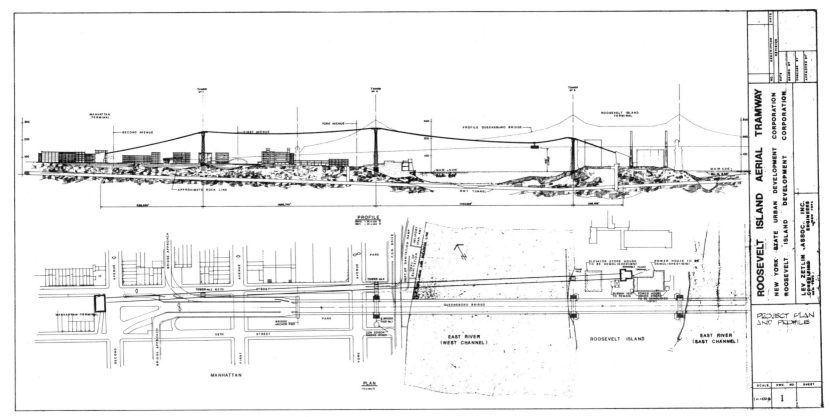

ROOSEVELT ISLAND AERIAL TRAMWAY

NEW YORK STATE URBAN DEVELOPMENT CORPORATION
ROOSEVELT ISLAND DEVELOPMENT CORPORATION

LEV ZETLIN ∘ASSOC., INC.
CONSULTING ENGINEERS
NEW YORK

PROJECT PLAN
AND PROFILE

SCALE | DWG. NO. | SHEET
1 in.=100 ft. | | 1

138

Aerial Tramway, New York City
Roosevelt Island Development Corporation; New York State Urban Development Corporation

The aerial tramway is planned as a public rapid transit system, connecting Manhattan's Upper East Side with Roosevelt Island. It will serve approximately 5,000 housing units planned for completion on Roosevelt Island in 1979. Lev Zetlin Associates is responsible for the preliminary analysis, site evaluation, structural, mechanical and electrical engineering design, and construction supervision.

The 125-passenger tramway cars will ride a two-track $2\frac{1}{2}$ inch diameter wire rope cable suspended from one tower on Roosevelt Island and two on Manhattan. The towers will rise approximately 200 feet above the East River. The cars will be propelled by a third traction cable at an average speed of 13.5 miles per hour. Total travel time for the 3,400-foot one-way trip is approximately 4 minutes.

The Roosevelt Island–Manhattan aerial tramway represents the first such system in the United States to be used for mass rapid transit.

140

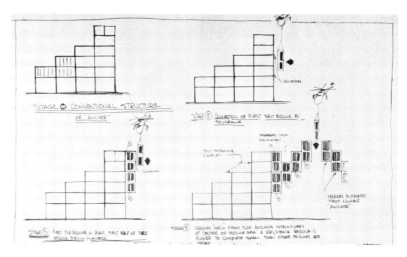

Stratasystem

The paper bridge structural system was used in conjunction with architects Eggers & Higgins to design a slum clearance project, actually a city above the slums, without removing the slums before or during construction.

The theory was to let the slum dwellers live where they were for the time being. A tower would be built and then a platform. On top of the platform buildings would be erected. The cost of the platform brings the cost of land up to that comparable to Fifth Avenue in New York City.

This is the stratasystem in which all the buildings are molecules. Each apartment of each livable area becomes a molecule in itself that would be mass-produced in the factory—with the characteristic that when joined they become a chain, like a polymer. A polymer is a man-made controlled chain of molecules. When these molecules bridge themselves over the slums, you will not need a platform.

Today people are much more sympathetic to such ideas than they were in the past. Five years ago when an exciting structural system was evolved, it was necessary to work within accepted engineering concepts.

The stratasystem of housing was kicked around by various government agencies. Ideas like this have to be realized on a gigantic scale. I still believe that housing can be built over the slums without a platform and if you can do that, there will be tremendous cost savings.

You cannot make instant rehab or a drastic innovation in these terms for low-rise, high-density housing.

Ours was a very straightforward approach—to replace old elements with new and open up larger spans working with everyday labor but use slightly more sophisticated elements, such as staircases, which became curved slabs instead of beams.

I don't think that rehab is going to solve a big problem because you are giving housing to people who are not particular about its upkeep. Nothing can stand abuse, not even housing. A precast concrete building can stand more abuse than lath and plaster but old buildings have to be repaired with lath and plaster. Ordinarily this is a beautiful material but in rehabilitation it is put into the hands of people who abuse it. The life span of rehabilitation housing is, therefore, limited.

I believe more in tearing down old slums and building new housing that can stand abuse. As long as a building has the same number, on the same street, and looks like an old building, it is going to be treated with that attitude by its users. But if people move into a new development, there is a change in their attitude. They treat it differently.

141

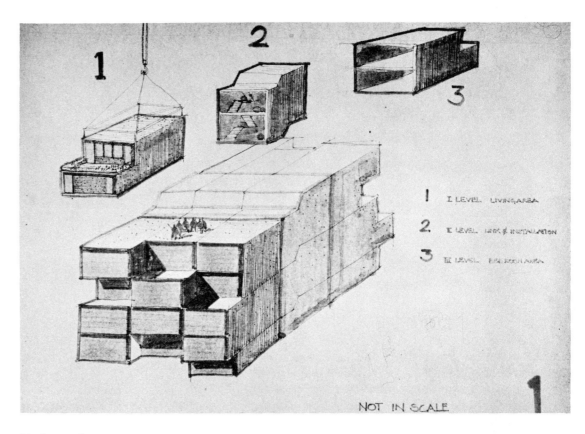

NOT IN SCALE

1   I LEVEL LIVING AREA

2   II LEVEL SHOP & INSTALLATION

3   III LEVEL BEDROOM AREA

Stratasystem: Renewal Without Relocation— A Design Exercise

Eggers & Higgins, architects
Lev Zetlin Associates, structural engineers

The architects developed a conceptual system to bring about urban renewal without relocation. The proposal, known as stratasystem, involves building new self-contained neighborhoods of 4,400 persons, each neighborhood constructed on platforms over streets, vacant land, abandoned, or still-occupied dilapidated buildings.

The housing would be supplied with an upper level of shops, while underneath the platform would be trunk space for the mechanical system. Added, as relocation progresses upward, are the parking level, stores, offices, and other community-supported facilities at grade. The stratasystem is nevertheless flexible enough to "descend" to parks, historical sites, and areas with existing housing restored.

The system, devised without a client or immediate promise of implementation, envisions a basic minimum area for application at 11 acres, or two New York City blocks. Six to eight of these neighborhoods, linked by pedestrian malls on the concourse or housing level and levels beneath, would form a community. Built on a modular basis, the housing is adaptable to any type of construction technique, whether conventional steel or concrete, or prefabricated methods. Neither high rise nor low rise, the modular townhouses rise in stepped increments. The rectangularly planned apartment buildings have dwelling units flanking a longitudinal corridor because of this organization's suitability to either conventional construction or innovative plug-in prefabricated modular units.

The system, which could be built on private land with air-rights leasing, would have to be government-subsidized for low rents. Yet the construction of the stratasystem community for 35,200 persons should cost $411 million, $25 million less than a conventionally designed project and without the problems and upsets of relocation.

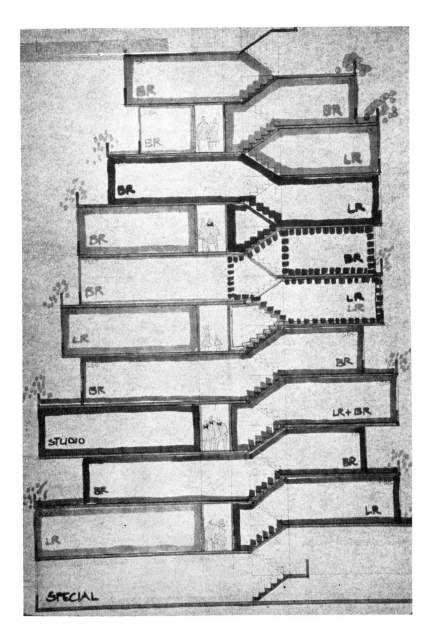

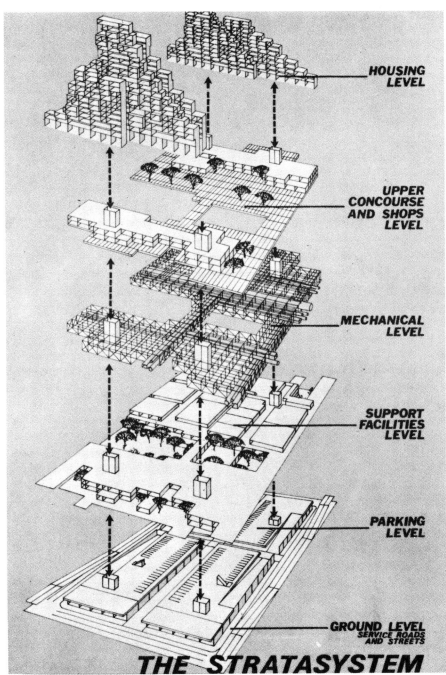

HOUSING
LEVEL

UPPER
CONCOURSE
AND SHOPS
LEVEL

MECHANICAL
LEVEL

SUPPORT
FACILITIES
LEVEL

PARKING
LEVEL

GROUND LEVEL
SERVICE ROADS
AND STREETS

THE STRATASYSTEM

143

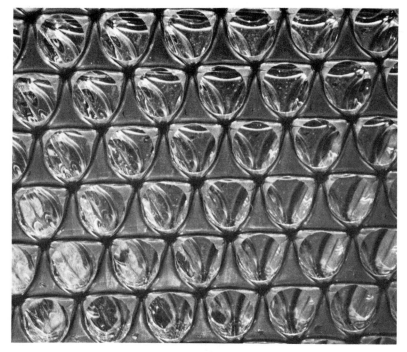

Plastics

Various plastics are beginning to assume an important role in building construction. The properties of plastics have been improving rapidly. Perhaps of more importance, those properties have become more homogeneous. In the past plastics were used essentially only as replacement materials for fixtures and finishes. They have now begun to assume structural functions. The usefulness of plastics in building has been increased by the introduction of the reinforced plastics employed profusely by the aeronautical and space industries.

In general, the application of plastics to building construction falls into two groups. The first is the substitution of plastic material for conventional building uses. This seems to be the tradition always followed in the past when new materials were introduced. The debut of precast concrete and aluminum into buildings was in the form of I and WF sections, imitating the shapes of structural steel in much the same spirit as the Greeks devised the shape of their stone columns from the wooden posts they replaced. The second application of plastics in the building process has been as unique complete structural systems. It is in this area that the possibility of innovative building form in this new material will emerge.

The first application as imitations of conventional structural components is not a creative engineering approach. It obviously limits full utilization of a new material. On the other hand, the application of plastics to entire structural systems will induce innovation in the building industry.

New materials inherently possess properties different from those of the materials previously used even if some of the properties of the new material, such as strength, are similar to the conventional material replaced. To utilize new material efficiently new structural systems suitable to their unique properties must be devised. Such structural uses utilizing a new material efficiently might well evolve very different forms and shapes than those we are accustomed to. This will change the shape of our built environment. The effect of such change will have to be interpreted by sociologists.

Because of the physical properties of reinforced plastics, they are most efficiently used resisting external loads through skin stresses. Long-term, time-dependent deformations might be a significant parameter to consider in designing a long-span glass-fiber-reinforced plastic structure. The concept of pneumatic prestressing might be an important contribution to its structural stability. Air pressure, dynamic devices, and similar nonstatic means to resist external loads are a potential means of achieving economical structures in plastic and other synthetic materials.

There are other developments than reinforcement in the field of plastics that are of significance to the structural engineering profession. Structural foam as a material has a great deal of potential. It can be manufactured in compositions similar to bone structure. Although its strength is not the same as glass-fiber materials, it can be made rigid with strong dense exterior surfaces to resist major stresses and spongelike interiors analogous to the human bone structure where stresses are reduced. Foam is much cheaper than a reinforced material and requires only one process in manufacture.

Structural foam is produced by chemical companies, which are not directly involved in construction or design. They look for fast, easy markets, mostly in the application of their products as substitutes. These companies know very little about complete structural systems.

As structural engineers become aware of new materials and a plethora of synthetic materials is available to them, they must seek methods of using these new materials in structural systems. Novel systems must be devised if need be. If the materials do not meet all the criteria required for structural systems, engineers must advise the manufacturers of the needs of the building professions. Such an interchange of ideas might initiate the improvement and utilization of new materials for the construction industry, spurring a trend toward badly needed innovation. Engineers may initiate a creative chain of ideas. Plastics and other synthetic materials are an ideal beginning for such a chain reaction.

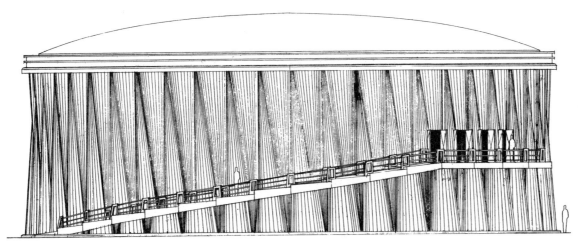

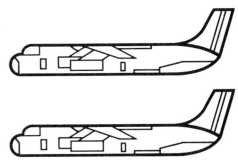

Portable Theater Developed for the
U.S. State Department, 1968
Lev Zetlin Associates, structural engineers

A new concept in totally integrated portable-theater design was created by the KOHM Group consisting of Edward Kook, Donald Oenslager, Cyril Harris, and Jo Mielziner. The research and study for the theater was made possible by a Ford Foundation grant awarded to the Arts of the Theatre Foundation.

The research resulted in a scale model of the theater and the publication of a brochure entitled "Porto Theatre." Illustrations shown here are from this publication.

The structure is round, has about 10,000 square feet of floor space, and is roughly 100 feet in diameter. In this case there were three main goals to be achieved. First, the structure has to be light enough to fit in an airplane. Second it should be assembled and dismantled by unskilled labor. Third, it should stand on any type of soil, roughly graded, and in any kind of weather, from monsoon zones to the North Pole.

The building would consist of three basic repetitive elements. Flat segments of a ring are used as footing, so the building does not require any permanent foundations. The second group of elements is the fluted wall sections. The third group is the slanting seat elements. The wall panels fit into grooves in the ring footing and are interconnected by gaskets under air pressure. A circumferential compression is imposed on the walls making them both rigid and watertight.

The sloping seat members wedge against the walls, creating a continuous closed structure. Segmental elements similar to the footings are used as ring members, as shown on top of the wall panels, to support a plastic air-pressured roof. Each component member of the structure serves both a structural and an architectural function. The building would weigh approximately 80 tons with all the equipment as compared to 1,200 tons if it were a conventional building.

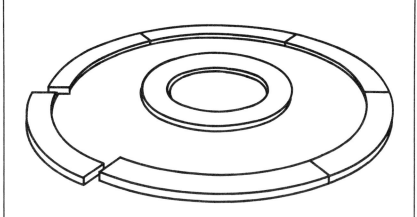

Inner and outer rings are laid out on the ground. Each ring is made up of conveniently short sections which interlock with each other.

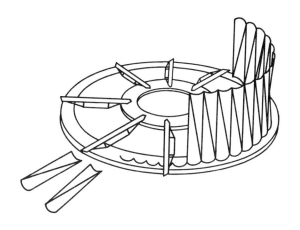

After seats and aisle units are assembled, wall units are set up in grooves in the outer ring. Note that seating structure locks into the foot of the stage at one end and into the wall at the other.

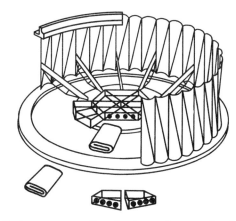

Before all the outer wall units have been raised and inter-locked, the component parts of the Light and Sound Canopy and all lights and speakers are assembled on the stage floor. Then the inflatable roof is unfolded and laid on top of the Light and Sound Canopy. Finally the top ring locks all wall sections together.

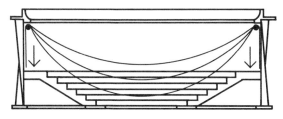

Men standing on the top ring pull up the uninflated roof which is then inflated by means of auxiliary blowers.

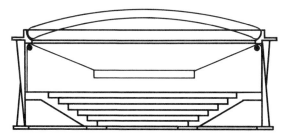

Light and Sound Canopy is pulled up into operating position.

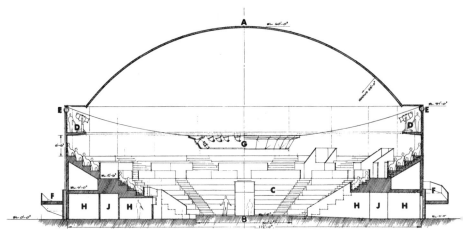

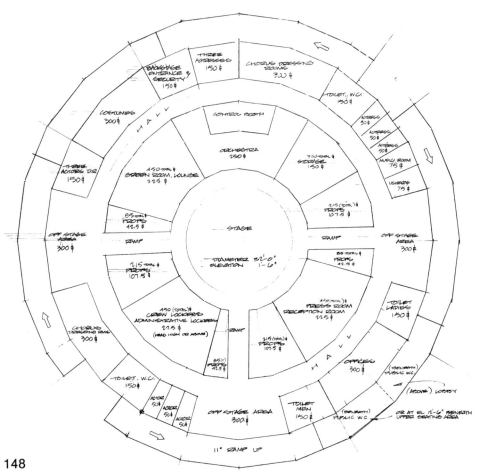

Schematic section of Porto Theatre
A. Inflated Dome.
B. Stage.
C. Seating Area.
D. Spotlight Gallery.

E. Hardware for Cables Supporting Light and Sound Canopy.
F. Ramp for Entering Theatre.
G. Light and Sound Canopy.
H. Dressing Rooms and Service Areas.
J. Internal Passageways.

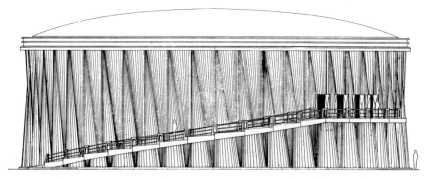

Exterior of Porto Theatre showing ramp leading from ground level to entrances.

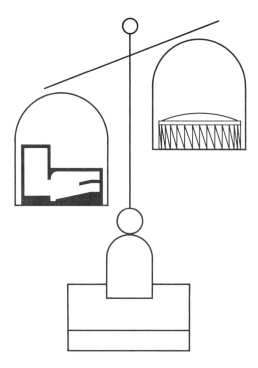

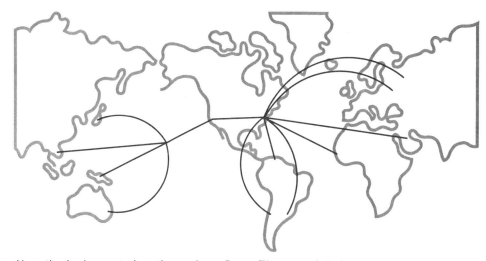

Comparison of approximate weight of Porto Theatre with that of a conventional proscenium stage theatre. The best estimate of the weight of a 1000 seat proscenium stage theatre is 1900 tons. Porto Theatre will weigh only 100 tons!

Hypothetical remote locations where Porto Theatre might be flown.

149

LaGuardia Airport Runway Pier Extension

One should look for structural systems and forms for buildings compatible with the property and special quality of the material. A salient feature of reinforced plastics is low weight-to-strength ratios. The suggested use of plastics shown here to increase the capacity of a runway pier in the LaGuardia Airport in New York applies this principle. Currently, this precast concrete pier is supported on steel piles. One way to increase the capacity of the pier if it is contemplated to use it for heavier planes than those for which it was originally designed is to decrease its dead weight. This could be achieved through buoyancy. In this case, continuous plastic, large diameter tubes generate the uplift.

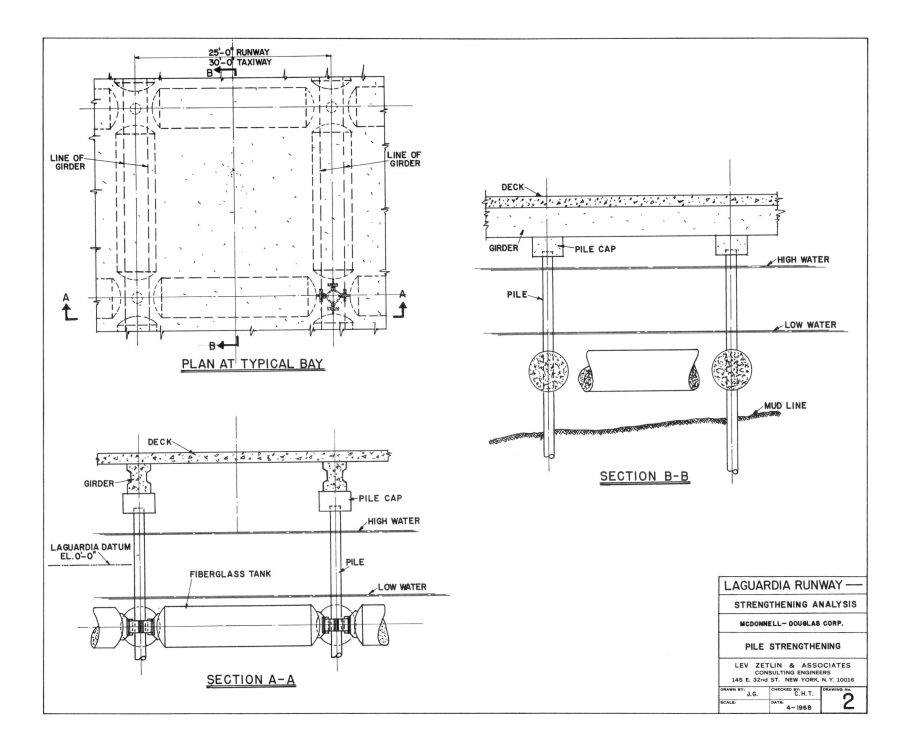

25'-0" RUNWAY
30'-0" TAXIWAY

B

LINE OF GIRDER

LINE OF GIRDER

A

A

B

PLAN AT TYPICAL BAY

DECK

GIRDER

PILE CAP

HIGH WATER

LAGUARDIA DATUM EL. 0'-0"

FIBERGLASS TANK

PILE

LOW WATER

SECTION A-A

DECK

GIRDER

PILE CAP

HIGH WATER

PILE

LOW WATER

MUD LINE

SECTION B-B

LAGUARDIA RUNWAY —

STRENGTHENING ANALYSIS

MCDONNELL— DOUGLAS CORP.

PILE STRENGTHENING

LEV ZETLIN & ASSOCIATES
CONSULTING ENGINEERS
145 E. 32nd ST. NEW YORK, N.Y. 10016

DRAWN BY: J.G.	CHECKED BY: C.H.T.	DRAWING No. 2
SCALE:	DATE: 4—1968	

151

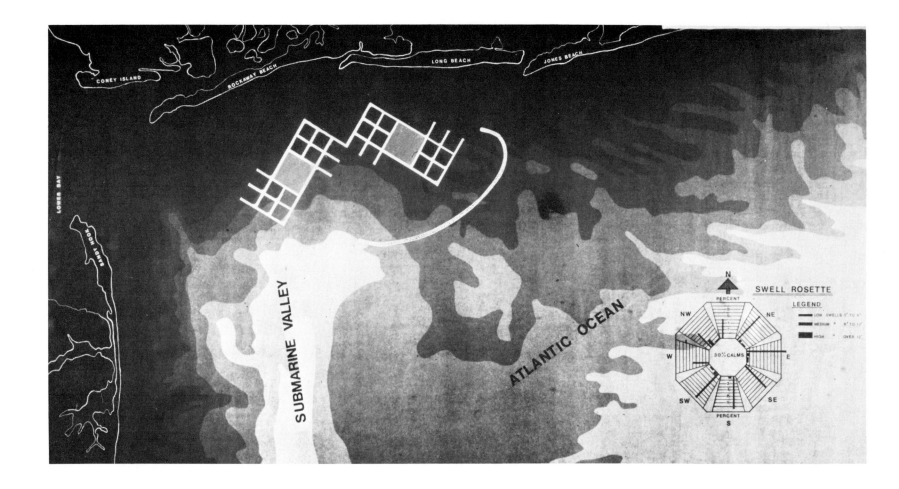

Offshore Buoyant Airports

Following the proposal for the buoyant tubes used to support the LaGuardia Pier, the Environspace Corporation, an affiliate of Lev Zetlin Associates, published a brochure in which they took the idea of buoyancy forces and airports one step further.

The brochure stated that the concept of offshore airports presented an exceptionally feasible solution to conserving land when developing airport facilities. They further claimed that floating airports were currently the only feasible solution to offshore airports in very deep water.

In shallow water, approximately 50 feet deep or less, the construction of an offshore airport using dikes or land fill would be more economical than a floating airport. As water depth increased, the cost of conventional construction methods would increase rapidly, making the potential of the floating airport more economically feasible.

The technical philosophy behind a floating airport is the use of buoyant forces to support the platform structure. Under certain conditions these buoyant forces could be used without floating the entire airport. This solution is potentially economical in medium water depths of from 100 to 200 feet.

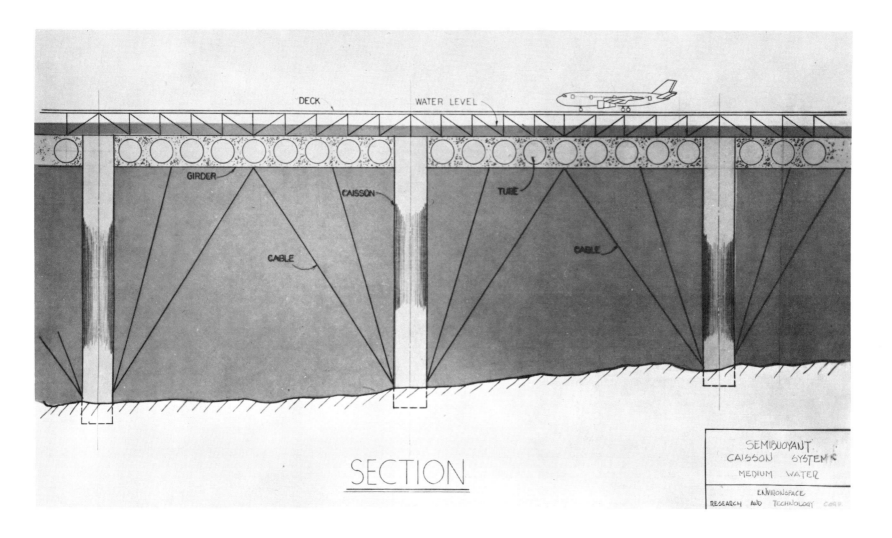

DECK

WATER LEVEL

GIRDER

CAISSON

TUBE

CABLE

CABLE

SECTION

Semibuoyant Caisson System

An intermediate solution is illustrated showing buoyant forces supporting a lightweight floating platform that spans more than 300 feet between large caissons. In medium water depths, the caissons eliminate the need for numerous massive anchors. The combination of caissons and cables results in an economical system that provides both stability and support to the entire airport platform.

153

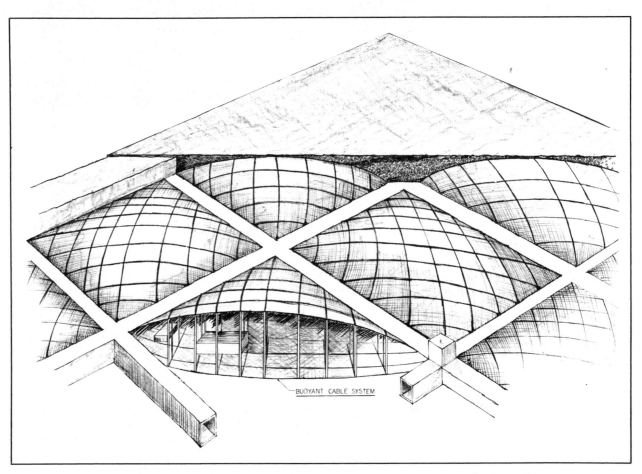

BUOYANT CABLE SYSTEM

Air Foundation on Buoyant Cable System

Here the designs incorporate the runway air foundation and a unique cable buoyancy system. The lightweight cable system provides the platform with both buoyancy and rigidity. In addition, the use of lightweight materials reduces the buoyant forces required to float the airport.

The airport, in turn, requires less enclosed area to develop the buoyancy, resulting in overall economy. The caisson system can also be used with this scheme. However, due to the overall light weight of the air foundation and the cable buoyancy system, the amount of anchorage required for this scheme is minimal. The system can be economically constructed in deep water.

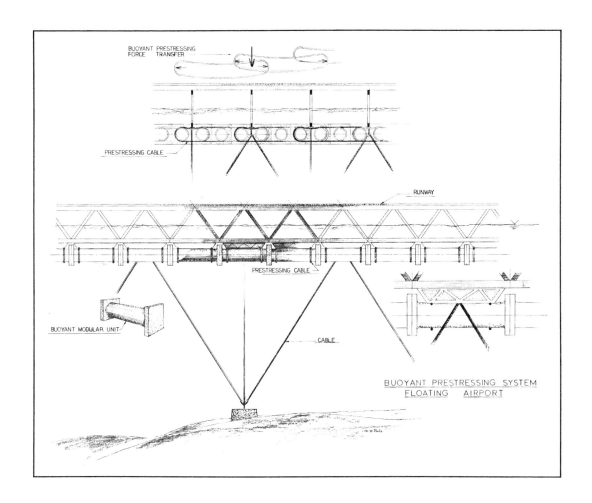

BUOYANT PRESTRESSING
FORCE TRANSFER

PRESTRESSING CABLE

RUNWAY

PRESTRESSING CABLE

BUOYANT MODULAR UNIT

CABLE

BUOYANT PRESTRESSING SYSTEM
FLOATING AIRPORT

Buoyant Prestressing System

The designer must capitalize on available forces to strengthen the structure if he is to develop an economical structural system for deep water. The deep-water design shown here employs natural buoyant forces to prestress the submerged platform as well as to float it. This results in the economical use of structural materials and permits use of a modular buoyant unit readily adaptable to industrialized mass-production techniques.

155

Tall Buildings

Technology of construction and design of tall buildings grew gradually from the technology of low buildings by adding tiers or floors, essentially by stacking a steel or concrete post-and-beam system—a rigid frame is classified as a post-and-beam for the purpose of this discussion—one on top of the other. This procedure has four main disadvantages: 1) Increase in the number of connections and in the number of structural components as the height of the building increases raises construction cost and duration of construction. 2) Conventional tall-building structural systems are subjected mainly to bending moments through the columns and beams; thus, all the material is not stressed efficiently. 3) As the height of a tall building is increased, the dead weight of the building uses a considerable portion of the structural strength of the columns on the lower floors. This not only puts a limitation on the height of the building, but the columns occupy large spaces on the lower floors. The high-strength steels available could not be used to a considerable extent to reduce the column sizes because of the lateral flexibility. 4) Lateral sway of tall buildings, as well as the gravity loads on beams and other frames within a tall building, are resisted mainly by bending moments within the structural system. These bending moments result in rotations within the axial elements; rotations depend on the modulus of elasticity of the structural material, which is usually structural steel. Since moduli of elasticity of low-strength and high-strength steels are almost the same, the load resistance of the conventional structural frames depends essentially on the moment of inertia of the component elements of the frame. Since the use of high-strength steels would reduce considerably the moment of inertia of the component elements, flexibility of the structural frame is increased. It is this reason that prevents large-scale introduction of high-strength steels in tall buildings.

In many structures, such as aircraft and machines, many of the problems outlined above have been solved through the use of geometry of the structural system. For example, one type of such development was in large-span structures where a solid beam developed through the years into a truss, then into a space frame, and then into a light-gauge hyperbolic-para-

156

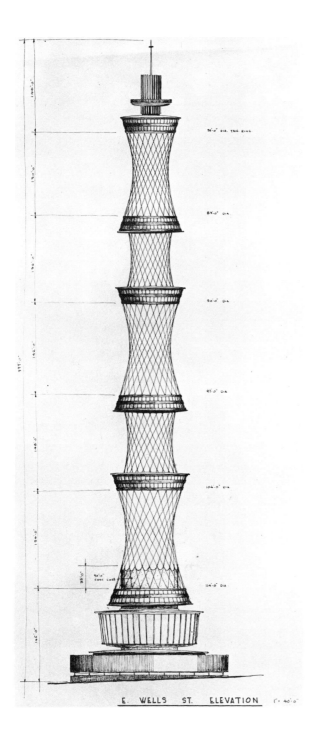

boloid skin. In such an example both the weight of structural material and the labor of putting it up have been successfully and drastically reduced as it has undergone the transformation from a solid beam to hyperbolic paraboloid.

With the present increase in population density and therefore the increasing need for tall buildings, an effort toward more efficient and economical construction is urgent. Introducing the effect of geometric configuration of the structural system into the design of tall buildings could be one of the most successful factors. If one can come up with a structural system whose rigidity is not so sensitive to the modulus of elasticity as a beam-and-post system (for example, if the entire tall building consisted of a honeycombed tube), one could achieve the prescribed goal.

Obviously, as efficient geometric structural systems that are different in form from the conventional ones are devised, the form of the tall building and therefore the architectural expression of the exterior, as well as the configuration of the floor plans, might be affected and be somewhat different from traditional planning concepts. In many cases the change is toward a better architectural solution. However, in every case the final adopted solution for the geometric configuration of the structural system should be one that results in an optimum compromise between the various needs of architectural planning, environmental control, and structural flexibility. The geometry of the structural system, rather than an indiscriminate use of the traditional tier construction, will contribute a great deal to this optimum solution.

Traditionally, a structure is subjected to permanent as well as temporary loads. Temporary loads are usually of various intensities. Normally, structures are designed for temporary loads of maximum intensity irrespective of the incidence of their occurrence. Therefore, for loads of high intensity, which occur rarely (i.e., earthquakes and hurricanes), structural material to resist such temporary loads is normally provided permanently in the structural system. A kinetic device built into a structural system could provide temporary resistance only when called upon. Provision of such a kinetic device could prove extremely economical. Significant economies could be achieved because such kinetic devices would reduce the expense of and the need for a multitude of connections required in a tall building.

Telescoping 80-Story Office Building

A breakthrough of tall building construction is proposed here in which all the exterior bearing walls are poured on the ground simultaneously with foam lining separating each exterior ring. This system therefore requires only one set of interior forms and one set of exterior forms to pour all the exterior walls of this 80-story building.

Each section poured at ground level is approximately eight stories high. After the concrete has hardened, all the exterior wall sections are posttensioned vertically. As a first stage in floor construction, all the precast floors are constructed inside the first interior ring of the wall. Then, all the remaining exterior walls are pulled up to the top of the first interior ring. At this stage the next group level of eight precast floors is constructed within the second interior ring. This process is continued until the whole building has telescoped to its top level.

The proposed system eliminates continuous delivery of small batches of materials floor by floor throughout the height of the building, enables most of the work to be done at one constant level, and saves a tremendous amount of formwork. Although the examples shown are of a circular building, the system could be adapted to any other geometric form.

PRESTRESSED HI RISE SYSTEM

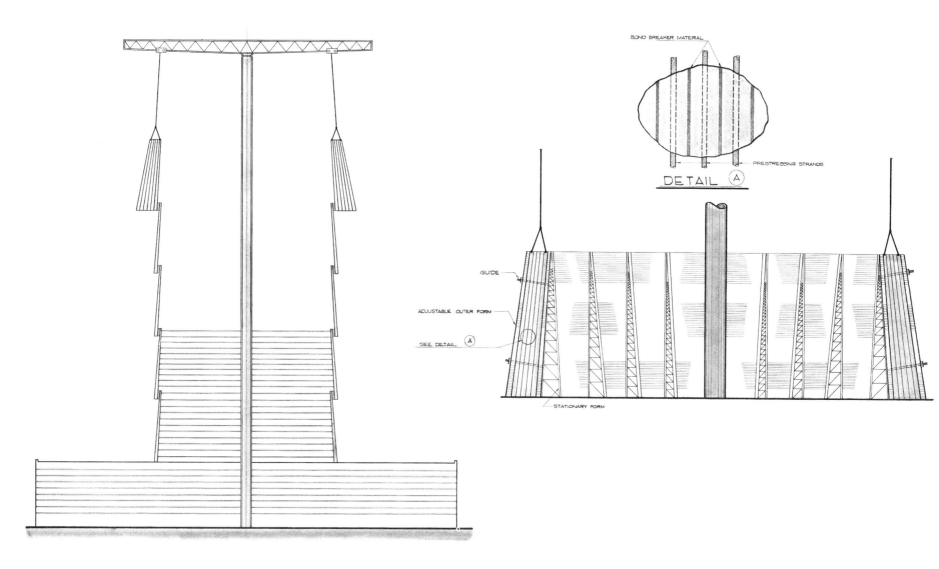

BOND BREAKER MATERIAL

DETAIL (A)

PRESTRESSING STRANDS

GUIDE

ADJUSTABLE OUTER FORM

SEE DETAIL (A)

STATIONARY FORM

PRESTRESSED HI RISE SYSTEM
ERECTION SEQUENCE

159

Vibration and Sound in Construction Planning

The control of vibrations and noise during construction operations and during the service life of buildings is becoming one of the most acute problems in modern engineering technology. Concerned reaction of communities to environmental problems and the use of modern construction materials as well as thinner and more flexible structural components, which aggravate the problems associated with vibrations and noise, increase the importance of finding solutions to the problems involved. Construction economy increasingly dictates the employment of less skilled field labor. Construction industrialization and the use of thinner structural members composed of nonconventional structural materials will increase in the coming years. This will further aggravate the problem of vibration and noise because of the sensitivity of such structural components to dynamic impulses.

The present trend to emphasize continuity of structural frames and the more abundant use of skin-type structural systems and components will continue. This will drastically affect the dynamic characteristics of structures. It is thus imperative for the engineering profession to include considerations of vibrations and sound propagation during the initial stages of the design of structural systems. This requires the designing engineer to acquire new skills and to relate such new skills to the traditional design and construction practice.

Since response to vibrations and to sound propagation of complete structures is a complex phenomenon, little of such response is known. Extensive theoretical as well as model and prototypical structure-testing procedures will have to be undertaken. Our knowledge of the responses of conventional structures to dynamic loads has been gained empirically. Such accumulation of knowledge served a useful purpose in the past because structural systems remained relatively unchanged.

It was possible by observing the behavior of one structure under dynamic load to derive conclusions and predictions by extrapolation of this behavior to similar structures to be constructed in the future under similar conditions. Such extrapolation was safe and reliable even though the exact mechanics of behavior and response was not known and a reliable method of analysis did not exist. With today's rapid change in technology, we can no longer extrapolate by observation. We must gain more knowledge. More research and more testing becomes necessary.

Until we develop better skills in ascertaining dynamic response to vibrations and to sound in relation to complete structures, we should use whatever information is available to us now. Our knowledge of analyzing and evaluating response to dynamic effects of uniaxial structural members is quite broad and such behavior of uniaxial members could be evaluated fairly accurately. The knowledge that we lack is the response of whole structures consisting of multitudes of such components. I suggest, therefore, that the engineer evaluate more closely the dynamic characteristics of individual structural components and then use value judgment on interaction of such components, basing such value judgment on available test data and theoretical knowledge which, though meager, does exist today.

Unfortunately, even a partial design approach such as this is not practiced.

The prevalent approach of the engineering profession to avoid detrimental effects of vibrations or of sound has always been first the elimination of the source from which these dynamic effects emanated. It is not common to design structural components so that their behavior is acceptable under adverse dynamic effects. Although it is desirable to eliminate the sources of vibration and sound where possible, to do so in urban areas would require a national effort. We should try to eliminate the source of objectionable vibrations and sound. Nevertheless, as engineers, we have the obligation to solve the problem at the target of the dynamic effect, namely, the project that we are designing. Since both vibrations and sound result from energy from a source, the logical approach is to design a structure that absorbs or dissipates the energy of vibration or of sound. We must consider the dampening properties within a structure. To eliminate the detrimental effects of vibrations or of noise by dampening the structure would obviously be tantamount to controlling the source.

The efficiency of dampening can be seen from the correlation of the amplitudes of vibrating mass with the frequency of the imposed dynamic force. Without dampening, the amplitudes become infinite—that is, the collapse of the structure becomes imminent. There are diminishing amplitudes with increas-

ing dampening and one could go down all the way to zero amplitude with critical dampening.

Dampening does not necessarily require a large expenditure for mechanical dampeners such as shock absorbers. Since dampeners are merely means to absorb or to transfer energy, it is possible to devise structural systems that have inherent dampening characteristics. For example, suspension structures that employ catenaries were known for their dynamic instability in the past. Prior to the exposure of the structural engineering profession to more scientific tools, a simplified empirical approach to eliminate dynamic instability was to increase rigidity or to add mass, such as concrete planks, to the suspension system. This approach is inaccurate, unreliable, and costly in construction. Sixteen years ago I introduced a system based on the principle of transfer of energy to stabilize a suspension structure. This system consists of a double layer of cables used in the Utica Municipal Auditorium. The two interconnected cables are designed to have two different natural frequencies that tend to diverge with imposed loading. This fact of the presence of two different natural frequencies within a system constitutes the perfect dampener because they constitute the means for a continuous flow of energy from one layer of cables to another. The resulting system is economical and lightweight since it does not require any added mass on top of the roof or rigidity beyond that needed to resist static loads.

This system has been used on several dozen large-span structures throughout the world. Approaches like these, utilizing broader scientific principles, will have to be used more often in the future design of structures to eliminate the detrimental effects of noise and vibrations.

In the case of rigid structures such as frames or skin structures, more attention should be paid to the design and employment of connections that have inherent energy-absorbing characteristics. It is obvious that a structural system whose

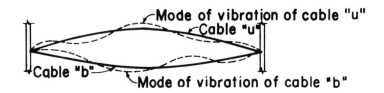

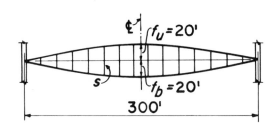

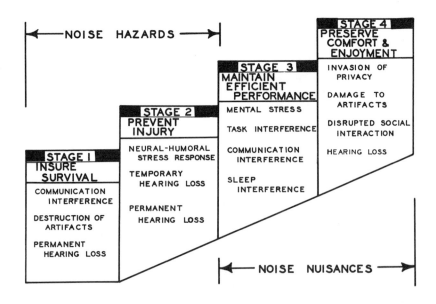

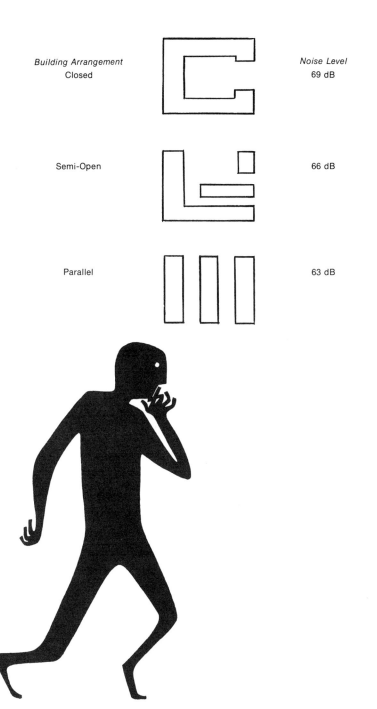

Building Arrangement
Closed

Noise Level
69 dB

Semi-Open

66 dB

Parallel

63 dB

components are all interconnected through self-dampening connections will have a very small capability of transmitting and amplifying mechanical vibrations or noise.

Referring to noise pollution, more studies have been made and more knowledge has been gained on this topic in the last ten years than in the 100 years preceding that period. Unfortunately, not too many design engineers made it their business to use this data as part of their design of the geometry of a structural system. Noise pollution is usually treated as an acoustical problem and its solution is referred to acoustical specialists. Thus, the problem is usually treated by attaching materials to and over the structural system, rather than examining the structural system itself. The geometry of the structural system, the structural material used, continuity of the system, and its dynamic response characteristics could contribute to noise control. For example, studies made on the geometry of buildings show that the geometry of the building itself could contribute to a difference in noise level of 6 decibels. Under normal frequencies at 60 decibels, conversation is possible, while 74 decibels corresponds to the noise of a vacuum cleaner. A 6-decibel difference is significant.

The health problem of noise can be disruptive to an organism's physiology as well as detrimental to emotional and social well-being.

While the design profession pays attention successfully to the geometry and cladding material of interior spaces, such as theaters and auditoriums, no regard for noise control is paid to the exterior finishes or the exterior geometry of the buildings. It is conceivable that successful envionmental solutions to noise pollution for communities or even cities could be achieved by concentrating on the exterior of buildings. This might prove to be cheaper, in the long run, than relocating highways and changing the mechanical components of vehicles.

Connections

I advocate we discard strait-jacketed basic engineering tenets as we now understand them. I propose we evolve new ones, appropriate to today's technology in today's world. We have engineering theories that do not express the flow of stresses accurately. Nor do they accurately represent the behavior of structures under stress. All they tell us is: if you design a structure with these formulae, it will behave like thousands of others designed in a similar fashion. One important assumption of modern engineering theory is that structures are divided into components. We design the components and then connect them. Every theory assumes that the material in that infinitesimal plane that connects the two members is the same material as the members joined. This is different than the design of connections. The connection between two members is always assumed to be a continuation of the two members; nothing can be further from the truth. Every connection, be it concrete, steel, or whatever, incurs slippage—which is what we

call rigid body movement, as opposed to elastic movement. In addition, the elastic properties are different from the adjoining members. If we examine this problem and pursue it, it will result in the evolution of extremely complex engineering theories. Although we avoid this eventuality, it is exactly what today's computers do best.

If you can analyze the true behavior of the connection, it will correspond to what actually occurs in the field. We will be representing the behavior of the structure accurately, and will not be forced to waste so much material. We waste mate-

rial today even knowing the problems are those of these connections.

The only salvation for our building problems in the future is prefabricated skin components. The problem is that everyone who connects shells assumes that the material is the same. Tests were conducted, results obtained, and somehow turned into formulae. Why do we act as ostriches, spending hundreds and millions of dollars on the wrong assumption, when we could have spent only part of that on making the right observation?

Rapid Transit Structural Systems

In 1971 the office of Lev Zetlin undertook an examination of systems of structural components for lining subway tunnels, viaducts, bridges, stations, retaining walls, cuts, overpasses, and related transportation structures. The project was undertaken for the Delaware River Port Authority. The objectives sought were ease of construction connections, minimum field labor, and construction time savings.

The components were mass-produced under factory conditions and production techniques. They were interchangeable and could be nested for shipping. The almost universal use of the components for rapid transit facilities reduced the construction operation to repetitive patterns, which speeded and economized construction.

Even though the motivating design philosophy of sophisticated design elements, simply erected, dominated the designs, this study differed from that undertaken for the airlines hangar facilities—which eventually resulted in the American Airlines hypar cantilever prototype structures. The elements here are modest, yet with possibilities for a far greater effect on the built environment because they would infiltrate the entire building process on a major scale.

Traditional methods of construction have served us well for numerous years. They are, however, primarily applicable to a set of rapidly changing economic conditions. The projected future economic climate dictates optimization in the economy of construction.

Too often engineers are called upon to innovate under conventional routine design circumstances. This forces the engineer to rely on handbooks. The opportunity to save millions of dollars in construction cost is lost.

Drastic cost-cutting cannot be accomplished by laboriously saving on construction material through sophisticated analysis of conventional construction components. A total design approach is needed that takes basic project requirements into consideration, and results in an optimized design concept. The form of the entire structure and its components should not be predetermined before studying the needs of the problem.

This was the overriding consideration as the Zetlin office undertook the examination of the problems of rapid transit structural systems.

CONOID

TENSION TIE

SEATING DETAIL

CONNECTING SHEAR DOWELS

ALIGNMENT LIP

ANCHORAGE

BASIC SHELL ELEMENT

FOOTING CAST IN PLACE

The Conoid

Weight is minimized by using the optimum geometrical form for resisting earth forces with this structural component. By combining in one element thin curved portions, which maximize strength, and straight-line portions, which permit ease of seating, cost-cutting through rapid erection of easily handled lightweight elements is achieved. The standard precast element can be used to develop various aesthetically varying systems of retaining walls for open cuts and retained embankments, as well as for bridges and underpasses. The basic form of the element lends itself to simple standard connections for various applications, thereby adding further economies.

167

RIB VIADUCT

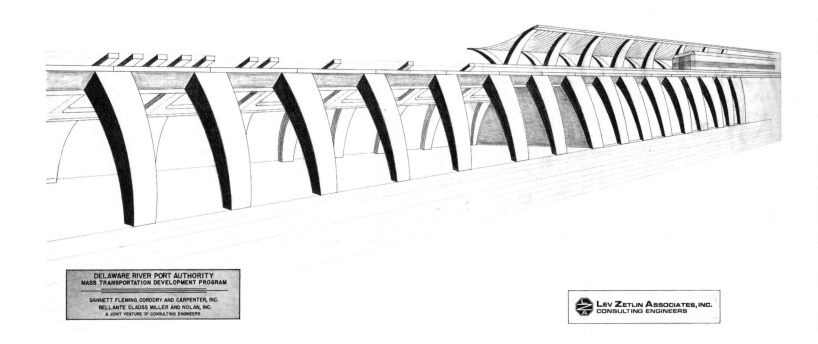

DELAWARE RIVER PORT AUTHORITY
MASS TRANSPORTATION DEVELOPMENT PROGRAM

GANNETT FLEMING CORDDRY AND CARPENTER, INC.
BELLANTE CLAUSS MILLER AND NOLAN, INC.
A JOINT VENTURE OF CONSULTING ENGINEERS

LEV ZETLIN ASSOCIATES, INC.
CONSULTING ENGINEERS

Rib Viaduct

The use of arches in this viaduct system provides for potential savings through the adaptable use of structural elements. The geometry of the system allows for the development of unique projecting supports to permit maximum flexibility to grade changes. The use of a connection system which would permit on-the-job adjustments by the contractor to eliminate costly watchmaking precision during construction is being developed.

168

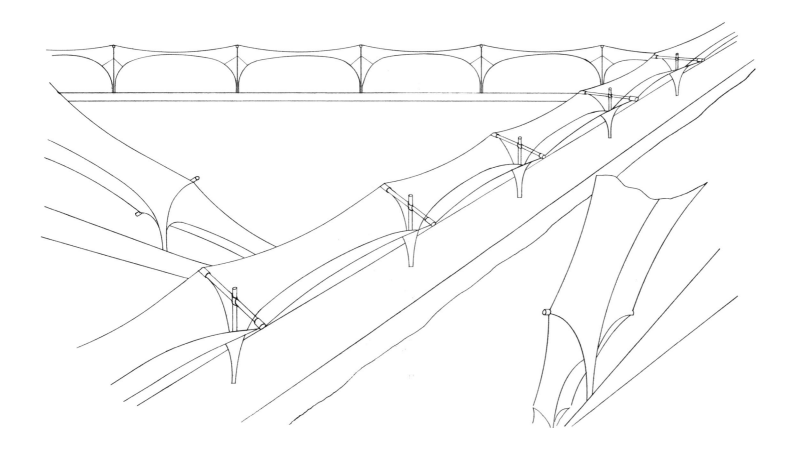

The Skin Shelter

The use of high-strength structural fabric and steel cable provides a lightweight structure for sheltering passengers waiting for trains at stations. The durable structural fabric is prestressed between the cables, providing a rigid, nonfluttering structural covering. The geometry of the system provides for rapid erection by literally pushing up the roof at the supporting post locations, thereby drastically reducing erection costs.

169

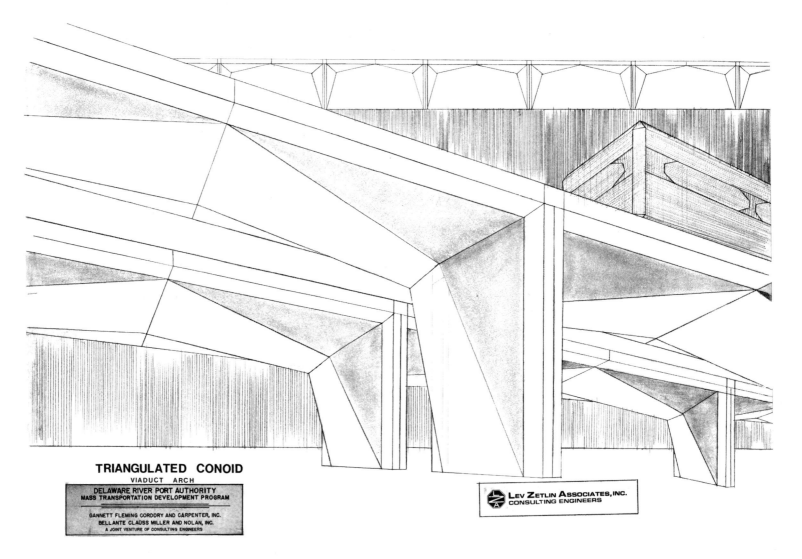

TRIANGULATED CONOID

VIADUCT ARCH

DELAWARE RIVER PORT AUTHORITY
MASS TRANSPORTATION DEVELOPMENT PROGRAM

GANNETT FLEMING CORDDRY AND CARPENTER, INC.
BELLANTE CLAUSS MILLER AND NOLAN, INC.
A JOINT VENTURE OF CONSULTING ENGINEERS

LEV ZETLIN ASSOCIATES, INC.
CONSULTING ENGINEERS

The Triangulated Conoid

Geometry provides for material savings in the development of a basic component for viaduct systems. The spanning element capitalizes on the depth usually allocated for hammerheads to provide structure which helps in developing spans between piers. This, with the use of large precast units, minimizes precise field operations.

The basic elements may either be shipped to the site or precast at the site and used with either precast ties or a cast-in-place slab. The boundaries of a formwork for a cast-in-place slab are built in, eliminating costly form building and stripping.

This standardized component can be used for retaining walls for both cuts and retained embankments, as well as for constructing underpasses and bridges. In this application it has similar advantages to those of the basic conoid element.

170

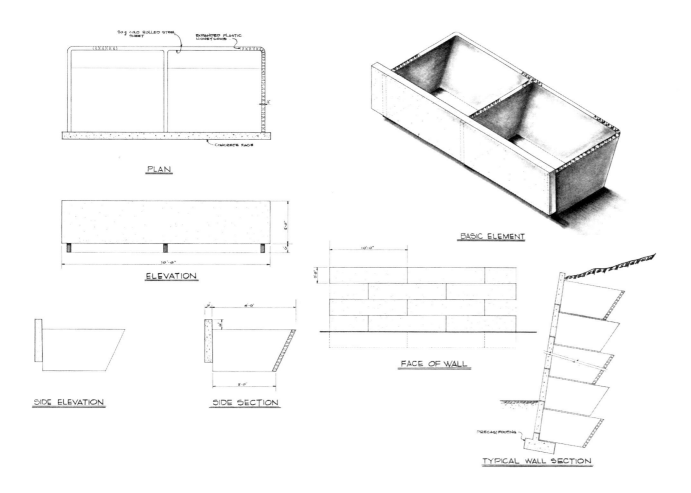

PLAN

20 g COLD ROLLED STEEL SHEET EXPANDED PLASTIC HONEYCOMB

CONCRETE FACE

ELEVATION

BASIC ELEMENT

SIDE ELEVATION

SIDE SECTION

FACE OF WALL

PRECAST FOOTING

TYPICAL WALL SECTION

Box Wall

This system reduces the amount of field labor and time needed to construct retaining-wall systems for either cuts or retained embankments. The large basic elements drastically reduce the amount of field operations needed as compared to conventional crib-wall construction and cast-in-place cantilevered walls. Design details permit proper interaction between soil and structure to assure a rugged, durable wall system. Standardization of elements adds further economies.

Lite-Wall

Use of lightweight modern expanded plastic materials permits the development of an exceptionally light prefabricated basic wall unit. This permits handling of even larger units, further increasing speed of construction and reducing cost.

171

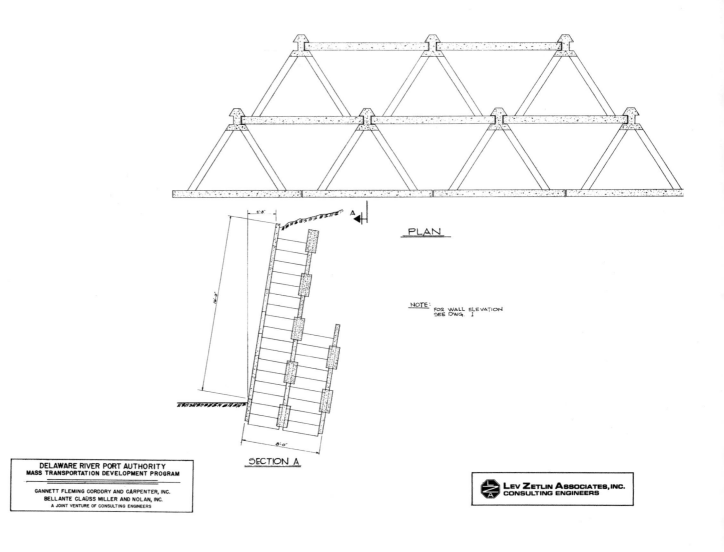

PLAN

NOTE: FOR WALL ELEVATION
SEE DWG. I

SECTION A

Tri-Wall

A modification of the basic box wall, this system provides three-point stacking to insure proper bearing between elements. For higher walls, the same basic prefabricated elements may be used for deepening the wall.

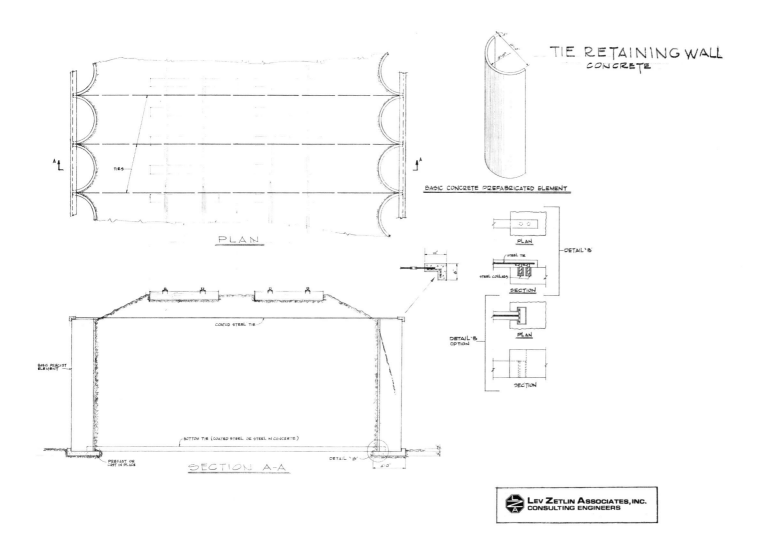

TIE RETAINING WALL
CONCRETE

BASIC CONCRETE PREFABRICATED ELEMENT

PLAN

PLAN

DETAIL 'B'

STEEL TIE

STEEL COLLARS

SECTION

DETAIL 'B'
OPTION

PLAN

SECTION

COATED STEEL TIE

BASIC PRECAST
ELEMENT

BOTTOM TIE (COATED STEEL OR STEEL IN CONCRETE)

PRECAST OR
CAST IN PLACE

SECTION A-A

DETAIL 'B'

LEV ZETLIN ASSOCIATES, INC.
CONSULTING ENGINEERS

Cylindrical Retaining Wall Units

Use of curved precast concrete elements, which provide for efficient resistance to soil pressures as well as act as their own counterfort, allows for the construction of retaining walls with one basic precast element. The basic conoid elements, or triangulated conoid elements previously discussed, may be used in this manner. Various connections and post-tensioning schemes have been worked out to simplify erection.

The basic elements can be used as either cantilevers or as a self-equilibrating system where they are tied to each other below tracks in a retained embankment, or over tracks, when used in developing cuts. For such self-equilibrating systems the use of lightweight materials such as light-gage steel or plastics is also possible, which can further reduce costs by permitting rapid erection through ease of handling.

173

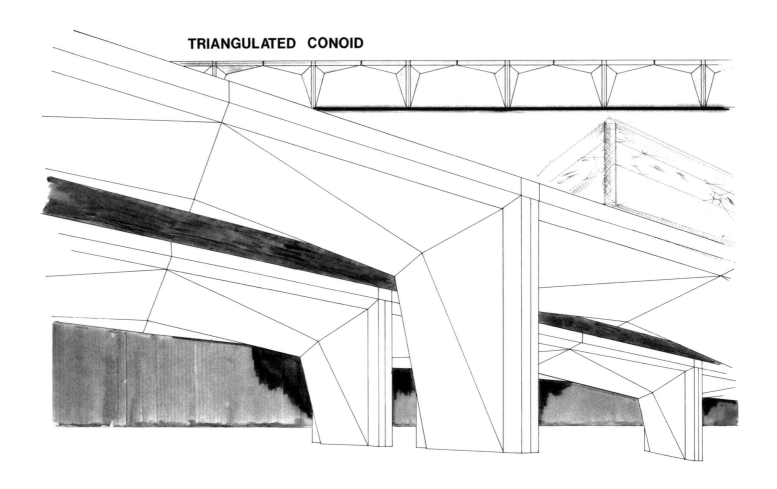

TRIANGULATED CONOID

Triangular Viaduct

This viaduct system is a study in the use of an innovative, triangu-
lar-shaped precast beam member. These members have the potential of
developing an extremely rigid diaphragm action when connected to each
other due to the type of trusswork system developed in cross section.
They also provide for efficient transfer of forces at main pier locations.

174

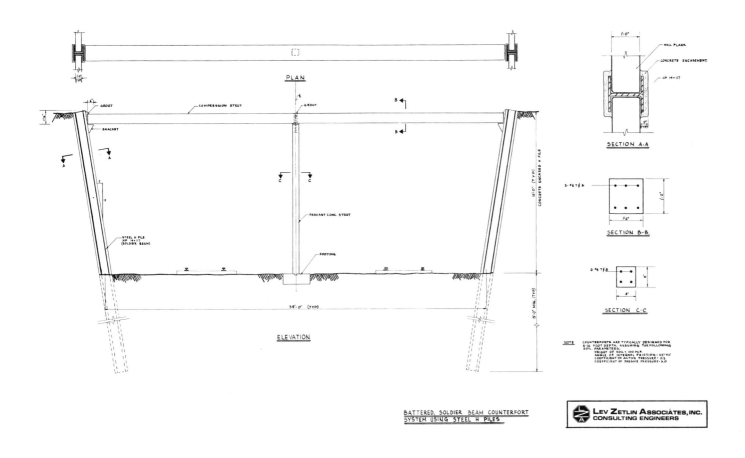

PLAN

SECTION A-A

SECTION B-B

SECTION C-C

ELEVATION

BATTERED, SOLDIER BEAM COUNTERFORT
SYSTEM USING STEEL H PILES

LEV ZETLIN ASSOCIATES, INC.
CONSULTING ENGINEERS

Optimum Span Viaduct

Structural spans for main viaduct precast deck elements are shortened
through the use of longitudinal hammerheads, as well as reducing costs
by putting maximum bending forces at locations where it is most economical to resist them, and minimizing the weight and size of components shipped to the site.

5 The Self-Fulfilling Prophecy

The forms of the future that Zetlin anticipated in 1966 are emerging in self-fulfilling prophecy. This is not surprising, for some of the studies shown here were underway in his office at that time. Others had already been built, and still others were the logical progression of innovations he had previously introduced into building.

The connection between prediction and reality can be seen in studies such as those undertaken for the six major airlines in 1967, and the building of the American Airlines hangars four years later. The American Airlines hangars had their origins in this study but were also directly related to the preliminary exploration of the hyperbolic paraboloid in Johnson's Nuclear Reactor for Rehovot, Israel, in the late 1950s.

The self-dampening cable system, beginning with the Utica Auditorium in 1955, runs like a taut thread through Zetlin's work. Ten years later it makes its appearance flamboyantly at the New York World's Fair in Johnson's New York State Pavilion, and in almost identical form in Salt Lake City almost two decades later.

It appears as a reversal of applying suspension bridge structures to buildings by using the Utica roof principle in a proposal for the Baltimore Inner Harbor Bridge in 1967. The steel bents and cables of the Travelers Life Insurance Company Building of 1964–1965 were extrapolated almost immediately into plans for a superstadium shortly after the building was erected. The most far reaching concept for Zetlin's cable use appeared in his cable system to transport ships across the Isthmus of Panama in 1972.

The modest paper bridge that made its appearance in Colorado in 1970 reemerges as the "Stratasystem" for renewing entire blighted city areas barely a year later. Small incremental changes that begin as evolutionary building change emerge later as major urban elements.

With this in mind we will examine the brainstorming session Lev Zetlin and his associates undertook for the major airlines. The project was ideal for Zetlin at this time.

It brought together all of the ideas that were percolating in his mind and those of his staff. The hangars were ideal as vehicles for structural brainstorming. The function is simple but the buildings were major structures in which, like bridges, engineering concepts would of necessity dominate the form.

HANGARS FOR FLIGHTS OF FANCY

Structural Research and Development Project
Maintenance Environment Housings for Boeing 747
and Supersonic Transport Aircraft
Prepared for American Airlines, Eastern Airlines, Pan American
Airlines, Quantas Airlines, Trans World Airlines,
United Airlines
By Lev Zetlin Associates, consulting engineers
Final Report: April 14, 1967

In 1967 Lev Zetlin undertook a Structural Research and Development Project for six major airlines: American, Eastern, Pan American, Quantas, Trans World and United. The report was a preview of structures to come. It grappled with the problem of major structures, new materials, the rising costs of construction; in short, it probed the capabilities of the traditional engineering profession and building industry to meet the unorthodox needs of the aircraft industry.

Building technology, which in many instances had not changed appreciably for thousands of years, was asked to adapt to the technology of the aircraft industry, which was changing daily.

The approach used was that of the virtuoso engineer capable of solving all problems by the genius of engineering concepts. There was no question at this time of the wisdom of ultramodern planes and antiquated transportation systems, of fuel shortages and noise pollution. These structures do not necessarily represent the solutions that Zetlin would propose today; however, they are remarkable for their ingenuity and prediction of the future. They reflect, as well as any study done in the Zetlin office, that period in the recent past when we all agreed that individual skill could solve multidisciplinary problems. We know today that problems such as these are only components of larger problems that concern the airplane, the runway, and the city itself.

The study's preface stated that breakthroughs in any technical field are achieved through revisions of the established traditional practices and search for new concepts. The study was made to improve the efficiency of modern-day structures and to reduce construction costs through conceptual research, relying on current construction practices and drawing from existing technology in other fields.

The report emphasized the juxtaposition of the building and aircraft industries during the previous half century.

Historically, when the first small planes needed a cover, they were brought into existing sheds of relatively small span. These sheds of 50 years ago were commonly constructed of trusses supported on columns of either timber or steel. The reason for this type of construction was that the sheds used to be built by relatively small individual contractors for whom this type of structure was the easiest to build. Not much thought was given to the engineering aspects of design of construction.

As airplanes grew larger, requiring larger span housing—by then called "hangars"—the previous structural system for sheds was still used by increasing the length of structural components. This same structural system persisted as the spans grew larger to accommodate an airplane of B-707 size.

Very little examination has been afforded on whether a structural system used in small sheds is suitable for large spans. As the spans grew, there were tremendous increases in weight and cost per square foot of the hangars, without significant increases in their flexibility or efficiency.

Experience and logic show that economical and more efficient structures are possible. Obviously, to achieve this, each structure and its efficiency should be examined and designed on its own merit, and not by extrapolating previous practices. Reexamination and scrapping of traditional practices has been the cause of breakthroughs in many fields of technology. Such reexamination of structural systems for hangars has been undertaken in connection with this study.

The report described the ideas that Zetlin proposed with technical descriptions of each. They were divided into four groups: 1) those to be constructed in the near future—1969, 2) those to be constructed in the mid-1970s, 3) portable hangars, 4) door structures.

The structures proposed for 1969 included materials and construction methods that were basically traditional, except that structural systems were designed that saved on the weight of structural materials and also facilitated and expedited construction time.

The structures proposed for the mid-1970s combined both traditional and more modern materials. More emphasis was placed on prefabrication and automated erection.

The study of portable hangars assumed that traditional material would be inapplicable to economic construction. However, portable hangars of any size could be built with traditional materials and methods. Emphasis was given to materials and fabrication methods that were predicted to be economical and prevalent in the mid-1970s.

The last section of the report on door structures involved ideas that could be extrapolated to structural components of entire airplane housing units.

It was admitted that fire-resistance of the various structural systems would have to be studied in further detail in the future. It was assumed that this would not present serious problems in the proposed structural systems.

All structures were designed for a 40 psf snow load, a 30 psf (100 mph) wind load, and a moderate earthquake zone.

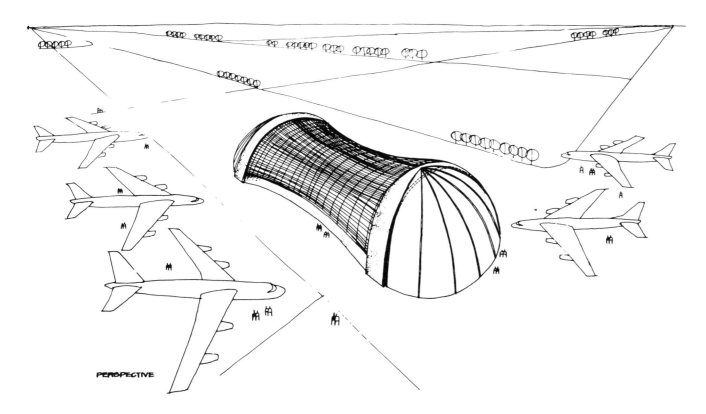

PERSPECTIVE

Proposed Hangar I-1

Structural Description:

This hangar consists of a saddle-shaped roof surface having anti-clastic curvature, whose surface is formed by two sets of orthogonal cables. The longitudinal set of cables are the "load cables," and have a span of 310 feet and a sag at the midspan of 40 feet. Because all of the longitudinal cables have approximately the same sag-to-span ratio, all have about the same load-carrying capacity. As a result, the cables near the high point of the roof carry the vertical snow load, and those near the side carry the horizontal wind load. The transverse set of cables are the "tie-down" or "prestress" cables which have a span of 160 feet and a rise of 40 feet. The network of cables, which is formed by the intersection of these two sets, forms the entire enclosure, thus eliminating the need for separate roof and walls.

The longitudinal set of cables is suspended between a parabolic re-inforced (possibly posttensioned) concrete arch at each end of the hangar. These arches are subjected to vertical loads which are comprised of the vertical component of the load-cable tension at each end of each cable, the weight of the arch, and the vertical reaction of the moveable door. In the horizontal direction these arches must resist the horizontal component of the tension in each load cable and the horizontal reaction resulting from wind loads on the moveable door. These horizontal forces tend to cause the arches to translate and rotate toward the centerline of the hangar. These tendencies are resisted by a horizontal reinforced concrete strut which follows the plan shape along each side. The bending moments in the arch, which are caused by its tendency to rotate under the action of the summation of all the horizontal forces acting on the arch, are transmitted into the side strut. The strut is also used to anchor the transverse "tie-down" cables. Because of the symmetry of the hangar about its transverse centerline, this combination of arches and side struts results in a self-equilibrating structural system for horizontal forces.

179

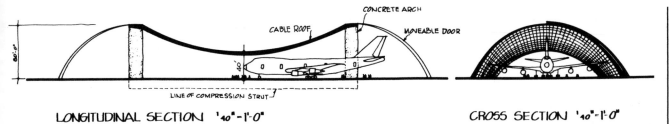

LONGITUDINAL SECTION '⅒"=1'-0"

CROSS SECTION '⅒"=1'-0"

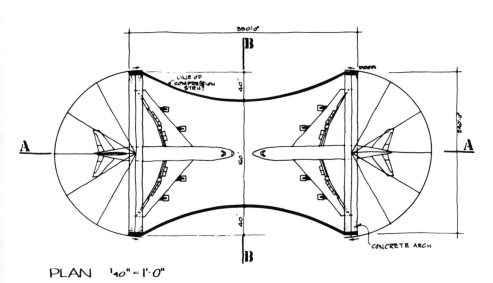

PLAN '⅒"=1'-0"

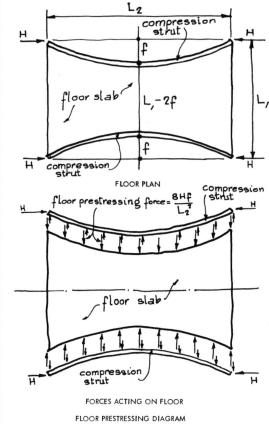

FLOOR PLAN

floor prestressing force$=\dfrac{8Hf}{L_2^{\,2}}$

FORCES ACTING ON FLOOR

FLOOR PRESTRESSING DIAGRAM

Since the strut is subjected to a combined axial compression force and bending moments about a horizontal axis through the strut cross section, the axial force acts as a prestressing force and reduces the amount of reinforcing steel required to resist the bending stresses. The axial force would also cause bending moments about the strut's vertical axis because the strut has a parabolic shape in plan. However, due to symmetry about the longitudinal axis, these bending moments can be eliminated by utilizing the hangar floor as a diaphragm. Another advantage of the plan shape of the strut is that the forces which the struts apply to the floor slab act as an external prestressing and therefore could be utilized to eliminate cracking and expansion joints in the slab.

The horizontal transverse "kick-out" force from the end arches could either be resisted by a tension tie in the floor structure or by the passive pressure of the soil and/or batter piles. If the hangar require-

ment at a specific location was for 4, 6, or 8 aircraft, the two plane units could be placed next to each other; as a result, the horizontal arch kick would be self-canceling at the interior abutments.

The basic plan shape of this hangar could be described as an "hourglass" with a semicircle attached at each end. The longitudinal section (top left) indicates that the sectional area is approximately one-half of the plan area. In other words, the entire enclosure approximates a surface of revolution. In plan, the wide portion of the hangar occurs at the wing tips of each plane and the narrow portion in the vicinity of the nose. If the entire aircraft were to be covered by the main cable roof structure, the structure would either be unnecessarily wide and high at the ends or the cable sags would have to be reduced, resulting in heavier cables. For these reasons the configuration placing the arches at the wing tips and using the movable leaf-type door was adopted.

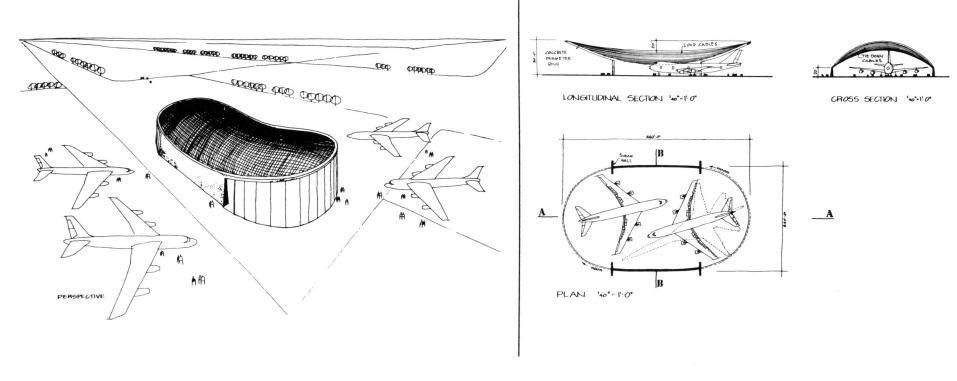

LONGITUDINAL SECTION '40"-1'-0"

CROSS SECTION '40"-1'-0"

PLAN '40" = 1'-0"

PERSPECTIVE

Proposed Hangar I-2

Structural Description

The roof structure for this hangar consists of a distorted "snowshoe" or "tennis racquet" type prestressed suspension system. The plan of the hangar is basically an oblong or oval. The roof is comprised of two sets of orthogonal cables which form a surface of double curvature. The longitudinal cables are the "load" cables and the transverse cables are the "tie-down" or prestress cables. The cables are spaced at 5'-0" centers in each direction measured in the horizontal projection of the roof.

The cables are suspended between a compression ring which conforms to the general outline of the hangar. The most economical plan configuration of this ring is parabolic. If a parabolic curve is used, the bending moments are minimized because the ring follows the pressure line of cable forces in the prestress condition.

Most of the roof forces are carried by ring compression, not bending. Since the ring acts mainly in compression and this compression results from an external force system, the ring is in effect prestressed by the roof forces.

When a prestressed cable system is suspended from the ring, buckling in the horizontal plane is for all intents and purposes eliminated. This elimination of buckling occurs because as the ring begins to distort, the transverse distance tends to reduce and the longitudinal distance tends to increase. As the longitudinal distance increases, the load cables are stressed and therefore restrain the distortion. In summary, the cables carry the roof load; the ring supports the cables, and the cables stabilize the ring, eliminating buckling and thus allowing the concrete ring to be utilized at maximum efficiency.

Two-way cable roofs derive much of their rigidity from their double curvature. In order to obtain this curvature, the parameter ring must be distorted out of the horizontal, as shown in the longitudinal section. The

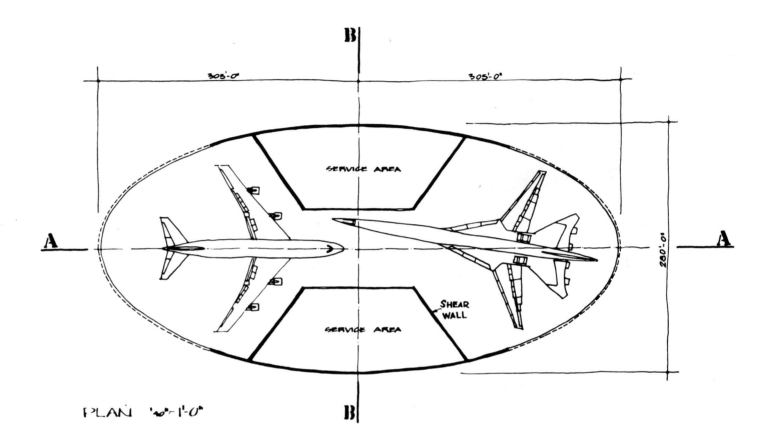

B

SERVICE AREA

A   A

280'-0"

SHEAR WALL

SERVICE AREA

B

PLAN '₁₆"=1'-0"

ring appears as a parabolic curve having a height of 80 feet above the ground at each end, and a minimum height of 20 feet at the center. The structural advantage of this shape is the arching effect obtained at each end over the doors, as shown in the cross-section. In addition, the ring cantilevers at each end of the hangar. By curving the ring up, as shown in the longitudinal section, a portion of the roof load is carried by compression. The major economy in the ring is attained due to the different configurations of the cable roof and the parameter ring. The ring would normally act as a pure cantilever; however, since the profile of the load cables is higher than the profile of the ring in the longitudinal section, the cables act as a tie-back to minimize the bending moments in the ring. In the extreme or optimum case, the prestress forces in the cables could be manipulated to completely eliminate these bending moments. It is this interaction of the components of the structure working together to carry the loads, that is, the ring supporting the cables, and the cables holding up the ring, that could result in an extremely economical structure. At the transition points in the geometry of the parameter ring, forces are developed which could be carried by the ring internally or could be transmitted down to the foundations through shear walls. There is a structural advantage in constructing a series of these hangars in a row, since there is no need for these shear walls at the connection between units because of the equilibrating effect of adjacent units.

From the geometric standpoint, the advantage of this structural system is that a minimum enclosed volume is approached. The highest point of the roof occurs at each end where the tail of each plane is situated. This high point continues in a ridge along the longitudinal centerline so that the high portion of the space follows the high points of the aircraft.

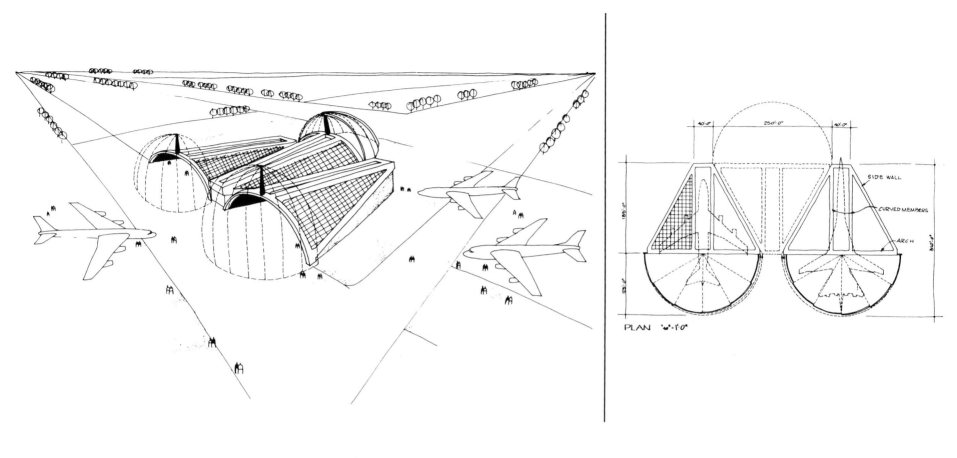

PLAN ⅛"-1'0"

Proposed Hangar I-5

Structural Description

The structural system for this hangar consists of a double-curvature pre-stressed cable roof suspended between a rigid framework. The framework consists of a circular arch that spans 240 feet at the wide portion of the structure. In addition, two curved members span 185 feet over the centerline of the aircraft. These members are supported on the arch at the high end and the side wall at the low end. Besides carrying the cable forces, these members eliminate the tendency of the 240-foot circular arch to rotate inward. The side walls slope up from a low point at the wide portion of the building to a high point at the narrow end. The configuration of these rigid frame members causes the plane between them to be a warped surface, thus giving the cable roof its double curvature. The two triangular side portions of the roof are the double-curvature cable spans. The central 40-foot span between the curved members is spanned using long-span open-web joists.

The modular layout for this hangar type consists of a repeating triangular-fixed structure and a semicircular movable door. The fixed portion has a maximum height of 55 feet. The high portion of the tail is covered by the movable door, which is 85 feet high. A door opening could be provided at the narrow end to allow the nose of a stretched, longer aircraft to protrude.

183

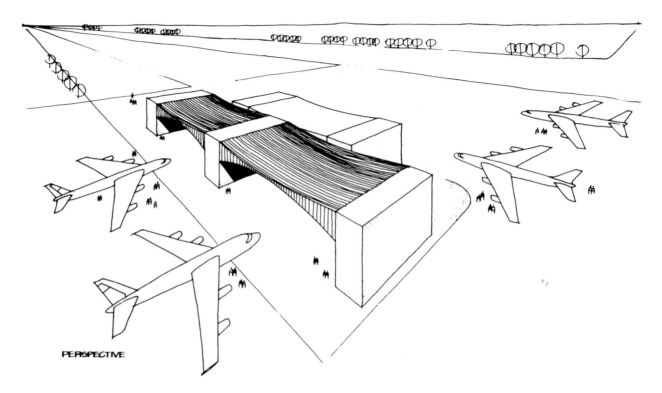

PERSPECTIVE

Proposed Hangar I-6

Structural Description

The structure for this hangar is based on a prestressed double-layer cable roof, and three different structural configurations for resisting the forces resulting from the cable roof scheme, with two using the weight of the support buildings plus mass concrete or rock anchors, and the third using the framing of the support buildings.

Prestressed Flutter Resistant Double Layer Cable Roof

(a) *Roof Structure:* The roof structure for this system consists of a double layer of strands which are prestressed against each other and connected together by hangers.

This type of cable roof derives its rigidity from the double layer of cables which enables the system to be prestressed. Deflections are controlled by prestressing the cables, not by adding material as is done in standard trusses. Fairly heavy concentrated loads can be hung from the

roof structure. Another advantage of this system is that undesirable dynamic instabilities, which are inherent in lightweight roofs, are eliminated by adjusting the values of prestress in the cables.

There are many varied configurations in which the cables may be used. Three different schemes have been studied for incorporation into this proposed hangar. The double-layer cable systems shown are spaced 10 feet o.c. with corrugated metal deck spanning between them.

The portion of the structure that covers the nose of the aircraft consists of a steel or concrete framed system that spans 60 feet at a height of 40 feet above the ground. Office and service areas could be placed in these towers.

(b) *Methods of Resisting Roof Forces:* The first two methods for resisting the cable forces from the roof incorporate the use of tie-backs which carry the forces down to the foundations. If the service tower is used at each side, as shown above, the tie-back locations would have to be coordinated with the room layout. For the cable configurations shown on the opposite page, a tie-back is required for each load and tie-down cable.

184

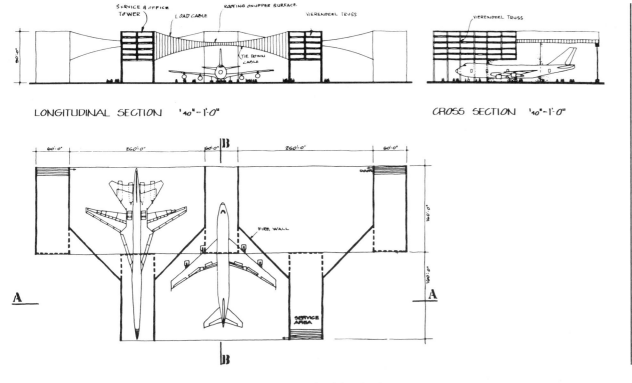

LONGITUDINAL SECTION   '40"-1'-0"

CROSS SECTION   '40"-1'-0"

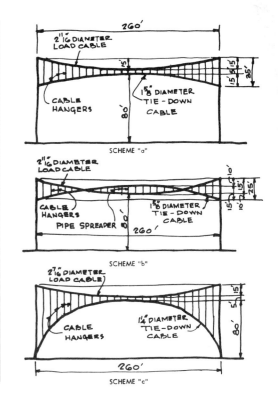

SCHEME "a"

SCHEME "b"

SCHEME "c"

Only one tie-back for the load cable would be required for the layout shown above. When no service tower is required, the tie-backs would actually be outside the building and would be carried down to a mass concrete "dead-man" or to rock anchors, if bedrock were relatively near the surface. The space between the tie-backs could be used for automobile parking and other facilities. The advantage of the scheme using the service towers is that the dead weight of the building is utilized to reduce the amount of additional weight required to resist the cable forces. The service towers could be constructed of reinforced concrete in order to maximize the magnitude of the column reactions while maintaining an economical structure.

The cable scheme shown in scheme "c" has the advantage over the other two in that the tie-down cable is brought directly to the foundation at the interior line of columns and the load cable is tied back to the exterior line of columns. This results in utilization of the dead-load reactions in both lines of columns to resist the roof forces. The other schemes use only the exterior line of columns.

The third method for resisting the cable roof forces utilizes the structure of the service tower. The floors of the tower at which the cables are connected act as horizontal trusses with a depth equal to the width of the tower. These trusses distribute the roof forces to the fire wall at the center of the hangar and the compression strut across the door opening.

Since the geometry of the aircraft is basically a long, narrow fuselage and wide-span wings located between the rear and the midlength of this fuselage, it becomes apparent that the use of a long-span roof structure to cover the entire plane could be wasteful of cost, floor area, and enclosed volume. Using this criterion the tail and wing areas are spanned by the long-span structure and the nose area is spanned by more conventional framing.

This layout lends itself to a modular system with expansion possibilities. Each unit is capable of housing a Boeing 747 or Boeing 707. If future aircraft, such as the supersonic transport and ballistic transport are constructed longer, the structure can be enlarged at either the wide or narrow portion. Furthermore, if more units are required, additional modules could be added.

185

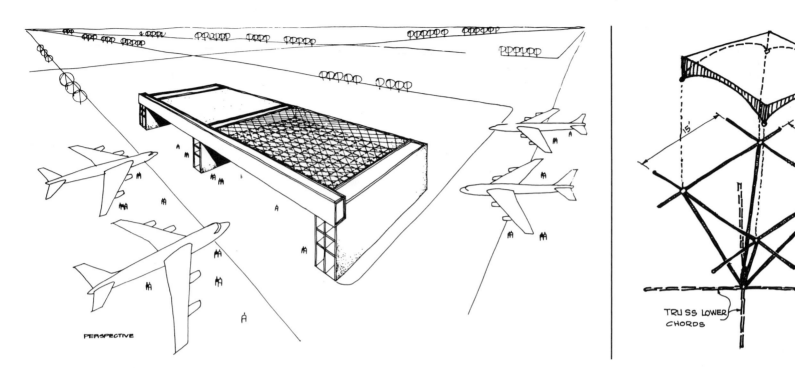

PERSPECTIVE

FIBERGLASS REINF. PLASTIC PANEL

TRUSS UPPER CHORDS

WEB MEMBERS

TRUSS LOWER CHORDS

15'

15'

Proposed Hangar I-14

Structural Description

The roof structure for this hangar is a two-way space truss consisting of A-36 construction pipes, having a constant outside diameter of 6.625 inches. A variation in pipe size due to varying axial forces is accommodated by changing the wall thickness. As a result, the connections at the panel points can be standardized to allow for mass production.

The two-way truss is comprised of inverted pyramids. The lower chord members run parallel to the sides of the hangar at a 21'-3" spacing, while the upper chord members are at a 45 degree diagonal with a 15'-0" spacing in each direction. The most economical two-way structure is one that is square and supported on all four sides with a firm support. For a hangar, one side must be open for the door; therefore, a truss must be spanned over the door opening. If the structure is elongated to 320 feet long to accommodate the Boeing 2707, the quantity of structural steel would be increased. If more than one unit is constructed in a row, some reduction in the amount of structural steel could be realized due to continuity over the interior service core or wall. Because the upper chords of the truss form a grid of 15' x 15' squares, it appears

that the use of a mass-produced roof panel could achieve substantial economics. For this reason, the 15' x 15' glass-fiber reinforced plastic roof panel shown was considered. The top surface is level and the under surface is spherical so that the panel is supported at each of its corners which coincide with the panel points of the truss. Supporting the roof panel at the panel points of the truss eliminates bending of the pipes and saves about 4 psf of structural steel in the truss. Because of the multiplicity of standard connections for the truss, the connections should be field-welded in order to simplify the details. If the truss is fabricated on the ground, welding would be facilitated. After the truss is completely fabricated, large capacity hydraulic jacks could be used to lift the roof into place. This erection procedure also eliminates the need for costly scaffolding and falsework.

If the hangar is designed to house one Boeing 747, the overall dimensions are 260 feet by 260 feet, resulting in a required floor area of 68,000 square feet per plane. For the Boeing 2707 SST, the size would be 260 feet wide by 320 feet long, or 83,000 square feet per plane.

The service towers are designed to carry the vertical roof loads from the roof trusses. If the service towers were not necessary at any point, they could be replaced with a single wall.

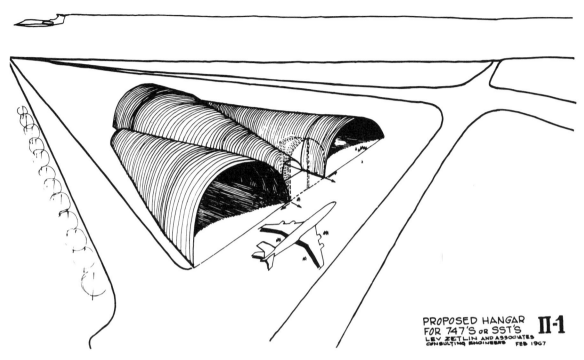

PROPOSED HANGAR **II-1**
FOR 747'S or SST'S
LEV ZETLIN AND ASSOCIATES
CONSULTING ENGINEERS   FEB 1967

Proposed Hangar II-1

Structural Description

The structural system for this hangar consists of a glass-fiber reinforced plastic shell. The geometry of the shell is that of a section of a circular cylinder, so that the radius of curvature at all sections is constant. The resulting shape lends itself to the mass production of elements, which is necessary if glass-fiber reinforced plastics are to be used economically. The shell has a maximum span of 240 feet at the widest portion and tapers down to 60 feet at the narrow end. Sections through the shell consist of corrugated $\frac{1}{4}$-inch-thick glass-fiber reinforced plastic with an overall depth of 48 inches. The voids would either be filled with foam or stiffened with a glass-fiber reinforced plastic strut in order to increase the section's resistance to local buckling.

An alternate section consists of elliptical tubes, 24 inches wide and 48 inches deep, with a $\frac{1}{4}$-inch-thick wall. In order to give the thin wall tube stability against local buckling, two methods are considered: (1) the use of foam or glass-fiber reinforced plastic struts, previously mentioned, and (2) utilization of a pneumatic system to prestress the plastic tubes.

The tubes are filled with a segmented inflated structure and air is pumped into it, inducing a logitudinal tension into the tube. In addition, the inflated structure gives radial restraint to the thin wall tube against local buckling. As wind loads, or snow loads, are applied to the structure, the induced tensile stresses resulting from the prestress would be altered by the resulting axial force and bending moments. Because long-term, time-dependent deformations (creep) might be a significant parameter in designing a long-span glass-fiber reinforced plastic structure, the concept of pneumatic prestressing could be an important contribution. From past experience with inflated structures, one objection to their use is the deleterious effect the sun's rays have on the fabric material. By enclosing the inflated structure within the glass-fiber tube, this disadvantage is eliminated.

The glass-fiber shell would consist of many mass-produced segments, either curved or straight. The actual size would be dependent upon the individual manufacturer. With present fabrication facilities, the size would be approximately 4'-0'' wide by 6'-0'' long. These pieces would be shop-bonded into an element 4'-0'' wide by 30'-0'' long. At the site an assembly line with an erection rig would be constructed, the elements would be field bonded in the complete arch, 4'-0'' wide, and

187

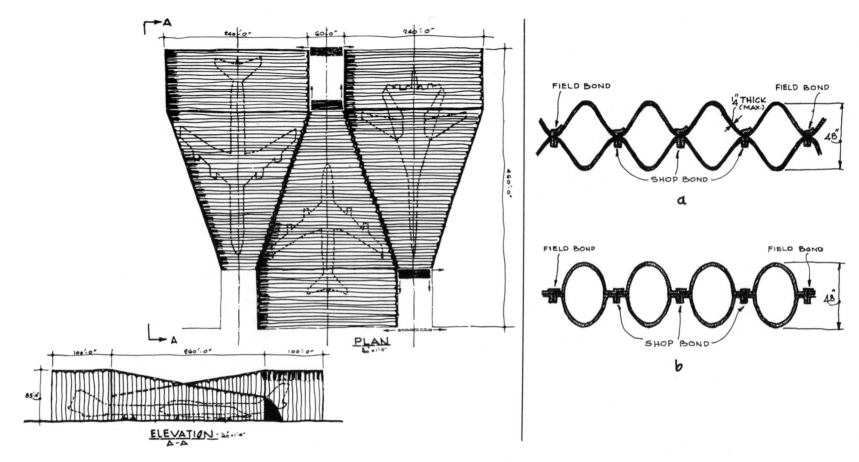

PLAN

ELEVATION A-A

FIELD BOND   ¼" THICK (MAX.)   FIELD BOND

SHOP BOND

a

FIELD BOND   FIELD BOND

SHOP BOND

b

the arches would be tilted up into a vertical position and bonded together to form the complete shell.

The hangar shape conforms to the aircraft in both plan and section so that a minimum floor area and enclosed volume is approached. As aircraft of the future are constructed, additional length can easily be added to the hangar at each end. The configurations shown are only one possibility. If a constant-height hangar is desired, a circular cylindrical shell of constant profile could be utilized. Since land is at a premium at the major airports, a combination of a fixed facility and a mobile facility might be desirable. This could be accomplished by using two constant height glass-fiber reinforced plastic shells. The overall length in the extended position would have to be approximately 320 feet. The fixed portion would be a 160 foot long, 240 foot span shell, while the mobile portion would also be 160 feet long with a slightly smaller span and height

to allow it to be slid under the fixed portion. Due to the large turning radius of the next generation aircraft, there would be difficulty in approaching and turning into a hangar if the amount of land was restricted. The advantage of a half-fixed and half-mobile structure is that the mobile portion could be slid out of the way while the plane is being hangared and then pulled back out over the plane. If space is at even more of a premium, the hangar could consist of two or three movable portions and one fixed portion. A controlling criterion for any mobile structure is a high strength-to-weight ratio; glass-fiber reinforced plastic has one of the highest. Another feature that could be utilized to achieve economy is the fact that the mobile portions could be designed with lower factors of safety for wind and snow, since the mobile structure could be placed under the fixed portion during severe weather conditions.

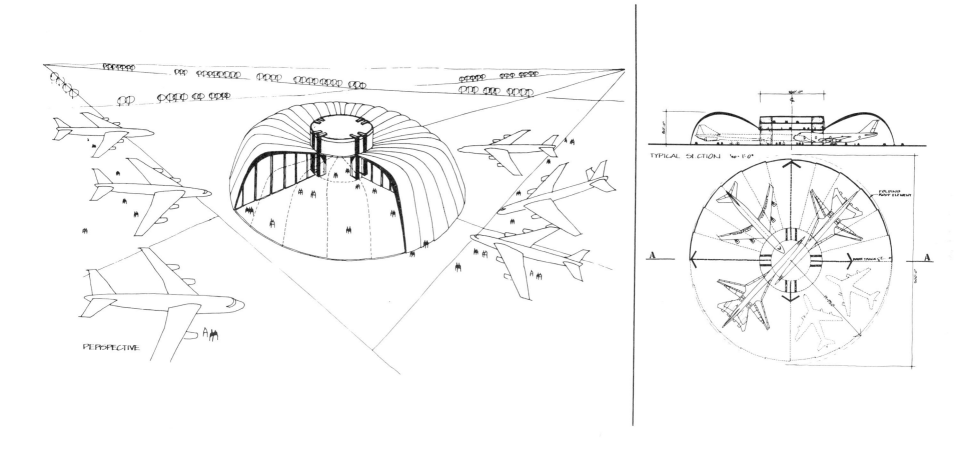

PERSPECTIVE

TYPICAL SECTION ¹⁄₁₆" = 1'-0"

FOLDING ROOF ELEMENT

DOOR TRACKS

A — A

Proposed Hangar II-2

Structural Description

The structure for this hangar consists of central fixed core areas, either concrete or steel, and a completely movable roof structure. Since weight is an extremely important parameter for any movable structure, the ma-

terial of construction for the roof construction should have a high strength-to-weight ratio. Glass-fiber reinforced plastic sandwich construction, or aluminum, fulfill this requirement.

The plan layout is a 500-foot diameter circle capable of housing four Boeing 747's or two Boeing 2707 SST's and two Boeing 747's, each of which occupies one ninety-degree quadrant. It is also possible to house two Boeing 707's in each quadrant. Service areas are placed in the central core, either at the ground level or at the upper levels.

189

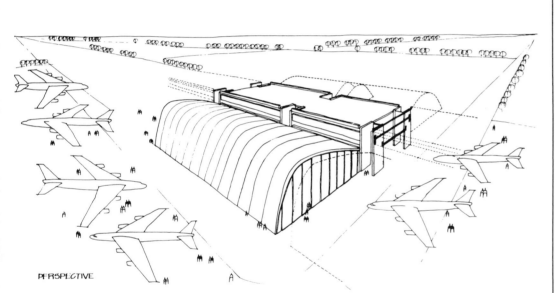

PERSPECTIVE

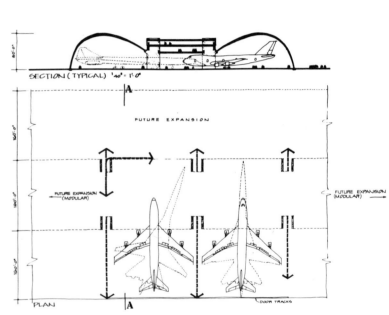

SECTION (TYPICAL) $\frac{1}{40}'' = 1'-0''$

FUTURE EXPANSION

FUTURE EXPANSION (MODULAR)

FUTURE EXPANSION (MODULAR)

PLAN

A

DOOR TRACKS

Proposed Hangars II-3 and II-4

Structural Description

Both Hangar II-3 and Hangar II-4 incorporate the same principle—a fixed rectangular core area and a movable roof structure that forms the doors. The difference between the two structures is that in the case of Hangar II-3, the roof spans from the door track at threshold to the central core,

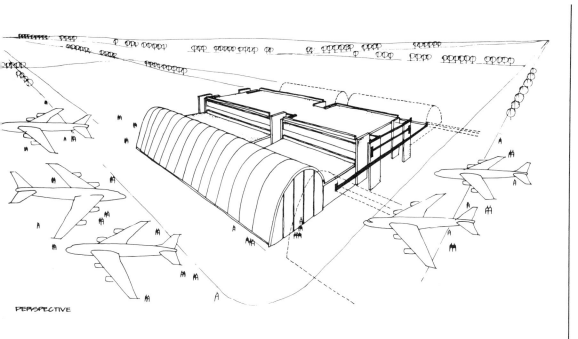

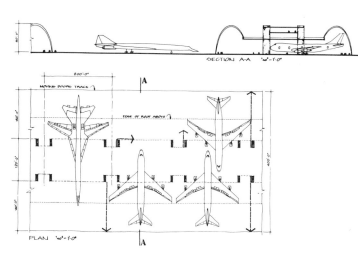

SECTION A-A   'w'=1'-0"

PLAN   'w'=1'-0"

while for Hangar II-4 a cantilever is extended from the core structure to reduce the span of the roof. The same criteria of high strength-to-weight ratio mentioned in the discussion of Hangar II-2 also applies here. As a result, glass-fiber reinforced plastics or aluminum should be utilized.

The advantage of these hangars over the circular structure utilized for Hangar I-2 is the facility with which future expansion can be accomplished. The central core can easily be extended in either direction and additional roof sections added at each end.

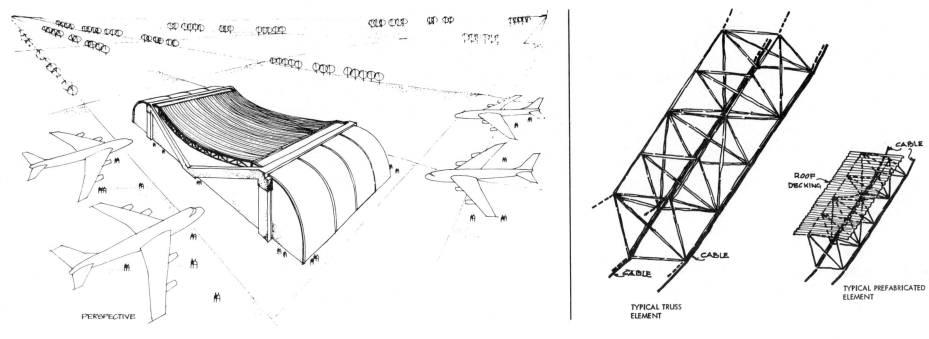

PERSPECTIVE

TYPICAL TRUSS
ELEMENT

CABLE

ROOF
DECKING

CABLE

CABLE

TYPICAL PREFABRICATED
ELEMENT

Proposed Hangar II-5

Structural Description

The main advantages realized through the use of cable structures are lightness of construction, and as a direct result, economy and easy erection. When a single cable is subjected to symmetrical loading distribution, the displacements of the cable are of the same magnitude as any other structural system. However, when unsymmetrical loads are applied, the displacements are large. There are many ways of eliminating these large displacements, such as using doubly curved surfaces, or prestressed double layer systems. These structural systems are pure cable structures known as ''suspended roofs.'' Another concept used in long span structures is that of ''cable supported structures.'' In these structures, loads are carried by the combined action of a flexural member—such as, truss, beam, or folded plate—and a cable. The double cantilever hangar is an example of this type of structure.

Hangar II-5 is an attempt to combine the advantages of a cable structure, lightweight and fast erection, with the stiffness of a truss structure. The structures consist of a 360-foot-long by 260-foot-wide main portion and a movable door that constitutes a 60-foot extension at each end.

The main roof structure consists of bridge strands, spaced at 10'-0'' centers, and spanning 280 feet between a 40'-0'' wide by 25'-0'' deep high strength steel box truss at each end. The cables would be strung first and then the prefabricated truss element would be placed on the cables and connected. The resulting system is one in which the dead load and any uniform live loads are carried by the cable while unsymmetrical loadings are carried by flexure of the truss. If the cable is connected to the truss at each of the panel points, the resulting structure would be a truss, which has a lower chord consisting of a high-strength cable. The roof forces are transmitted to the foundation by the side compression strut.

This hangar, which has overall dimensions of 480 feet wide by 260 feet long, can house two Boeing 747's in a nose-to-nose position or two Boeing 2707 SST's in an overlapping nose layout. The 747's could be positioned in an overlapping nose layout, thus eliminating the need for the extension until the 2707's become operational. The floor area per plane required, with the extension, is 62,500 square feet. The end trusses, from which a crane system could be supported, are 70'-0'' above the hangar floor. The sag at the midspan of the cable is 28 feet, which results in a clear height of 57 feet at midspan.

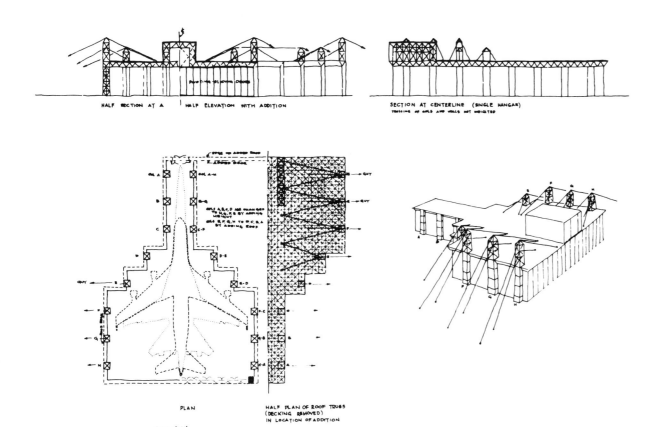

HALF SECTION AT A | HALF ELEVATION WITH ADDITION

SECTION AT CENTERLINE (SINGLE HANGAR)
TRUSSING OF GIRLS AND WALLS NOT INDICATED

PLAN

HALF PLAN OF ROOF TRUSS
(DECKING REMOVED)
IN LOCATION OF ADDITION

SCALE 1"=40'

Proposed Hangar II-7

Structural Description

The truss evolved as a method of spanning large distances using a minimum quantity of material. However, most trusses are constructed as one-way. For an aircraft housing, the plan is basically square or comprised of squares. As a result, two-, three-, or even four-way truss systems can be used. The advantage of multidirectional space truss is the utilization of all components of the roof structure to carry loads. In addition, the bending moments, and therefore, the stresses, in a multidirectional system, are less than a one-way system.

This hangar is an example of a space-truss structure. The wide portion and the narrow nose portion are spanned by the same basic structure: a space truss consisting of members which are all 10 feet long. The depth of the truss is 7.07 feet with all diagonal web members at 45 degrees. In order to obtain relatively similar sizes of truss members, guy towers are added at the wide portion with guys connected to the space truss. These guys supply support to the long-span truss and result in truss member sizes that are all in the same range. The guy towers also act as columns to support the roof. In order to reduce the dead load of the truss, the consideration of aluminum as the material of the truss might provide economy.

The structure has a clear interior height of 40 feet, except at the 80-foot-high tail slot. The layout of each hangar lends itself to a modular type of expansion. Service areas could be included by widening the 40-foot-wide nose pocket.

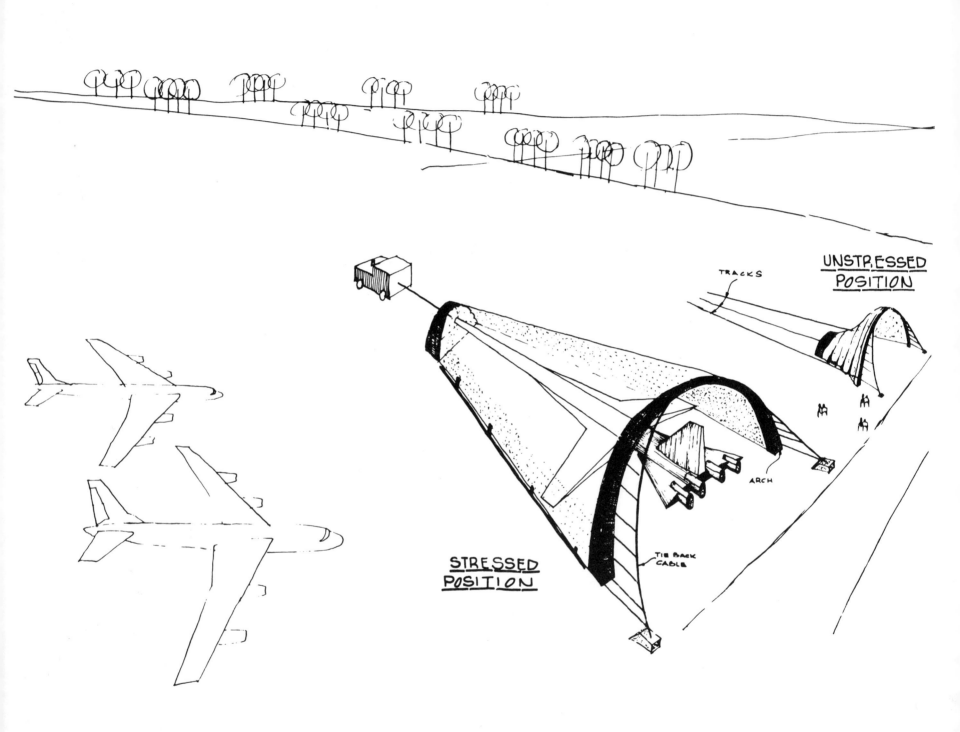

UNSTRESSED
POSITION

TRACKS

ARCH

STRESSED
POSITION

TIE BACK
CABLE

PORTABLE STRUCTURES

Introduction

Because of the tremendous increase in size and number of aircraft, and the limited space at the major airports, many traditional concepts of aircraft maintenance will have to be revolutionized. In addition, since the efficiency of an aircraft is directly proportionate to its time spent in the air, the reduction of the amount of time expended on routine maintenance and checks is of paramount importance. At many airports, much of this maintenance time is spent transporting the aircraft from the terminal to the hangar facilities, which are located a significant distance away. In order to reduce this time, the concept of portable maintenance units becomes desirable. The six configurations described in this section are a result of this concept.

Portable Structure III-1

Structural Description

An elastic membrane and a fixed position arch are the main components of this structural system. The fixed arch has a span that depends upon the aircraft or portion of the aircraft to be covered. If the span of the arch were small, the arch could be designed so that any tendency to overturn is resisted by its foundations. For a long-span structure, the arch would be supported by a tie-back cable, which resists the forces arising from the elongation of the membrane. The elastic membrane would hang in an unstressed position when the unit is not in use. When it is desired to house a certain aircraft, the tractor, which is normally used to pull the plane, would be connected to the abutment. This abutment, which is mounted on a track down the centerline of the hangar, is then connected to the aircraft. The edges of the elastic membrane are also connected to a continuous track along each side. The line of these edge tracks and the centerline track converge at a point. As the aircraft is pulled forward, the elastic membrane forms an envelope in which to perform short-duration maintenance. Locking positions would be situated at points along the central track. These locations would be coordinated with the different classes of aircraft to be housed.

The advantage of a collapsible structure is that when the facility is not in use, the area can be used for parking or maneuvering aircraft into other adjacent hangars. For a minor repair job, the collapsible unit could be used at the terminal in order to eliminate the need to transport the aircraft to the hangar area. In addition, the variable size lends itself to servicing different classes of aircraft with the same unit. A Boeing 2707 SST is shown completely covered. It might be desirable to cover only the tail section for the SST since most of the servicing would be performed there.

A smaller version of this system might be adaptable to a completely portable tail assembly enclosure or wing covering. Instead of the arch being in a fixed location, it would be mounted on wheels and either be capable of resisting the membrane forces through its own geometry or utilize a tie-back that would be connected to "dead-men" built into the apron at service areas. This unit could then be placed over the fuselage or wing and the membrane stretched over the working area.

195

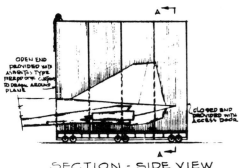

OPEN END PROVIDED WITH ASBESTOS TYPE FIREPROOF CURTAIN TO DRAPE AROUND PLANE

CLOSED END PROVIDED WITH ACCESS DOOR

SECTION - SIDE VIEW
SST PLANE

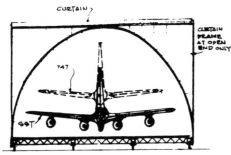

CURTAIN

CURTAIN FRAME AT OPEN END ONLY

747

SST

SECTION A-A

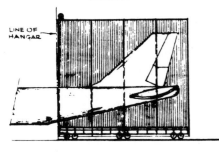

LINE OF HANGAR

SECTION - SIDE VIEW
747 PLANE

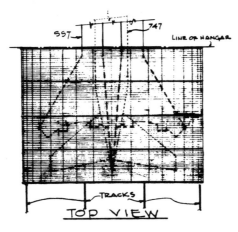

SST   747

LINE OF HANGAR

TRACKS

TOP VIEW

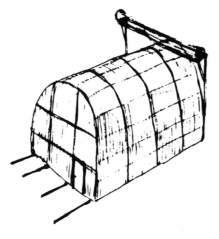

Portable Structure III-2

Structural Description

The structure for this portable unit consists of a glass-fiber reinforced plastic cylindrical shell mounted on a platform constructed of structural steel girders and open-web joists. In order to reduce the weight, it might be desirable to replace the steel girders with aluminum or even possibly glass-fiber reinforced sections, which are now manufactured by a few companies.

The glass-fiber reinforced plastic shell is comprised of a repetitive section, which would be mass-produced and connected together by bonding or mechanical means. The size of the repetitive element for the 120-foot span is a "zee" shaped section with a 15-inch depth and 12-inch legs. The thickness of the piece is 0.1 inch. When the "zee" shaped pieces are assembled to form the shell, the voids are either filled with a foam for insulation or are left open to allow electrical and mechanical systems to be incorporated.

The configuration shown is capable of enclosing the tail of a Boeing 747 or Boeing 2707 SST. The unit measures 70 feet high, 120 feet wide, and 70 feet long. Another application of this unit would be to extend an existing hangar facility and thus enclose the tail of any aircraft longer than that for which the facility was designed.

The scheme shown is for enclosing the tail only, since the Boeing 2707 SST has its engines at the tail. For the Boeing 747 or any other aircraft that has wing-mounted engines, a portable unit of different dimensions would be used to cover the entire wing. In fact, it would even be possible to have several portable units of different shapes to enclose the entire aircraft. With this system, the entire hangar could be brought to the aircraft as opposed to the conventional method of bringing the aircraft to the hangar.

The floor of the unit would be used to mount any heavy working platforms or equipment. Light scaffolding required to work on the tail assembly could be hung from the glass-fiber reinforced plastic shell.

One possibility of mounting the unit is to place it on steel wheels that operate on steel rails. This would be a favorable system when the unit is operated at fixed locations, such as an extension of an existing hangar. The weight of the unit is approximately 250,000 pounds. If more flexibility in operation is desired, the unit could be mounted on wheels or possibly even an air-cushion system.

Portable Structures III-3 and III-4

The main difference between these units and the unit described in the preceding section is that these consist of two halves that operate from each side of the plane. The advantage of this system is that since the unit is divided into two parts, the weight of each individual part is less. If these units are utilized at a new facility to enclose the tail of an aircraft, the structure can be designed as being supported on the structure over the door and at the ground. This structure would be a series of curved members with a lightweight covering. Rigid frames would be utilized for the other configuration.

If the roof structure of an existing hangar is not sufficient to support the additional weight of the unit, the units can be designed as self-supporting box-type structures. The opening on the inside wall for the fuselage complicates the structure and results in a slightly heavier structure than would result if the opening were not present.

Another possible application of this type of structure is its use at the terminal for minor maintenance of the tail assembly of SST's, Boeing 747's, or any other aircraft.

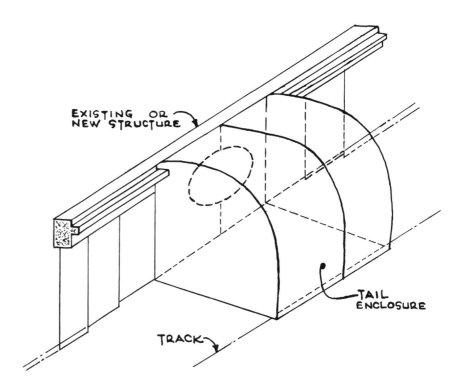

Portable Structure III-5

If it is desirable to perform a routine, short-duration repair or checks, at the terminal, on the engines of a Boeing 747 or any other aircraft with wing-mounted engines, the unit shown might prove advantageous. The unit consists of a rectangular box, about the size of a conventional trailer truck, which is mounted on rubber wheels. The unit is large enough to allow easy access to the engine and possibly might have a carriage, built up from the floor, to carry the engine in case it has to be removed completely. The structure shown consists of a fixed unit, which has slots in each side to allow the wing through, and a rotating closure unit that is mounted on top of the fixed unit and swings down to completely enclose the engine. Since the outboard engines are higher than the inboard, a hydraulic system is included for adjusting the height of the unit.

A variation would be to utilize two separate units, each having a slot in each side, which are brought from the front and back of the engine to form the enclosure.

Portable Structure III-6

Another possibility for extending an existing hangar, which is not large enough to house future aircraft, or for short-duration maintenance jobs at the terminal, is the use of "accordian" type collapsible structures. The structure would stack against the wall of an existing terminal or hangar to serve as a tail-assembly service unit. For the case of extending an existing hangar, some means must be provided for either raising or transporting the stacked structure out of the way while the aircraft is entering the hangar. In either case, a guide trace would be used at the base of each side.

The structure for the unit would consist of a folded plate shell having the profile of a gambrel-type roof. Since weight is a significant problem, glass-fiber reinforced plastic should be used for the folded plate panels. The joints between the panels would have to be flexible hinges. Structures of this type have been constructed on a smaller scale using paper-laminated foam board and taped joints.

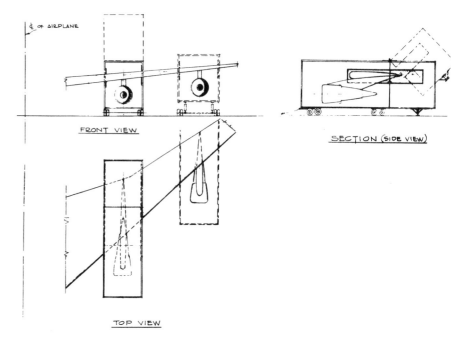

FRONT VIEW

SECTION (SIDE VIEW)

TOP VIEW

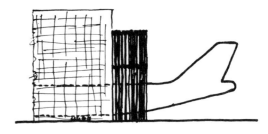

SIDE VIEW – COLLAPSED POSITION

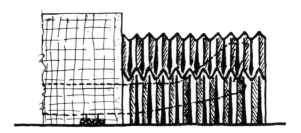

SIDE VIEW – OPEN POSITION

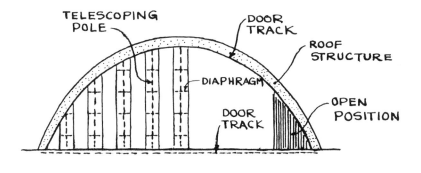

TELESCOPING POLE

DOOR TRACK

ROOF STRUCTURE

DIAPHRAGM

DOOR TRACK

OPEN POSITION

FRONT ELEVATION

INFLATED STRUCTURE

DOOR TRACK

CLOSED POSITION

TELESCOPING POLES

OPEN POSITION

PLAN

DOOR STRUCTURES

Introduction

Although there are many geometric shapes which can be used to attain economic advantages in the structural system of a hangar, a major problem that arises is the fact that the door opening is no longer rectangular. The use of a standard sliding door with vertical leaves becomes impractical and complicated when the door opening is anything but rectangular. Since many of the proposed structures in the report result in unusual shaped openings, consideration has been given to novel systems for door structures.

Door Structure IV-1

A door system that is adaptable to any shape opening must be capable of movement in both the horizontal and vertical directions. The door structure shown is one possible structural configuration that conforms to this requirement. The main components of the system are an inflated tubular membrane and a spring loaded, or hydraulically operated, aluminum telescoping pole which is situated in every other inflated tube. A collapsible diaphragm mechanism, which is connected to the telescoping pole and operates in sequence with the action of the pole, is incorporated to eliminate the possibility of puncture of the membrane by pinching during the operation of the door. When the door is closed, the wind pressure is resisted by the inflated structure with the telescoping poles acting as a guide. As the door is opened, the telescoping poles, which act along a track at the top and bottom of the door opening, begin to collapse with the springs maintaining a pressure against the tracks. When the door is completely opened, the diaphragms connected to the poles are collapsed and the entire door system is stacked at each side.

The advantages of this door system are that it is adaptable to any shaped opening, it is not affected by displacement or settlement of the hangar structure, or by misalignment of the tracks, and only a single track is required at the top and bottom. This door system could be used for Proposed Hangars I-1, I-2, I-3, I-4, and II-1.

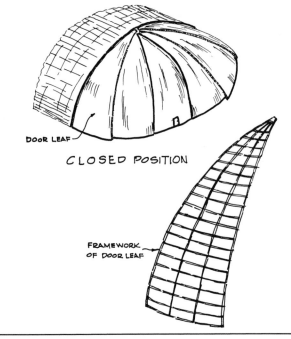

DOOR LEAF

CLOSED POSITION

FRAMEWORK OF DOOR LEAF

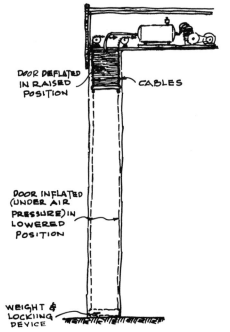

DOOR DEFLATED IN RAISED POSITION

CABLES

DOOR INFLATED (UNDER AIR PRESSURE) IN LOWERED POSITION

WEIGHT & LOCKIING DEVICE

Door Structure IV-2

Another possible door configuration for a circular, parabolic, or elliptical-shape opening is a half-dome structure which consists of four separate leaves on each side operating on four separate tracks. The four leaves at each side converge into a weldment at the top, which is mounted on a vertical pin that allows rotation of each leaf. This type of door is shown on pages 179 and 180. For the size door shown in these figures, which is 80 feet high and has a 120-foot radius in plan, the structure is approximately 18 inches thick and consists of about 12 psf of structural steel—if this material is used. Since weight is important, aluminum or glass-fiber reinforced plastic could also be used. An advantage of this type of door is the fact that additional apron area is available for maneuvering large aircraft into the hangar. Proposed Hangar I-5 also utilizes this door system.

Door Structure IV-3

The door system shown consists of an inflated tubular structure, similar to the inflated portion of Door Type IV-1, which is supported by the structure over the door. In its closed position, a locking device at the floor resists the horizontal reaction due to wind. A mechanical system which is attached to a counterweight at the base of the inflated structure by cables is used to raise and lower the door.

Door Structure IV-4

Because the doors contribute to a major portion of the cost of a hangar installation, there seems to be justification for attempting to combine the door and roof structure or a part of the roof structure. In addition, if the door system has curvature, the resulting structure requires less material to resist wind forces. The circular three-hinged arch-door structure shown is based on this concept of combining the roof and door into one structure. The door, which operates along tracks at the structure over the opening and at the base, consists of approximately 30 foot-long sections, which stack one over the other at each end of the door opening. The hinge at the midheight of the door allows for differential settlement between the supporting structure and the ground without inducing stresses in the door structure. The actual structure of the door is a corrugated sinusoidal glass-fiber reinforced plastic shell having an overall depth of 24 inches and a skin thickness of $\frac{1}{4}''$. This type of door structure is shown in the figures relating to Hangars II-5 and II-10 or could also be used for Hangar I-8 instead of the tail enclosure shown.

The hangar structures shown here are the result of the brainstorming sessions Lev Zetlin and his associates conducted to solve this simple enclosure problem.

It is exciting in terms of sheer dispersion of ideas. There was no preconceived commitment to any one system of spatial geometry; cables, arches, trusses, space frames, inflated and membrane structures were used singly and combined and adjusted to the configurations of the giant aircraft.

This is a virtuoso display of engineering which would never grace the galleries of the Museum of Modern Art, but might well make the front pages of the newspapers and trade publications.

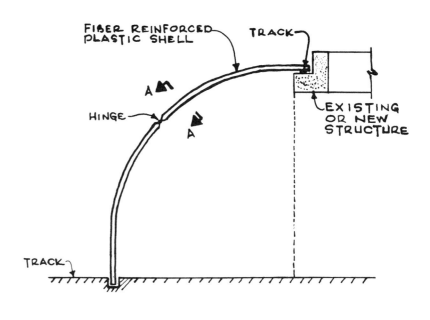

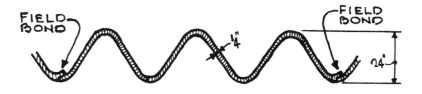

Underwater Exploration

The very nature of civil engineering is such that it is involved with the construction of large structures within the economic resources of our society. In this light, civil engineering must look at underwater exploration and the structures that it requires.

Underwater Resources

Two questions arise immediately in underwater exploration: what type of ocean resources can be economically recovered and when and why, and should the physical extraction system be located underwater? The most important resource being recovered from the sea today is crude oil. Over 16 percent of the world's oil production, or about 6 million barrels per day, are produced offshore. This percentage is expected to increase to 33 percent in ten years and 50 percent in twenty. The additional world-wide expenditures for offshore production are expected to reach $25 billion over the next decade. This represents a considerable commitment to the utilization of offshore resources. This commitment is currently centered on the problem of new recovery systems for depths over that of the present platform systems, from depths of about 340 feet to 1,200 feet, where considerable oil reservoirs are known to exist.

In addition to the recovery of crude oil, the recovery of essential minerals from the ocean requires the creation of new ocean civil engineering systems. Two minerals besides salt, magnesium and bromine, are recovered on a large scale from the ocean. About 90 percent of the total U.S. production of magnesium comes from the ocean. Nodules of feromanganese are among the most common components of the ocean floor. Trillions of tons of ferromanganese nodules are believed to exist here. Manganese nodules are particularly lucrative. They can be mechanically separated from the ore so that large excess bulk material does not have to be transported for further processing. At present, the most economical way of mining the ore is by dredging. Of the several dredging methods, all used are potentially dangerous. Dredging alternatives are needed.

The basic method today of recovering ocean resources is by surface operations. The oil industry may be leading the way to a safer, more economical approach to the recovery of ocean resources through the development of subsea production systems. The greatest natural hazard to recovering ocean resources is the sea state. Surface systems are, therefore, highly vulnerable. Wave pressure is greatest near the surface and re-

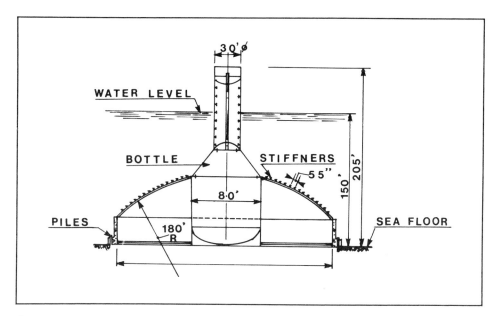

duces exponentially with depth. By locating production systems deep below the surface, they are virtually isolated from sea turbulance. This is particularly important in light of the problems of economic offshore drilling associated with deep rigs; as they become more massive they become extremely unstable. The costs for deep drilling rigs are increasing.

It has been estimated that during the next ten years over 10 percent of all offshore wells will be located in depths of water over 300 feet. It is in this range that subsea production systems are presently economical. With time, as subsea production systems are perfected, they will be competitive with surface systems in even shallower depths.

For the recovery of mineral resources from the ocean in depths of less than 150 feet, dredging is presently the most efficient method. Most techniques commercially considered consist of lifting the ore to the surface for processing. Submarines and undersea tractors have generally been rejected because of their limited lifting capabilities.

Deep water dredging presents several hazards by nature of its essentially "blind" pattern of movement. This can result in the collision of the dredging equipment with subsurface traffic, wrecks, cables, buoys, and any dumped explosives. These factors together with the sea state vulnerability of the surface-

orientated systems make the recovery of ocean minerals excessively risky. Subsea production systems have not been so rigorously applied to mineral recovery as they have been to the recovery of oil.

Subsea Storage Units

The subsea storage unit recently installed in the Arabian Gulf off Dubai marks a new trend in ocean construction. This large vessel, shown here, was submerged in 160 feet of water and is a by-product of the new era of the oil supertanker. Pipeline economics was the primary factor leading to the decision to build an offshore storage tank. If the storage tank had not been located at sea in the oil field, it would have been necessary to pump the oil 58 miles to a land-storage terminal and then pump it back to sea 10 miles where the water depth is sufficient to accommodate supertankers. This cost would have exceeded the cost of the one-half-million barrel undersea storage tank. The Dubai undersea storage-tank design is an example of the use of the concept of an oil-water interface storage tank. Oil, lighter than water, floats on top, allowing the oil to be contained in an open-ended cylinder extending to a greater depth than the oil contained.

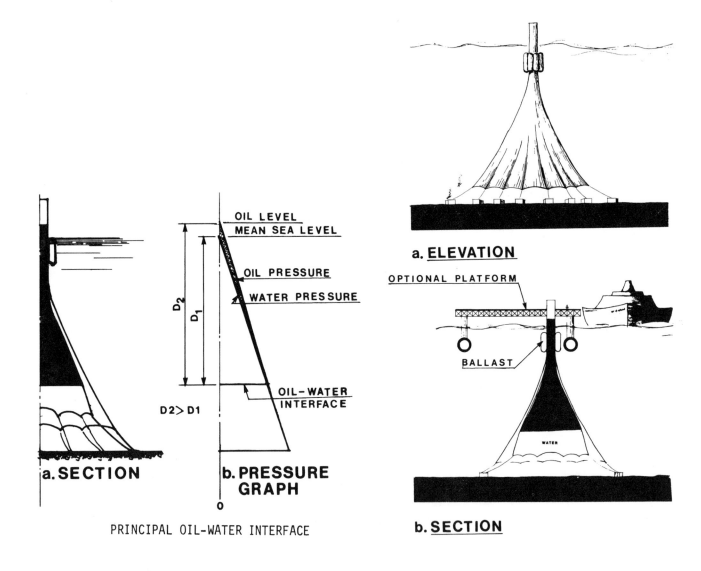

a. **SECTION**

b. **PRESSURE GRAPH**

OIL LEVEL
MEAN SEA LEVEL

OIL PRESSURE

WATER PRESSURE

OIL-WATER INTERFACE

D2 > D1

PRINCIPAL OIL-WATER INTERFACE

a. **ELEVATION**

OPTIONAL PLATFORM

BALLAST

WATER

b. **SECTION**

Membrane Storage Tank

The storage tank at Dubai represents a simple approach to the utilization of the principle of the oil-water interface. A lighter storage tank is shown. This oil-water interface storage tank utilizes membrane walls of this stainless steel, aluminum, or glass-fiber reinforced plastic. The tank can deform slightly to form a plane stress state for any hydraulic loading. This illustrates the hydraulic principle on which the oil-water interface storage tank is based. The oil surface is at a higher level than sea level. There is an excess hydraulic head in the oil compared to the sea level. There is, therefore, a net outward pressure inside the tank which is slowly balanced with depth by the hydraulic pressure of the water. At the level where both pressures are

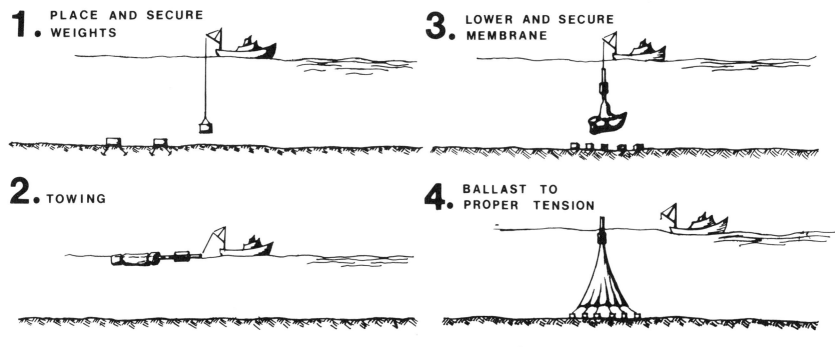

1. PLACE AND SECURE WEIGHTS

2. TOWING

3. LOWER AND SECURE MEMBRANE

4. BALLAST TO PROPER TENSION

MEMBRANE STORAGE TANK CONSTRUCTION SEQUENCE

equal, there is an oil-water interface which is always within the depth of the storage tank.

The use of membranes for large enclosures is among the most recent breakthroughs in the area of structural engineering.

Membrane forces and modularity allow the use of materials normally considered structurally weak.

The concept of a membrane undersea storage could be combined with a complex for undersea exploration combined with tankers; membrane undersea storage tanks can make offshore oil-storage terminals within the vicinity of an oil field economically feasible. Because of the relative portability of membrane structures, the membrane storage tank does not have to be abandoned once the well is no longer economical to run.

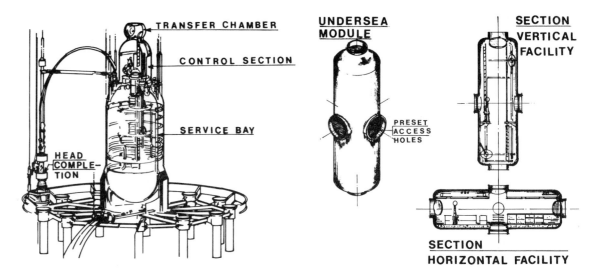

TRANSFER CHAMBER

CONTROL SECTION

SERVICE BAY

HEAD COMPLE-TION

UNDERSEA MODULE

PRESET ACCESS HOLES

SECTION VERTICAL FACILITY

SECTION HORIZONTAL FACILITY

Subsea Production Systems

With requirements for a technology in deeper water the oil industry has taken the first step toward eliminating fixed platforms, with the initiation of subsea well completions. This concept has been enlarged to make the enclosing of conventional equipment inside a pressure chamber—either on the ocean floor or at some intermediate depths—accessible to divers.

A next logical step in the development of an undersea production system is to place subsea processing equipment, separators, pumps, and other items beneath the ocean surface. Mobil Oil Co. and North American Rockwell have developed a prototypical system of sea floor satellites performing most of the functions of a conventional offshore platform. A submarine work-boat enables men to perform maintenance of the subsea systems. An isometric drawing and a section taken through the Mobil/NAR Satellite is shown here. System operation and maintenance philosophy emphasizes maximum use of automatic oil field components coupled with workmen performing a variety of corrective maintenance tasks. The system utilizes a large atmospheric enclosure which contains the well-control equipment, manifolds, and a maintenance station for a number of wells drilled on the periphery. A complete manned access and life support system is provided to permit normal shirtsleeve working conditions. A subsea test program for the Satellite is planned. The problem of the Satellite system is that the Satellites are specially designed for each circumstance. To make undersea production economically viable, a greater degree of standardization must be achieved.

Undersea Module

An undersea module must be developed that can be used for a multitude of functions, from storage tanks and ballasts to control rooms and living areas. A typical single module is shown above. It can be used either as a tank or employed vertically or horizontally as habitable space. By attaching fittings at predetermined locations, the module can become a submarine. With special attached arms it can be used as an undersea work-boat or a transfer chamber to bring work crews from the surface. A number of modules can be combined together to form a small complex such as a well completion system, or a larger complex such as a habitable production system.

The sea-floor production system is equally usable for processing minerals from the ocean's bottom. This particularly applies to the manganese nodule, which can be separated mechanically. There is no economic justification for lifting the ore to the surface to process it there to return most of the ore residue to the ocean floor.

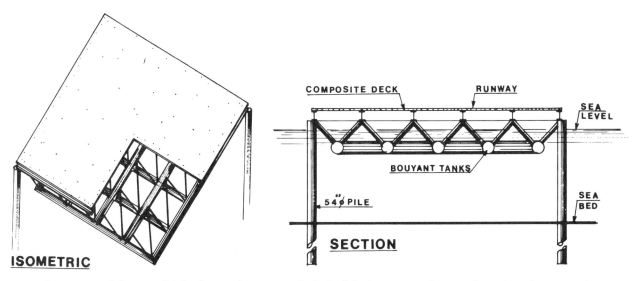

COMPOSITE DECK **RUNWAY** **SEA LEVEL**

BOUYANT TANKS

54" Ø PILE **SEA BED**

SECTION

ISOMETRIC

The material from which the undersea module is fabricated becomes a challenging task for undersea design. Presently, high strength steels (HY 80 and now for deeply submerged systems HY 130) are used for pressure hulls. Aluminum has also been used successfully because of its relative inactivity in the presence of pure sea water. Glass and plexiglass are potentially usable because of their chemical inertness. All of these materials have a high ratio of collapse stress to density. For these materials, which are used as approximately 1-inch-thick solid-plate pressure hulls, the plate is normally stiffened by ring stiffeners. From experience with buckling phenomenon, to prevent buckling, a more uniform stiffening—such as provided by honeycomb materials—produces better results than individual ring stiffeners. The technique has been applied to light-gage metal sheets to eliminate buckling. The technique allows complete utilization of the allowable compressive strength of the material.

Preliminary indications are that prestressed concrete could be a very economic material for underwater constructions. To solve the waterproofing problem, the concrete would have to be properly protected by coatings such as epoxy resin.

Concrete does not have to be thick. Ferro-cement ship hulls are normally constructed 2 inches thick and the technique is applicable to undersea construction, particularly the undersea module shown.

It is possible that an underwater production system could

be combined with a membrane storage tank to achieve a complete self-contained well operation. A second alternative for storage is in using the undersea module as a storage tank, floating slightly below the low water level of the ocean, where it would be relatively undisturbed by the sea state. The supertanker can then either fill itself up or, alternatively, replace and tow the oil-filled modules.

There are new concepts still in an embryonic stage of development that offer great future opportunities for major civil engineering contributions to undersea structures. The most important of these is the harnessing of wave energy for electric power. The energy contained in waves is enormous. The pressure of a 30-foot wave is almost 1 ton per square foot. Transferring this energy into mechanical and finally electric energy introduces an enormous new potential. With this energy available, sea industries become economically feasible. An example is the extraction of pure water from sea water, which requires a considerable output of energy. Energy sinks made from undersea modules may provide an unlimited source of clean hydroelectric energy.

These concepts for undersea exploration structures represent only the immediate ideas of the undersea exploration structures. Other ideas, such as undersea farming, are only now being investigated. The need for simple, economical undersea structures will be an exploding area to which civil engineering can make significant contributions.

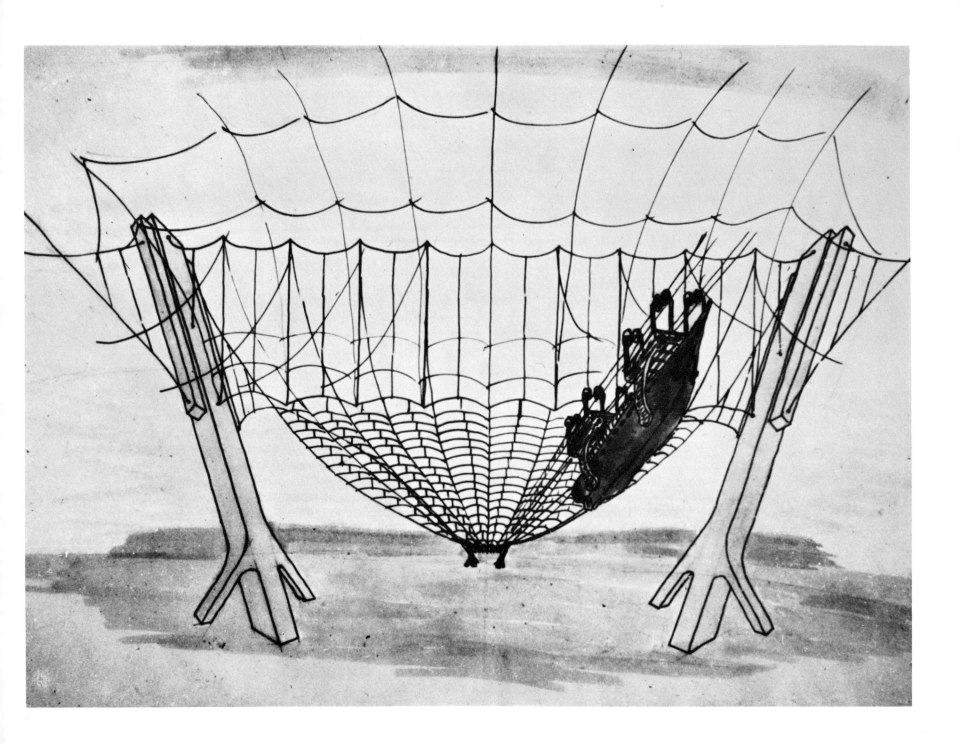

The Panama Canal

Canals have important political significance. The Suez Canal helped create the British Empire. Panama was only a district in Colombia but the effect of building the Panama Canal made it a nation.

The Russians used the slave labor of a number of camps to build the canal to the North Sea. The question is, which was first, the camps and the available labor or the need and then the camps? The historical ramification of canals is suffering. You need thousands and thousands of people to build a canal.

In 1970 Congress considered building a new Panama Canal. Our progress in thinking was to blow the canal out of the ground with an atomic bomb. That would save some labor. We know that it will take eight or ten years to build and it would cost between $8 billion and $10 billion. The question is, Is it right in 1970 to think in terms of ditches? Since we built ditches to connect oceans before, we think we should do it now. This is the inertia of past thought.

The only way that a canal apparently can be conceived is to move dirt. The purpose is not to move dirt but to move ships from one ocean to another.

Suppose I came up with a scheme to pick up the ships and carry them over? A ship is designed structurally so that it can be picked up. We could move ships as we do people on a ski-lift. We could move them from ocean to ocean without locks to adjust to the difference in elevation between the two oceans and it could be done at one-tenth of the cost of moving dirt.

My proposal also has salvage value. If the Panamanians decided they did not want the canal we could always dismantle the towers. The towers also have other uses. They could be

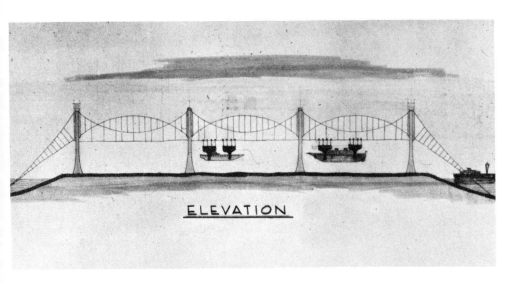

ELEVATION

used as structures for small cities, observatories or a number of other uses.

When faced with a new problem, we only consider old solutions. We dug a canal once so for canals we only think in terms of digging another ditch. Bombs are available so let's blow it out instead of digging it out of the earth.

I presented this cable scheme to Ambassador Mundt who was negotiating with the Panamanian government. It is 1,000 feet above ground and designed like a big fishnet. You can move ships in three or four lanes. It picks up the ships and brings them to the underbelly of this mesh, moves them across and drops them down in the other ocean.

The ship is transported suspended by the cables. It is a rigid mesh, the same system we have used on a number of buildings. The towers could be used for a number of other constructive purposes: for buildings, for industry, for meterological observations. This mesh would cost only $3 billion and could be built in five years.

It could be mass produced in 50 locations throughout the world, brought in on reels and erected very quickly. Since a level canal is contemplated, it would be full of marine life going from one ocean to another and we do not know what the inference would be. These ecological ramifications and those of an atomic blast would be eliminated.

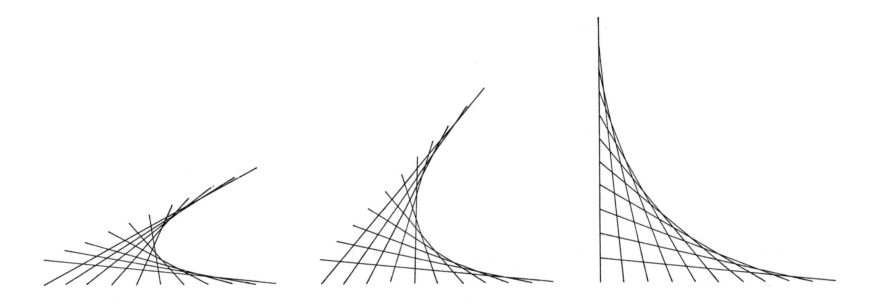

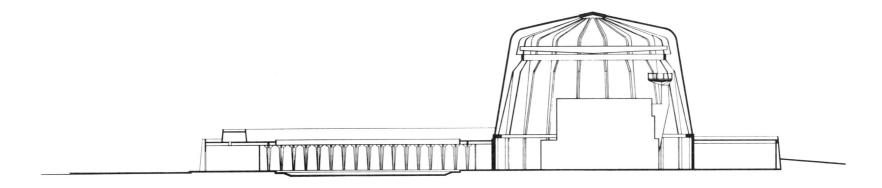

Theme and Variations

The Nuclear Reactor in Rehovot, Israel is an example of Zetlin's theme-and-variations method of design. All ideas once invented are later reexamined, refined, and used again. The modest hyperbolic panels of the Nuclear Reactor's walls find their expression a decade later in the tremendous cantilevers of the American Airlines terminals, in a market roof for Montreal, and in thin shell transportation units. The hypar is not a terminal form for Zetlin. Zetlin must know how it works, scientifically; he will not test it with "a hundred peons standing on its surface" but through mathematics, until it emerges as a new form justifying a new theory. But even this is a by-product of the design. The hypar must satisfy many conditions other than its form. It must emerge as the optimum solution balanced against materials, labor, erection, transportation, and spatial needs.

The Nuclear Reactor, designed early in his career, typifies Zetlin's way of thinking. He was working under the best of conditions. The architect, Philip Johnson, was talented with the objectivity and rationality of a George Bernard Shaw. He knew what he wanted without formal prejudice but with strong formal preference.

Nuclear Reactor *Rehovot, Israel*
Philip Johnson, Associates, architects
Lev Zetlin Associates, structural engineers

There are hundreds of parameters that determine the final conditons that influence the shape and form of a building. If only one is examined, such as aesthetics, an optimum solution will not evolve.

For example, the Nuclear Reactor illustrates a cooperation between architect and engineer. Johnson did not like the usual "bosom" form in which most nuclear reactors were built. The engineer convinced him that this form was in fact the least efficient and had been derived from a meaningless convention.

The architect asked, What is the best form? The engineer said a round building with a slightly curved roof. Johnson wanted the form to have a corregated surface. His design was a round building with a slightly curved roof. It took the architect and engineer until almost the completion of the design to find that a form could be created to resist torsion using hyperbolic parabaloids. The engineer was forced to think in these terms because of the architect's formal requirements. The architect's idea was not frozen. He was given a solution, realized its potential and accepted it.

If the engineer tells the architect the best way to build his building, he will probably not build it that way. However, if the engineer tells the architect what the parameters are and states the conditions, the architect may accept them.

The way the final form should be created is that the architect should start with a blurred form and the engineer with exact data. The two should come together.

Conclusion

Zetlin's rationale is drawn together like the assembly of a jigsaw puzzle. We are clued to the position of various pieces by a recognizable familiar configuration randomly fitting into place. Yet the picture in its entirety is unfamiliar. It is easy to see but difficult to comprehend in its complexity. It seems vulgar and obvious compared to established refined ideas, as the new invariably does.

For Zetlin the experience of engineering is personal and direct. He has freed himself from fixed patterns of thought and prejudice. Engineering in his hands is not a pure occurrence but a complex activity endlessly adjusted to requirements, opportunities, restraints, and the forces of everyday life.

When industrialization eliminated handcraft and the cottage industries at the beginning of the Industrial Revolution it did so by replacing individual working methods with standardized machine operations. As a result, all feet were fit to standard patterns. The rationale was that fewer people would go barefoot even though no one's shoes would fit comfortably. The idea of simple machine operation at the expense of human inconvenience, once accepted, governed the patterns of industrialization. The first industrial machines were muscle machines, designed to replace the labor of man and beast. They extended man's strength to that of an elephant but did nothing to extend his mind at all.

As a result, practical engineers and technicians designed standard solutions for simple machine operations. Ingenuity was coupled to and limited by the capabilities of machines that were the human equivalent of hulking idiots. Engineering and technology were dominated by brute-strength and solutions conceived in terms of machine muscle power.

Engineering handbooks were written to further standardize the process and to eliminate the necessity of constant calculation. Handbooks assembled proven answers and, in effect, defined solutions.

This attitude continues to prevail. For example, the problem of a new Panama Canal suggested to handbook engineers that they find a more efficient way to move dirt. Their solution was to substitute blasting for digging. Zetlin did not propose a canal at all. The problem as he saw it was not to move dirt but to move ships.

To assume that the problems of the built environment are purely formal presupposes that they are limited to the province of engineering, aesthetics, technology, and industry. But building is no longer an isolated activity any more than we are restricted to machines that can only extend muscle power. Building today, from design to use, is part of a complex social, economic and political system. We now have machines that can extend the human brain by considering a great number of complex variables simultaneously. Our thinking machines can help solve complex building problems if we are not too muscle-bound to use them.

The singular virtuoso engineer and egocentric architect are remnants of the age of industrialization and as such are valuable and historically interesting. But another form of architecture and engineering is emerging with no connection at all to virtuoso tradition.

The age of great discoveries such as those of Edison are over, says Zetlin. They were contemporaneous with the singular great architect and engineer. Engineering today is like the search for oil. All of the easy-to-find fields have been discovered. Today prospectors must search with great skill and sophistication, reexamining the old fields and methods to make new discoveries.

Zetlin does this in his search for the optimal problem solution. Optimization is the key because it cannot be discovered until all the conditions of the problem are known and visualized as a whole. Architects and engineers have always sought to do this. Yet the variables, in an increasingly complex society, grew beyond the ability of any single mind to comprehend.

Today machines that extend the human mind are aids in achieving this complex comprehension. The result is not more efficient Industrial Revolution solutions but an entirely different approach to problems and one without precedent.

The engineering shown in this book has a life of its own, born of the optimization of problem parameters. It is not engineering that relies on brute strength.

To merely say that form is no longer the primary concern of architects is to state an accepted idea. The concept of architecture as process is now an idea in good currency, recognized as one whose time has come and is, therefore, probably no longer true at all. We are entering a new age of design driven by as yet undefined motivations.

There are two ends of the spectrum from the trades to science in thinking and doing in the built environment. Science is not engineering, its solutions are limited to too narrow a range of practical knowledge, as Zetlin has pointed out. On the other hand, trade technology is not engineering; it suffers from an overabundance of practical restraints.

For example, the self-dampening cable system that Zetlin applied so successfully to buildings and now proposes for a major bridge at Baltimore and a superbillion-dollar Panama Canal ski-lift has been in use for decades in the overhanging electric power cables for electric train systems. It took Zetlin to scientifically exploit the implications of this technical device.

There are as many practical everyday vernacular trade solutions to enrich the profession of engineering as there are engineering solutions to stimulate the world of science. Scientific theory is enriched by engineering practically as fine art is nourished by a rich vernacular.

We do not learn all we know from science if we are scientists, engineering if we are engineers, or trade practices if we are tradesmen. Each is a different area of involvement, none more essentially important than the other, since they are interdependent. Although society reveres the scientific scholar the most highly and pays the tradesman the most handsomely the worth of any activity is eventually measured by the ability of the man who practices it. This Zetlin knows. His peculiar strength is in his interdisciplinary approach and absolute lack of pretense.

The best solutions are often found by breaking the rules. Those who follow the rules by definition perpetuate them. Zetlin says that he has learned to seek out the most difficult solution and experience has shown him that it is usually the best. This is the exact opposite approach to that of Industrial Revolution engineering.

New juxtapositions are emerging in almost every area. A changed flow of forces is passing through the society as we now recognize new concepts in the transfer of stresses in building structures. The old linear theories in engineering are disappearing as they are in our social, political, and economic institutions in favor of those that visualize the building and the world as a whole.

The idea that the designer has a preconceived idea and works with known conditions, known materials for preconceived ends, and that this is the only way that man can design or has designed from primitive aborigines to Detroit car stylists, is an outworn prejudice.

There has always been another design method: spontaneous design that emerges from gathering together and arranging all the parts and letting them inspire the solution wherein the elements themselves create the form. The form is not predictable until the parts are arranged. Not even the desired results are known because these may change in the arrangement of the parts. This idea is probably one of the oldest design methods known to man. It probably started when he picked up an interesting rock and found it made a good spearhead as he happened to fit it to a piece of wood. The idea of purpose emerged with the material and the conditions. Uneducated builders build in this fashion all over the world today with found material as the most primitive man fashioned his shelter from fallen trees, mammoth and whale bones.

The idea of suggestive design is almost totally contrary to industrial planning as we practice it. Zetlin seems to be returning to the older design method as he assembles the bits and pieces of labor, materials, transportation, client preferences, and user need and combines these with his information and knowledge. Not only does he question every premise of engineering in the problem solving, but by doing so questions the premise of how we design. Zetlin's approach is not primitive. His design method is on the scale of McLuhan's global village and is a far cry from the village tom-toms. We do not know the shape of the built environment of the future but we can be sure that it will be nothing like the ill-fitting forms of the Industrial Revolution. They are sure to be scientific and unfamiliar. They will fit human idiosyncrasy rather than be governed by design egocentricity as they are today, if we are to survive.

Credits

Photos and drawings on the following pages are courtesy of Lev Zetlin Associates:

12 (center), 13 (center), 20, 44, 45, 46, 47, 48, 49 (bottom), 51, 52, 53, 54, 59, 61, 62, 64, 68, 69, 72, 73, 74, 76, 78, 79, 80, 81, 88, 89, 90, 91, 102, 105, 108, 109, 114. 115. 117, 120, 121, 122, 123, 124, 125, 126, 127, 129, 138, 139, 140, 141 (right), 142, 143, 150, 151, 152, 153, 154, 155, 158, 159, 162, 163 (top), 166, 167, 168, 170, 171, 172, 173, 174, 175, 179, 180, 181, 182, 183, 184, 185, 186, 187, 188, 189, 190, 191, 192, 193, 194, 196, 197, 198, 199, 200, 201, 203, 204, 205, 206, 207, 208, 209, 210, 211

Photos and drawings on the following pages are by Forrest Wilson:

11, 12 (left), 12 (right), 13 (left), 21, 22, 23, 24, 25, 26, 27, 28, 29, 30, 32, 33, 34 (right), 40 (bottom left), 43, 49 (top), 50, 75, 132 (left), 133 (left), 135 (left), 136 (right), 144 (left), 145, 161 (top), 163 (bottom), 164 (right), 165 (right), 212

10 (top): Photo by Gene Washnik/Courtesy of Lev Zetlin Associates
10 (bottom): Photo by Morley Baer/Courtesy of Lev Zetlin Associates
13 (right): Photo by Ken Korsh/Courtesy of Lev Zetlin
14: Fuji Group Pavilion, Yutaka Murata, Architect, Tokyo Japan; Photo courtesy of Expo Osaka
16 (left): Toronto City Hall, Toronto, Ontario: Viljo Revel—John B. Parkin Associates, Associated Architects and Engineers; Photo courtesy of John B. Parkin Associates
16 (right): Temple of Amen-Mut-Khonsu, Luxor, circa 1390 B.C.
17: Cables and central tensile ring of Salt Lake City Civic Center; Lev Zetlin Associates, structural engineers; Photo by Wagner International Photos, Inc.
18: Kabah, Yucatan. 1960; Photo by Forrest Wilson
31: Courtesy of American Iron and Steel Institute
34 (left): Courtesy of French Government Tourist Office, 510 Fifth Avenue, New York City 10020
35: Sculpture by Ken Snelson; Photo by Forrest Wilson
36: Niagara Falls Convention Center, Niagara Falls, New York: Philip Johnson and John Burgee, Architects; Photo by Ezra Stoller Associates, Inc., © ESTO; Courtesy of Philip Johnson
38: Courtesy of American Iron and Steel Institute
39 (left): Courtesy of Aluminum Company of America
39 (right): Courtesy of General Motors Corporation
40 (top left): Theme Pavilion; Courtesy of Dominion Bridge Company Ltd.
40 (top right): American Cement Corporation office building under construction in Los Angeles: Photo by Julius Shulman, courtesy of Daniel, Mann, Johnson & Mendenhall, Architects
40 (bottom right): Photo by Jim Rankin/Courtesy of Armco Steel Corporation
41 (top): Courtesy of American Iron and Steel Institute

41 (bottom): Photo by Jim Rankin/Courtesy of Armco Steel Corporation
42: Russian precast housing system, Moscow; Photo by Forrest Wilson
55: Photo: Shunk-Kender
56: Photo: Shunk-Kender
57: Copyright © 1971 by Valley Curtain Corporation; Photo: Shunk-Kender
60: Courtesy of Munson-Williams-Proctor Institute
63: Photo © by Ezra Stoller Associates/Courtesy of Philip Johnson, Architect
66: Courtesy of Philip Johnson, Architect
67: Courtesy of Philip Johnson & John Burgee, Architects
70: Interior of American Airlines superbay hangar; Photo by Morley Baer/Courtesy of Lev Zetlin Associates
77: American Airline superbay maintenance facility, Lev Zetlin Associates, structural engineers; Photo courtesy of American Iron and Steel Institute
82: Photo by Wagner International Photos, Inc.
84: Courtesy of Bethlehem Steel Corporation
85: Courtesy of Bethlehem Steel Corporation
86: Courtesy of Bethlehem Steel Corporation
87: Courtesy of Bethlehem Steel Corporation
92: Drawings by Fred Freeman, based on design by Lev Zetlin Associates
93: Drawings by Zetlin & Westermann, Engineers and Architects
94: Drawings by Zetlin & Westermann, Engineers and Architects
95: Drawings by Zetlin & Westermann, Engineers and Architects
96 (top): Courtesy of New York State Department of Public Works
96 (bottom): Courtesy of Philip Johnson, Architect
97: Photo by Max Levine-Parkway Studios
98: Photo © Ezra Stoller Associates/Courtesy of Philip Johnson
99: Photo © Ezra Stoller Associates/Courtesy of Philip Johnson
100: Photo by Blakeslee-Lane, Inc.
103: Photo by Gene Washnik
104: Boissonnas residence, French Riviera, France; Philip Johnson, Architect; Lev Zetlin Associates, Structural Engineers; Photo courtesy of Philip Johnson
106: Sidney Opera House; Photo courtesy of Australian Information Service
110: Courtesy of United States Steel Corporation
111 (left): Courtesy of United States Steel Corporation
111 (right): Courtesy of American Iron and Steel Institute/Steel Products News Bureau
112: Courtesy of International Paper Company
113: Courtesy of International Paper Company
116: Habitat; photo by Panda Associates Photography and Art Services/Courtesy of Expo Corporation
118: Courtesy of Lawrence Halprin & Associates

119: Courtesy of Lawrence Halprin & Associates

128: Courtesy of Lev Zetlin Associates and *This Week* magazine

130: Takara Group Pavilion, Osaka; photo courtesy of Expo Corporation

134 (*right*): Habitat; photo by Forrest Wilson

134 (*left*): Housing system; drawing by Yona Friedman, Architect

135 (*right*): Wooden sectional unit being lifted into place; Photo by Tom Mitchell, Jr.

136 (*left*): Hans Rucker living environment; Photo © Gerald Zugmann

137 (*left*): Panelized building method; photo courtesy of O'Connor Lumber Company

137 (*right*): Courtesy of Sikorsky Aircraft, Division of United Aircraft Corporation, Stratford, Connecticut

141 (*left*): Courtesy of International Paper Company

144 (*right*): Archcraft by Williams, Troy, Michigan

146: Courtesy of KOHM Group

147: Courtesy of KOHM Group

148: Courtesy of KOHM Group

149: Courtesy of KOHM Group

156: Courtesy of French Government Tourist Office, 610 Fifth Avenue, New York, New York 10020

157: Kinetic tower design; drawing by Lev Zetlin Associates

160 (*top*): Model of World Trade Center; Photo courtesy of the Port of New York Authority

160 (*bottom*): State University of New York at Potsdam, H. & P. E. Building; Design by P. Gugliotta; 5 space frames up to 150' x 220' clear span, edge supported 10 psf.; Photo courtesy of P. Gugliotta

161 (*bottom*): SUNY Potsdam, H. & P. E. Building; Photo courtesy of P. Gugliotta

164 (*left*): Photo by Mr. Taisuke Ogawa; © 1970 by Shinkenchiku-Sha Co., Ltd.

165 (*left*): Photo by Mr. Taisuke Ogawa; © 1970 by Shinkenchiku-Sha Co., Ltd.

177: Airline logos courtesy of American Airlines, Eastern Airlines, Pan American Airlines, Quantas Airlines, Trans World Airlines and United Airlines

213: Nuclear Reactor, Rehovot, Israel; Philip Johnson, Architect, 1961; Drawing courtesy of Philip Johnson

214: Courtesy of Philip Johnson

215: Courtesy of Philip Johnson

Excerpts on pages 44–47 from "A New Look at Flat Plate Construction" by Professor Seymour Howard, *Architectural Record,* May 1961 appear with permission of *Architectural Record,* a publication of McGraw-Hill, Inc.

The extract on pages 78–79 from "Hangar Features Stressed Skin Hypars" by Charles H. Thornton and Richard L. Tomasetti, *Civil Engineering,* November 1970 appears with permission of *Civil Engineering,* the official monthly publication of the American Society of Civil Engineers.

Index

About the Author

Although Forrest Wilson describes himself as "an extremely common man," his background is anything but common. It includes both hard, practical experience and broad theoretical knowledge. Mr. Wilson is currently Assistant Dean for Architecture and Planning and Professor and Chairman of the Department of Architecture and Planning, School of Engineering and Architecture, The Catholic University of America. Formerly he was Director of the School of Architecture, Design, and Planning at Ohio University, and before that an Assistant Professor of Architecture at Pratt Institute.

The former editor of *Progressive Architecture,* Wilson has also served as designer and construction superintendent on numerous building projects. His earlier background includes practical experience as a draftsman, sculptor, construction worker, and ship's carpenter. Wilson has written ten books and more than 200 articles on various architectural topics.

This book was phototypeset in Melior and Helvetica with Melior display by York Graphic Services, York, Pennsylvania, and printed by offset lithography and bound by The Book Press, Brattleboro, Vermont.